Interactional Leadership and How to Coach It

All leaders make choices, but not all leaders are choice-focused. In *Interactional Leadership and How to Coach It: The art of the choice-focused leader* Michael Harvey presents an important new theory of leadership which demonstrates how to coach successful choice-making.

This clear, wide-ranging book integrates business and psychology, exploring the art of choice-focused leadership through neuroscience, cognitive psychology, existential philosophy and leadership studies. Interactional leadership helps leaders to make informed decisions throughout the 'achievement cycle' of strategy, resourcing and delivery, and emphasizes the importance of psychological balance. The book features chapter-long case studies which provide unique insights into the leader's inner world and clearly illustrate how the tightrope of leadership can be mastered. Harvey draws important lessons about decision-making from corporate leaders, politicians and even Shakespeare's tragic heroes, and addresses the leader's ethical responsibility for major issues facing us now and in the future. The interactional model also focuses on coaching the multiple roles of leadership, such as global leader, team leader, innovator, entrepreneur and chair of the board.

Accessible and practical, *Interactional Leadership and How to Coach It* is an ideal guide for coaches, leaders, students, trainers of coaches and anyone involved in leadership development and recruitment.

Michael Harvey is one of Europe's most experienced leadership coaches. Based in London, UK, he is an organizational psychologist and the author of *Interactional Coaching: Choice-focused learning at work* (Routledge, 2012).

Interactional Leadership and How to Coach It

The art of the choice-focused leader

Michael Harvey

LONDON AND NEW YORK

First published 2015
by Routledge
27 Church Road, Hove, East Sussex, BN3 2FA

and by Routledge
711 Third Avenue, New York, NY 10017

Routledge is an imprint of the Taylor & Francis Group, an informa business

© 2015 Michael Harvey

The right of Michael Harvey to be identified as author of this work has been asserted by him in accordance with sections 77 and 78 of the Copyright, Designs and Patents Act 1988.

All rights reserved. No part of this book may be reprinted or reproduced or utilised in any form or by any electronic, mechanical, or other means, now known or hereafter invented, including photocopying and recording, or in any information storage or retrieval system, without permission in writing from the publishers.

Trademark notice: Product or corporate names may be trademarks or registered trademarks, and are used only for identification and explanation without intent to infringe.

British Library Cataloguing in Publication Data
A catalogue record for this book is available from the British Library

Library of Congress Cataloging-in-Publication Data
Harvey, Michael Denis Bagenal, 1952-
Interactional leadership and how to coach it : the art of the choice-focused leader / Michael Harvey.
pages cm
Includes bibliographical references and index.
1. Leadership. 2. Decision making. 3. Executive coaching. I. Title.
HD57.7.H388574 2015
658.4'092—dc23
2014024754

ISBN: 978-0-415-74207-8 (hbk)
ISBN: 978-0-415-74225-2 (pbk)
ISBN: 978-1-315-73716-4 (ebk)

Typeset in Times
by FiSH Books Ltd, Enfield

Printed and bound in Great Britain by
TJ International Ltd, Padstow, Cornwall

To my mother and father

Contents

About the author   ix
Preface   x

PART 1
What is interactional leadership?   1

   Prologue: the choice-focused leader   3

1 The Achievement Cycle and the art of leadership choice-making   9

2 The psychology of interactional leadership and its ethical and multirole dimensions   17

3 The psychology and neuroscience of choice and the philosophy of interactional leadership   28

PART 2
Coaching the choice-focused leader: interactional leadership coaching in practice   39

4 Coaching the non-resourcing leader: 'Dracula' in the boardroom: the case of Blake S.   41

5 The practical techniques of interactional leadership coaching   53

6 Coaching the non-strategizing leader: 'zombie leadership': the case of Arjun J.   62

7 Coaching the non-delivering leader: 'blocked at every turn': the case of Deborah K.   70

PART 3
The multiplicity of leadership roles – and how to coach them 79

8 The global leader, the entrepreneur and the chair of the board: coaching across the spectrum 81

9 The team leader: creating the dialectical team 91

10 The potential leader: coaching the rising star and the gender gap in leadership 100

11 The thought leader: coaching creative and intellectual leadership 110

12 The influence of the group in leadership: coaching the board 120

PART 4
Interactional leadership in the public domain 131

13 From Steve Jobs to Hamlet: the art of the choice-focused leader in business, politics and literature 133

PART 5
Choosing the future: leaders and coaches 147

14 Engaging with choice: ethical issues for leaders and leadership coaching 149

15 Coaching difficult leaders: the paradox of leadership coaching 160

16 Choosing the future: what decisions lie in store for leaders and their coaches? 168

References 180
Index 188

About the author

Michael Harvey is one of Europe's most experienced leadership coaches. He is also an organizational psychologist, whose previous career roles include university teacher, corporate manager, media entrepreneur and psychotherapist. He has a first-class degree in psychology from London University and Master's degrees in psychotherapy, organizational psychology and English literature. He lives and works in London and can be contacted at michael@interactionalcoaching.com.

Michael is the author of *Interactional Coaching: Choice-focused learning at work* (Routledge, 2012).

Preface
The current crisis in leadership: how can interactional leadership coaching help?

So far in the twenty-first century, our leaders have not exactly covered themselves in glory. Banking scandals and governmental economic mismanagement have led to the one of the worst recessions in history, at the same time as we have witnessed a proliferation of unethical behaviour, from politicians' expenses to corporate and public sector corruption, not to mention the rank criminality in financial services which has landed some former high-flyers in prison. Trust in political, corporate and financial leaders has probably never been lower. So it is inevitable that we talk about a crisis in leadership. It is not the first time, of course. James MacGregor Burns (1978) in his influential book on transformational leadership used the term back in the 1970s and perhaps there has always been a sense that leadership is in crisis. Given the responsibilities they wield, leaders inevitably occupy a place not too far from the edge of some abyss or other, even if today there seems to be a new depth of uncertainty about their role in society.

Leadership is isolating, this is part of the problem. The leader is different from most people. She is picked out from the crowd for a role which carries unique responsibilities. This can make normal behaviour and productive relationships extremely difficult. I remember experiencing this isolation in my own modest career as an entrepreneurial leader, running an innovative media business in the late 1980s and early 1990s. It was often hard to talk openly with employees, colleagues or customers, without upsetting the delicate balance which held the enterprise together. I longed for a confidential, independent dialogue which would help me to articulate my thoughts and resolve my choices. A fledgling vision of coaching developed for me at that time, long before I knew of the existence of the practice (mainly in the USA in those days). My subsequent formal training as a psychotherapist and organizational psychologist was increasingly motivated by this desire to help others break out of the isolation of leadership and as a leadership coach I have been working towards this goal for the best part of 20 years.

I now realise that leadership is isolating because of the choices a leader has to make. The sheer quantity and interconnectedness of these choices and the consequences which they entail provide the real challenges of leadership. In coaching, it is possible to deal with complex business and psychological decisions because it is a relational experience which adapts itself to a leader's unique situation.

Providing a theory of all-round leadership choice-making is more difficult. Many conventional theories concentrate on a single aspect of leadership and present this as the whole, so ignoring the spiral of roles within roles in a leadership situation. It is this multidimensional, interlinked, time-based reality of leadership choice-making, which I have tried to represent in this book, both practically and theoretically.

To do so, I have drawn on a wide range of sources, including existential and dialectical philosophy, leadership and management studies, psychotherapy and organizational psychology and other disciplines as far-reaching as neuroscience, political science and even literature (my first academic pursuit). This multidisciplinary approach is not designed to complicate leadership but, on the contrary, to simplify it, by providing a consistent conceptual superstructure which reproduces the experience of leadership practice. In other words, it attempts to provide a theoretical framework for the interactional reality with which effective leaders need to engage. The practical side of this is conveyed by a rich mix of extensive case studies and shorter vignettes drawn from my coaching practice, which, together with public examples from corporate and political life, show a variety of leaders struggling to get in touch with their situations – and with themselves – in order to bring about successful change.

Tomorrow's future is being chosen today. Leadership choices affect many people and in this still relatively new century of ours, there is an immense need for leaders who can change lives for the better in the corporate, public and political spheres. Leaders need to master the art of balance which paves the way for positive choice-making. Helping them do so is the ambition of this book. Interactional leadership theory and coaching cannot guarantee that bad decisions will not be made. Sadly, nothing can do this. But the fusion of good theory with good practice is the best hope we have for supporting leaders in their endeavor to positively resolve the many choices which confront them – and which have consequences for us all.

Who is this book for?

This book is intended as a contribution to the study of contemporary leadership, as well as to the practical literature of executive coaching. As such, it should be of interest to all those who lead and who aspire to do so, across a wide range of leadership roles. Those who develop, train and recruit leaders will also benefit from this book, as will human resources professionals and, of course, students, teachers and practitioners of executive coaching in all its varieties.

Contents of the book

Part I: What is interactional leadership?

The Prologue introduces interactional leadership through the striking example of the choices facing a chief executive and in Chapter 1 we explore the nature of human choice as it relates to organizations and their leaders. What does it take to make informed decisions throughout the whole of the Achievement Cycle of strategy, resourcing and delivery? In Chapter Two we complete the interactional '6D model' by looking at the psychological factors involved in leadership. I also describe the influence of ethics and multiple roles in this balancing art. Chapter 3 examines psychology and neuroscience to reveal the extraordinary complexity of human choice-making and how this chimes with the holistic, interactional view of the world presented by existential and dialectical philosophers. 'Oppositional logic' is based on inclusion and synthesis rather than mutual exclusion and, in this spirit, I touch on the field of leadership studies and suggest the bridges that can be built between the interactional approach and other leadership models.

Part 2: Coaching the choice-focused leader

In Chapter 4, we turn from theory to practice and a case of a TV boss, nicknamed Dracula by his staff, who struggles to turn his bold vision into an organizational reality. He is an example of a non-resourcing leader, who needs to fundamentally change his choice-making style in order to have a chance of commercial success. Chapter 5 sketches the practical techniques of interactional leadership coaching in each of the interactional dimensions and the way it deals with challenges to effective choice-making.

Chapter 6 features a 'zombie-like' banker, who has good resourcing skills but lacks the vision to find his own way in a bank dominated by his profit-driven boss. Chapter 7 represents a third variation on fractional leadership, a leader with good strategic and resourcing skills but one who is failing to deliver the results her public sector agency urgently needs. Her coaching challenge is to find the executional skills necessary to bring about effective change.

Part 3: The multiplicity of leadership roles

In Part 3, we examine the wide variety of leadership roles. What can the interactional model tells us about global leadership and what it takes for an entrepreneurial leader to successfully start a business? We also look at the role of the chair of the board and its influence on the chief executive's choice-making. In Chapter 9, we move on to team leadership, with contrasting examples of managers attempting to build successful, 'dialectical' teams.

Chapter 10 concentrates on the leaders of the future, examining the hard choices which rising stars often have to make. I highlight an extreme imbalance in the world of leadership, the underrepresentation of women in top jobs, and illustrate one talented young woman's struggle to decide what kind of leader she wants to be. In Chapter 11 we move on to the role of thought leaders in managing innovation and inspiring their staff. I also present a case study of an academic historian desperately searching for the inspiration which created his earlier success.

Finally, we explore the influence of the leadership team on a leader's choice-making. Group-based coaching can improve this, as shown by two examples of leadership teams which have become incapable of acting effectively. How are these problems mirrored on the world stage in foreign policy group decision-making? For the answer we look at George W. Bush's decision to invade Iraq and Barack Obama's choices when the US located the hiding place of Osama bin Laden in 2011, as well as noting the importance of 'leading upwards'.

Part 4: Interactional leadership in the public domain

In Chapter 13, we examine how well-known corporate leaders like Steve Jobs and James Dyson and Enron's Jeffrey Skilling fit into the pattern of interactional leadership. Some bosses triumphantly overcome their whole-cycle biases; others are limited or even destroyed by them. The precariousness of the leadership tightrope also applies to the world of politics, as an analysis of the careers of recent British prime ministers shows. I conclude this panoramic view of leadership by arguing that the fate of Shakespeare's tragic heroes is directly linked to their choice-making styles.

Part 5: Choosing the future

In this final section, we turn towards the future and the issues facing leaders and leadership coaching in the coming decades. In Chapter 14, we examine the ethical dimension of leadership in an organizational world, increasingly stained by scandal, unethical practices and illegal wrongdoing. I outline the ethics of coaching from an interactional standpoint, compared to conventional coaching ethics, and illustrate some of its practical applications in coaching leaders. In Chapter 15, we focus on 'the paradox of leadership coaching', the challenge of working with difficult leaders who desperately need coaching but avoid it. The 'Soprano syndrome' and other risks involved in coaching manipulative, bullying leaders are vividly illustrated by an unusual case study.

In our final chapter, we move on to a wide-ranging and potentially controversial discussion of the choices facing leaders in the foreseeable future. We explore the dialectics of the future in the arenas of climate change, aging, population growth, economic inequality and new technology. How might these issues impact our corporate and political leaders and how can coaches make their contribution to improving the historically unprecedented choices which will determine our future?

A note on case studies

All the case studies featured in this book are based on real coaching cases, carefully anonymized to protect the privacy of the client and his or her organization. For illustrative purposes, composite elements from different cases have sometimes been included.

Acknowledgements

Many people have influenced me in writing this book, especially the clients whom I have coached over the years and the colleagues and human resources professionals with whom I have had many illuminating conversations. Particular thanks go to Martin Travers for his careful and insightful reading of the text and to Ismail Asmall for his advice and support during the formative stages of writing. I'm grateful to Toma Pople for the diagrams in the Prologue. I also want to thank my wife, Helen, for her helpful editing and my children, Frances, James and Patrick for their forbearance and much needed encouragement. Finally, my thanks go to Joanne Forshaw, Susannah Frearson and the entire team at Routledge.

Michael Harvey
London, May 2014

Part 1

What is interactional leadership?

Prologue
The choice-focused leader

What is interactional leadership?

All leaders make choices but not all leaders are choice-focused. The concept of choice-focused, or interactional, leadership is really not complicated. It simply refers to leaders who are sufficiently in touch with reality to act on it effectively. It is the philosophical definition of reality, in all its complex, multiple dimensions and changing forms, which is more of a problem. Perhaps that is why a commonly accepted definition of good leadership has eluded thinkers and practitioners from Plato onwards. So I want to begin this book not with theory but with a concrete situation, which I hope gets to the heart of the real challenges of being a leader.

Carl is the chief executive of an international telecoms company. As we meet him for the first and only time, he is sitting in his luxurious office, high above the glittering River Thames, bright and early one Monday morning. Carl's head is already buzzing with issues. There is a strong rumour of a possible hostile takeover by a long-standing rival, which he dismisses with snort of anger. He ponders whether to give the green light to a major project to develop a new type of mobile phone. This, he hopes will prevent him from having to close down several manufacturing operations throughout the world, which are reporting continuing production problems. Can he obtain the funds from his bankers for the project? He checks the latest interest rates forecast, before reading several emails from irate shareholders urging him to downsize the company, at which he feels a surge of frustration. He thinks about finishing his speech for an industry conference, attended by many City analysts, in which he wants to promote his new vision for online security, and boost his company's sagging share price.

Turning to his diary, Carl sees he has a disciplinary session that morning with his marketing director, who is facing a recurrent bullying complaint. Somewhat uneasily, Carl decides to delegate this meeting to his human resources director. There is a potentially fractious lunch with his chairman and a final interview for a much-needed new finance director. And he sighs, as he realises that he is scheduled to have dinner with an influential customer at the same time as his daughter's school play. He imagines his wife's fury if he misses yet another family event. He glances at his watch: 7.45am. His working week has barely started.

In this snapshot, what I would ask you to notice, first of all, is the sheer range of interactions which frame Carl's world. There are interactions with people, such as his employees, his customers, his shareholders, his chairman and his wife. There are interactions at the level of ideas, as represented by his plans for online security, and material interactions, like potentially closing down factories or creating new products. Carl's financial interactions encompass the entire world economy, as he ponders whether he can afford a huge loan, as do his business interactions, as he dismisses the rumour of a takeover by a multinational rival. And there are also interactions at the more impenetrable levels of knowledge, in terms of what Carl knows and does not know – or prefers not to know.

These interactions make themselves apparent to Carl as matters of interpretation with implications for action. In other words, they enter his consciousness as choices. There are choices about strategic development, choices about funding, about how to respond to frustrated shareholders. There are human resources choices, involving the selection of a crucial leadership team member and perhaps the dismissal of another one. There are personal choices about his values and beliefs (e.g. his resistance to downsizing), which are also influenced by his emotions (his disdain for his putative takeover rivals) and his family relationships. There are choices about delivery, in relation to production hold-ups and to the many people in his company's vast supply chain.

But not all of Carl's choices are fully conscious. There are choices which he seems to be avoiding, such as dealing with his marketing director's problematic behaviour or the reorganization of his overseas factories. And of course, there are always other choices which he might be making but is not. What is certain, is that all these choices are flowing into and through and past Carl's consciousness at a furious pace, in a seemingly continuous present, which has potentially huge implications for the future of many people (not least for Carl himself).

In short, Carl is making – and not making – choices. He is a leader, what else would he do? But is he making balanced, effective choices? The answer, unfortunately, is: no. By the time Carl entered coaching with me, the snapshot, which I have imaginatively reconstructed here from our conversations together, was a distant memory. All that remained of his career was for him to manage a dignified exit from his company.

In our sessions, Carl realised why he had fallen off the leadership tightrope. In part, it was due to his confused strategy in relation to new products and his mishandling of aspects of the production process. He had allowed the failings of his marketing director to go unpunished, which had soured relationships within his management team, and he had done nothing to repair the conflict with his chairman, which had turned a potential ally into a foe. Above all, Carl realised – what everybody knew by then – that he had been too emotional in dismissing the possibility of a takeover by the rival company, because this eventually took place, costing him the job he loved. Carl was highly intelligent, knowledgeable, energetic and even charismatic. But he was not adept at the art of balancing choices. In short, he was not a choice-focused leader.

This book is about the art of choice-focused leadership and how to coach it. It is about helping leaders to manage the interactions of the world they find themselves in so as to bring about positive results. This requires them to be successful in many of their key choices. Former supermarket chief executive Alan Leighton (2012) is probably correct in saying that an effective leader only needs to get 70 per cent of his 'tough calls' right; except, it has to be said, if too many of the 30 per cent he gets wrong are the ones that really matter (which was Carl's fate). Navigating the shifting border that separates success from failure, buffeted by powerful interactions which come at him from every angle (including from within): this is the leader's true challenge. Mastering it requires the exceptional expertise in choice-making that I call interactional leadership.

The dialectic of organizational achievement and psychology: leading in 6D

Interactional leadership theory attempts to generalize about choice-making and the interactional reality in which a leader has to make his or her choices. Some might say this is impossible, a view which the sheer number of theories of leadership which have been produced throughout history might seem to endorse. The multitudinous times and places of leadership certainly complicate a conceptual account of the subject, as do its many different realms in business, the public sector, government, science, religion and the arts. The plenitude of metaphors for leadership sounds another warning. General and servant, symphony conductor and jazz musician, sports coach and circus ringmaster: this is only a tiny sample of the conflicting images of leadership which have been used over the years. Some might even say that the practice of leadership coaching endorses a kind of situational relativism, in that it highlights the uniqueness of a leader's personal and professional context. And yet in spite of this profound diversity, I believe there are some structures and categories which we can use to frame leadership, which makes the tasks involved in practicing and coaching it a little easier. This is certainly the intention of my approach: to provide guidelines for leaders and coaches, while never obscuring the fact that leaders' choices are their own.

At the core of the interactional leadership model is the relationship between two concepts. One is the Achievement Cycle, the combination of strategy, resourcing and delivery which lies behind any successful organizational process. The other construct in this dialectical, dual-core relationship is the Interactional Self, the psychology of the leader, made up through the dynamic relationship of self and others in time, which draws on existential and cognitive psychology and interactional forms of thinking (which I'll say more about in Chapter 3). Constructive interaction between the Achievement Cycle and the Interactional Self produces positive results and a new reality. Two other factors are ubiquitous in this model, which has emerged out of my experience of coaching leaders for the best part of twenty years: the ethical frame of leadership (an extension of general choice-making) and the multirole of leadership.

Fundamentally, interactional leadership amounts to a process of leading in six dimensions (6D), as illustrated in Figures 1 and 2 on the next two pages.

On the left of Figure 1, you will notice the Achievement Cycle, representing the business-based, organizational reality of leadership, on the right, the Interactional Self, which is a philosophically-informed psychology of leadership. The leader's success depends on her ability to fuse these structures together through her choice-making. Figure 2 provides an alternative visualization of exactly the same model, which emphasizes the fluid and dynamic nature of this balancing act. In Chapter 2, I'll say more about the psychology of the balancing art of leadership but first let us turn to the kind of choice awareness involved in becoming an effective leader and the meaning of the Achievement Cycle.

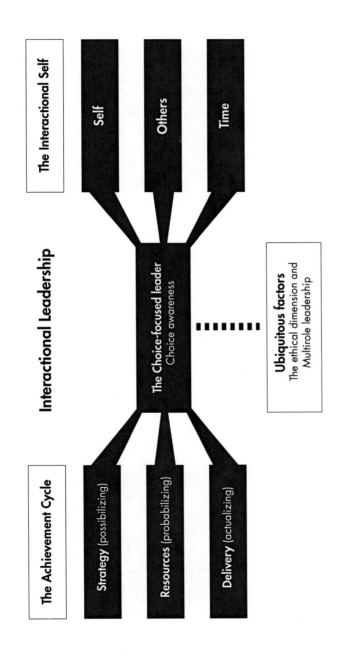

Figure 1 The Interactional Leadership model

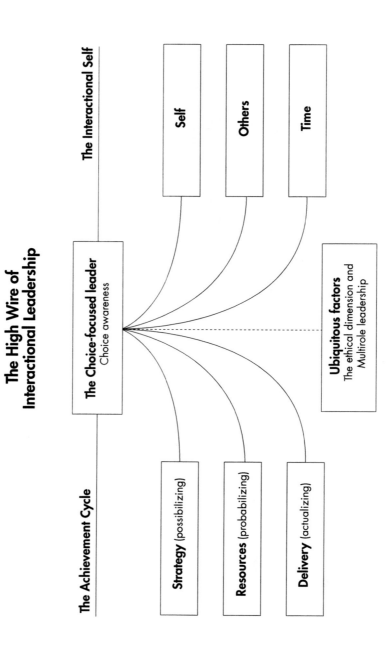

Figure 2 The Interactional Leadership model (High Wire version)

Chapter 1

The Achievement Cycle and the art of leadership choice-making

The hierarchy of choice

Life is about choosing. From the interactional standpoint, we make ourselves through our choices every hour of every day. Existentialist philosopher, Jean-Paul Sartre (1958: 448) expresses this profound idea when he says, 'to be is to choose oneself'. But not all our personal choices are of equal significance. Some are relatively trivial, forgotten almost immediately; others play a major part in determining who are and who we will become. In this latter category are our choices about what we believe in, who we love and want to live with, whether we want to become parents and how we want to earn our living. Nor are all of our choices within our immediate control. We are propelled into the world at a certain time and place which is not of our choosing, with specific familial, social, economic, cultural and biological attributes, but it is up to us what we make of the factors which make us.

In life's hierarchy of choice, leadership has an especially elevated status. In the main, the typical organization is structured around the amount of choice-making freedom its employees are granted. Unskilled workers largely follow routines and timetables which have been chosen for them. Administrative employees have more discretionary power and, as we rise through the organization's executive ranks towards senior management, we find that different degrees of decision-making translate into ever more significant distinctions of power and responsibility.

At the top of the organization, with the greatest range of choices, sits the leader. On behalf of others, she makes choices which can have huge consequences for the lives of many people, perhaps for tens of thousands, in the case of a corporate leader or many more, when it comes to political leaders. These choices not only influence everyday lives but also create the shape of what is to come. In a very real sense, leaders choose the future.

Of course, there is a case in organizations of every kind for redistributing some of these choices down the hierarchy – and at times I'll make that case, because, apart from anything else, it is often in the interest of leaders to do so. But the truth is that we appoint our leaders to make the choices which we cannot make ourselves, partially for practical reasons, and partially, if we are honest, because many of these choices are extraordinarily challenging. As voters, we retain some influence on governmental and public sector polices, and as employees, consumers and shareholders we may have a small say in the direction of corporations. But when the waves of a long economic boom finally crash to the shore, and the decisions of the good times – with their lavishly generous margins of error – give way to the painfully tight decisions of the bad times, we realise just how important these delegated choices really are and how necessary it is to help leaders get them right in the future.

The anatomy of choice

Choice-making is an art not a science. Although the term 'choice science' is increasingly used and scientific studies are giving us more information about this most complex of human activities (as we'll see in Chapter 3), in my view it seems unlikely that choice-making will ever be something that we can completely predict or learn by rote. It will always be intimately bound up with the exigencies of a particular human experience. Nevertheless, choices can be usefully analysed in various ways, in terms of their content (which I call the dimensions of choice), process, method, order and outcome. They can also be seen in terms of degrees of conscious awareness, as it is often prereflective choices, which have not been fully identified by consciousness, that have the most impact.

Possibilizing, probabilizing and actualizing

From an interactional viewpoint, the choice-making process is a three-stage transformation of a possibility into an actuality. The first stage of this cycle, possibilizing, is about stretching the boundaries of the imagination, playing with many options, coming up with wide-ranging creative solutions and using one's imagination to go beyond the status quo. The next stage, probabilizing, is about increasing the likelihood of an idea becoming a reality by making realistic choices, anticipating the resources which are necessary, and devising an action plan that turns the possible into the probable. The final stage, actualizing, is about making the plan happen and doing all that is required to make an idea real. Interactional choice-making therefore involves more than rational decision-making. As philosopher Renata Salecl (2010: 42) says 'the idea of rational choice, transferred from economics, has been glorified as the only choice we have.' In fact, real choices involve emotion as well as thought and are indissolubly linked to action.

The choice cycle has many implications for leaders. For example the leader who is strong at possibilizing may be better at coining bold ideas than at making things happen. The probabilizing leader may shy away from developing adventurous ideas, being too concerned with probabilities to challenge the status quo. He may engage in incremental thinking or what has been termed 'the science of muddling through' (Lindblom, 1959), which can be described as too much probabilizing and not enough possibilizing. Throughout this process, a leader has vital decisions to make about the 'how' of choice-making and the 'who'. Choice-making styles range from a unilateral approach, in which the individual leader has the final say on everything, to a multilateral style, in which the group makes all the decisions that matter.

All this implies another balancing act which the choice-focused leader needs to master, prioritization, or the principle of renunciation. This is the ability to focus on what is truly significant and reject what is not. Spread your attention too evenly across your objectives and you may fail to actualize the most important ones. As Steve Jobs once said: 'Deciding what *not* to do is as important as deciding what to do' (Isaacson 2011: 336).

Choice awareness

Underpinning the art of balancing choice is choice awareness or 'optative awareness', the interactional leader's knowledge of her own values and strongest desires. Optative awareness develops into a strong sense of what works and what doesn't and a feeling for when equipoise in a situation has been reached or has started to come apart. This 'super-reflective' consciousness (Harvey, 2012) involves a high level of attention and bears some similarities to what cognitive psychologist Daniel Kahneman (2011) terms 'slow thinking', which can often see through the rapid biases and short cuts which dominate ordinary consciousness. Choice-focused thinking also includes meta-choices or the ability to choose how to choose. It may feature simultaneous recognition of the forms of decision-making appropriate to a particular decision and the content involved in it. A leader cannot 'have eyes in the back of his head' – as one entrepreneur complained to me during a particularly vicious bout of infighting among his shareholders – but the accomplished choice-focused leader can at times achieve a kind of context-bound 360-degree vision. For this reason, he can rightly be called a virtuoso in choice-making.

The best possible choices are the most informed. Nothing can guarantee a positive outcome but the choice-focused leader engages in processes that are more likely to produce positive outcomes than poor decision-making processes. As human beings, we cannot know what is unknowable in a situation and the role of chance in determining the course of events should never be underestimated. Ineffective leaders do not get every outcome wrong. Sometimes that most precious of leadership attributes, good luck, comes to their aid or the sheer frequency of their poor decisions increases the possibility of a lucky strike. But we should beware of 'the pernicious effects' of hindsight which, as Kahneman reminds us (2011: 203), erroneously leads observers 'to assess the quality of a decision not by whether the process was sound but by whether the outcome was good or bad'. By failing to balance their choices, and by selecting the wrong content, uninteractional leaders increase the likelihood of making unreflective, unconsciously biased decisions, and this significantly raises the probability of poor overall outcomes

The Achievement Cycle

The achievement cycle is the principal theatre in which the choice-focused leader operates. It involves strategy, a future-directed set of possibilities, resources, all that makes more probable the success of that strategy, and delivery, which actualizes it by turning it into an organizational reality. The cycle can be seen as a dialectical opposition between strategy and resources, which enables a leader to produce a new reality. We can call this type of leader, a strategic actualizer, a vision resourcer or a realiser of possibilities. It comes to the same thing: making the right choices throughout the achievement cycle is at the core of interactional leadership.

Strategy: choosing the future

Strategy, the first dimension of the achievement cycle, outlines the way forward for the organization. Through it, the leader taps into the future, creating a path into the unknown which others are invited to follow. This ability to take a clear stance towards the future, to be ahead of the group, even if only by a small distance, is what often marks out a leader. Whether she initiates the strategy herself or facilitates others to do so, she must own it. This is the 'where' stage of leadership – the identification of a destination, a direction of travel. It also involves 'why', the ability to justify one particular destination as opposed to another.

Leaders assume positions of authority through their future designs. These are expressed in the visions, prospectuses, manifestos and business plans, which form the basis on which a leader's subsequent performance will be judged. There will always be an element of subjectivity in our opinion of a leader's strategy, depending on whether we agree or disagree with her intentions. However, some components of a strategy can be evaluated relatively impartially such as its direction, clarity, originality and scope.

'Directional' strategy is often the most clear-cut way in which leaders can be seen to choose the future. John F. Kennedy's audacious decision in 1961 to land a man on the moon within a decade typifies this kind of forward thinking. As psychologist Daniel Gilbert (2007) points out, humans are unique among primates in being able to imagine a future and we spend a fair proportion of each day thinking about it. But leaders do more than think about the future – they act on it. They make the choices which form it, for good or ill. Take Nelson Mandela, who maintained his startlingly clear vision of a multi-racial South Africa for half a century until he achieved his goal, during which time he withstood the opposition of an oppressive apartheid regime and the struggle for supremacy of rival political parties. One of Mandela's fellow prisoners at Robben Island succinctly described the future president's great strength, when he said, 'We couldn't see a future – it was blank. But Mandela always could' (Sampson, 1999: 214). In the corporate sphere, we witness the same uncanny ability to force the future into being in Steve Job's innovations at Apple and Pixar or James Dyson's transformation of dual cyclone technology. It is a facet of choice-focused leadership which we will return to many times.

But directional strategy has its dangers. Mandela's unflinching firmness of conviction cost him 27 long years in prison. He always remained flexible in his outlook but a leadership vision can become ossified and rigid. If your eyes are too tenaciously fixed on the horizon, you can miss the threats and opportunities that are under your nose. Leaders who become too convinced of their own visions and lose touch with the reality of their situations may pay a heavy price.

For this reason, leaders often adopt 'positional' strategies. These involve getting yourself in the right place, at the right time, to find a vision. It requires the ability to recognize opportunities when they present themselves. This can be an exhilarating experience, as one public sector leader explained to me: 'It felt like walking in the old town of a city, full of overhanging buildings, stumbling from one dark street to another. Suddenly you turn a corner and a long vista to the mountains opens up.'

In practice, leaders often combine directional and positional strategies in their strategic portfolio. This can be sensible but it brings with it the danger that your strategy becomes muddled, or too nuanced to allow for forward momentum. Leaders without clear strategies can end up passively following a course simply because it has always been followed or because someone else insists on it. This can lead to 'zombie leadership', based on a failure to choose the future, as we'll see in the case study of a banker in Chapter 6. At the same time, having too much strategy can be as unproductive having too little. The multi-strategizer may place himself in the lap of the gods as much the non-strategizer, his excessive number of goals being only another form of indecisiveness.

The choice-focused strategist learns how to strike the right balance between proaction and reaction. This is important because many of the best corporate strategies actually emerge by mistake, like Honda's historic breakthrough into the US auto market in the 1960s, which has been described as a triumph of 'miscalculation, serendipity and organizational learning' (Pascale, 1984: 51). (It was achieved by means of the 50cc motorcycle which initially Honda's strategists had totally ignored.) Pharmaceutics is another field which abounds with products that were intended for one purpose but achieved success in another, such as Viagra, which was originally developed as a treatment for hypertension. Leaders need to learn to operate in the ambiguous territory between success and failure and not let their creative problem-solving be overwhelmed by it. Knowing when to open up to the possibilities of a strategic change and when to maintain a closed attitude and persevere with the existing vision: this is a vital interaction which the choice-focused leader has to learn to negotiate.

Resources: transforming the possible into the probable

The interaction between a strategy and the resources available for accomplishing it is probably the most important of all the dialectics of achievement. Good resourcing turns a possibility into a probability and increases the chances of positive results. Inadequate resources can cripple a strategy, while inadequate strategizing often squanders the full potential of the resources available. Striking the right balance is crucial.

This resourcing dimension is itself multidimensional, involving many choices. Transforming high-level ideas requires a workable action plan and, almost certainly, appropriate financing. Many promising strategies are brought low by insufficient capital expenditure, stop-start cash flow and uncertainty around future investment. Physical resources may also be necessary in the form of office and manufacturing space, data processing facilities, logistics and communication resources. Licensing agreements, copyright and patents will need to be organized, if they are not to undermine a strategy. I well remember a coaching client whose entire career in charge of a technology company was dogged by a Byzantine patent dispute, worthy of Dickens' Circumlocution Office, which ultimately caused this ambitious innovator to quit his job in frustration. Resourcing of this kind can be an on-going struggle and a vital, if unglamorous, aspect of the leader's role.

Above all, the resourcing stage is about human resourcing. It is people who execute strategies or fail to do so, although the systems in which they are organized play a large part in this. Many of the basic functions of managerial competence are choice-related: delegation, selection, rewarding, promotion, and so on. The leader has to make choices which ensure that the right number of people are available for a project, that they are in the right state of mind and have the technical and interpersonal skills necessary for achievement.

One of a leader's key human resources is her executive team. As we'll see throughout this book, one of the greatest favours a leader can do herself is to form a management team and a board that gives her the best possible synthesis of support and challenge. If the scales are correctly weighted, the quality of the leader's choice-making can be improved; if it is wrong – as it often is – the executive team may be reduced to nothing more than a rubber stamp for the leader's desires.

In the wider organization, corporate culture also plays a role in determining the probability of strategies being put into practice. The choice-focused leader needs to create positive outcomes in this elusive arena, which reflect the choices employees make when not under the direct control of others. Organizational mood, the emotions that motivate or demotivate employees, can also be influenced by a leader's communication and the example she sets, especially in the field of innovation.

Nor is resourcing confined to the boundaries of the organization itself. Social capital, community good will, corporate responsibility and brand reputation: these are all potentially creative or destructive forces for leaderly ambitions. The opposition of a local community, consumer group or section of the media can be enough to severely dent a strategy's chances of success or wreck it altogether. Resourcing is a complex process but one which the interactional leader has to get to grips with. As we'll see repeatedly in this book, it is a stage of the achievement cycle which can topple the most talented leaders.

Delivery: executing the strategy

The final stage of the achievement cycle is about action. In the end, delivering results is always the measure by which a leader is most likely to be judged. 'You can't eat strategy', as former head of Daimler-Benz, Jurgen Schremp, puts it (Vlasic and Stertz, 2000: 381). Delivery is the completion phase of leadership, the 'what' stage which provides the substance of achievement, as an idea is finally transformed into a concrete reality.

If the match between strategy and resources is good enough, the results will follow. As long as a leader continues to monitor the delivery phase, perhaps fine-tuning it from time-to-time, she will reap the rewards of success. If she has created, or inherited, superb operational systems and a high-performance culture, it may look like the results are delivering themselves (although woe betide the leader who starts to believe this!) But what if her strategy and resources don't interact so productively? In this case, she may have to adjust the balance, toning down the objectives to meet with the actual level of resourcers or boosting resources to the level to which it is now apparent that the original strategy requires. Both courses call for determination, agility and sure-footedness under pressure, quite possibly amid criticism from all sides.

Sometimes, however, the problem lies not with the strategy or the resources but the leader's inability to actualize them. This capacity to make things happen is for many people the essence of what defines a leader. I call this 'action focus', the ability to make quick, accurate decisions under intense pressure. Experience often counts here, especially paradigms of past success and failure which enable speedy pattern recognition that confirm or disconfirm a possible course of action. Energy, resolution and leading by example also play a part in action focus. At times, there' is no substitute for the sheer will power a leader needs to overcome organizational inertia. Sometimes crossing the finishing line requires inspirational communication or even a bold declaration of the consequences of repeated failure. It usually means understanding the real motivations of the personnel involved in executing a strategy, as we'll see in the coaching case of Deborah K. (Chapter 7).

Sadly, not every leader reacts to failed delivery by throwing herself into the heart of the action or even by acknowledging the existence of a problem in this area. Some leaders adopt evasive tactics, concealing their poor performance behind a smoke screen of public relations spin. They may blame others in order to divert attention from their own responsibility or manipulate results to buy time. This form of non-delivery opens the door to unethical behaviour and the kind of wrongdoing, with which we have become so familiar this century. In particular, leaders whose strengths are primarily strategic may find it difficult to break out of the realm of the possible and engage with the bedrock of their organizations. But expertise in delivery is always a vital to choice-focused leadership. Combined with strategic and resourcing skills, it enables a leader to 'funnel' from the possible to the actual; drilling down into the reality of his situation to ensure that the achievement cycle is successfully completed.

The breadth of whole-cycle leadership

Effective choice-making throughout the achievement cycle is a continuous process. No sooner has one cycle ended than another begins. In fact, this serial process also occurs in parallel, as many such cycles are usually going on simultaneously, at different stages of completion. Whole-cycle skills enable the choice-focused leader to manage the multiple strata of her situation in what we might call the geology of achievement. That is why the achievement cycle recurs throughout this book, informing many of the aspects and roles of interactional leadership which we will examine. In coaching, leaders often recognize the significance of this construct instantly – it seems to intuitively relate to their experience – but in reality it is only half of the story. Effective choice-making at the top also requires psychological attributes, without which a leader will almost certainly fall from the high wire. It is time to explore the Interactional Self and the part played by the ethical and multirole dimensions in the balancing art of leadership.

Chapter 2

The psychology of interactional leadership and its ethical and multirole dimensions

A leader may be endowed with unusual power and responsibility but she is also a person with unique experiences, beliefs, values, emotions and personality characteristics. Every day, she interacts with other people, who are endowed with the same range of individual differences. These psychological dimensions of leadership are not always obvious to the outside world. Corporate and political leaders often jealously guard their privacy, making it difficult to detect the deep mechanisms by which they make their choices. One of the great advantages of the coach's approach to leadership is that he knows something about this psychological process from the inside. The confidentiality and openness of the coaching relationship enables a leader to reveal emotions, dilemmas, fears and conflicts which the outside world, and even her inner circle of colleagues, may never perceive. Balancing these potentially disruptive personal and interpersonal factors against the demands of the achievement cycle is another challenge for the choice-focused leader.

The interactional self

The idea behind the interactional self is that we define ourselves in relation to the choices we make, consciously and unconsciously, during our interactions with ourselves and others in the dimension of time (Harvey, 2012). In this chapter, we explore how these dimensions influence the leader's choice-making and look at the two additional dimensions which are ubiquitous throughout the six dimensions, the ethical frame of leadership and the multi-role. We also consider the way metaphors can help us to visualize the art of leadership balance.

Self: the personal dimension

At the core of the self are our deepest desires. 'What do you really want?' is a question that takes us to the heart of what it is to be human. The clearer we are about our desires, the easier it is to make choices that involve our values and beliefs. Unacknowledged desires, below the level of reflective thoughts, can bias our judgments, making it difficult to arbitrate between the aspects of a dilemma.

For leaders, dilemmas such as the conflict between an individual and a group, principle and expediency, creativity and profit, are a daily occurrence, which require exceptional clear-sightedness to resolve.

Unconscious biases can also take the form of assumptions about the world which have become so habitual that we are no longer aware of their existence. The insidious limitations of our rationality can also sabotage our choice-making, as we will see in the next chapter. The truth is that complete self-knowledge is never possible. We always remain ambiguous to ourselves, to some degree, but it is vital to continue to make the effort to arrive at the best possible choice. Being able to bring to the surface one's deep-lying thoughts and desires is a crucial aspect of optative awareness.

Our unique emotional patterns also influence our choice-making. Anger, frustration, anxiety or demoralisation can radically distort a leader's ability to frame a decision. Being able to recognize the onset of a bout of irritation or a mood of despondency is a priceless resource. In the drive for leadership, the exceptional qualities which take a leader to the top, and the intense pressure he experiences there, can lead to other psychological problems. One of these is a compulsive attitude to work, which can cause physical and mental exhaustion, as in several cases of high-profile financial leaders in recent times. Depression may also be a factor in the leader's psychology, a condition which it may be hard for him to admit to, or even to recognize, especially if he is weighed down with work.

Personality factors also play their part in influencing the leader's ability to make the right choices, such as resilience, the ability to cope with setbacks, which leaders often have to learn the hard way. Interactionally, personality attributes are viewed in terms of oppositions such as dominance versus supportiveness or confidence versus doubt. Consider the importance of self-confidence. It is often a leader's distinguishing characteristic, enabling her to take an inspiringly decisive stance towards the future, while other people falter or fear the worst about what is to come. Although doubt can be productive if it means questioning the genuinely questionable, failing to display the right amount of confidence at any stage of the achievement cycle can be detrimental to a leader, in the eyes of her followers. On the other hand, no trait is more dangerous than over-confidence. Some leaders' confidence feeds on past achievements to such an extent that they believe that they are capable of anything; worse, they try to shape their organizations so that nobody can effectively challenge this belief.

The hubristic story of Fred Goodwin, the former chief executive of the Royal Bank of Scotland (RBS), exemplifies the way justifiable self-confidence – Goodwin's talent for acquisitions helped to transform a provincial bank into a global financial institution – seems to have turned into a domineering sense of superiority and refusal to tolerate any opposition. This resulted in the disastrous acquisition of debt-riddled Dutch bank ABN Amro and other mistakes, which in 2008 ended Goodwin's career in banking and landed the British taxpayer with a £45 billion bill (Martin, 2013). 'The scale of bad decisions' made in the Goodwin era was still causing multibillion-pound losses six years later, according to one of his successors as CEO (RBS, 2014). Psychological imbalances don't come much more expensive than this.

Others: the interpersonal dimension

The interactional self is also formed by our interactions with others. The leader's interpersonal relationships are crucial to all that he does at work. The choices he makes about who to interact with in an organization, and how to do so, will go a long way to determining the success or failure of his ambitions.

The interactional map

The interpersonal dimension can most easily be defined by a leader's interactional map. This is his real organizational chart, tracing the multiple dimensions of the relationships that matter to him and giving some indication of their positive or negative status. One of the biggest shocks for a new leader is just how extensive this map is. It may feature twenty or more different constituencies or groups of interactors, including the main board, the executive team, the staff, customers, shareholders, regulators, competitors, community representatives and the media. Its complexity can be bewildering, with overlapping, interweaving, multifaceted connections, offering numerous opportunities for unbalanced choices. There are so many people to please but no leader can please them all. 'Don't carry the donkey' is the moral of a fable by Aesop (1998) about the man so susceptible to criticism about his treatment of his mule that he ends up carrying it to market. 'The moment you decide, you divide,' as former prime minister Tony Blair said (2011: 28). And yet incurring the displeasure of those who really matter is the surest way to fail as a leader.

Making and implementing key interpersonal choices takes competence. It means analysing the people around you and deploying the skills of communication, persuasion and networking, which enable you to get the best out of them. These interpersonal skills breathe life into a strategy and often determine whether reciprocal relationships, based on trust, can be established. Suspicious, competitive – even slightly paranoid – leaders often struggle to trust others, which makes it difficult for others to trust them, a negative spiral which is counter-productive at any stage of the achievement cycle.

Distrustfulness makes it difficult to really listen to others. This is a drawback because listening expertise is a resource that choice-focused leaders draw on extensively. It gives them clarity about what is happening in a situation and possible insights as to what should happen next. Nothing frustrates and demoralizes employees more than a leader who, at best, seems highly selective in what he hears. Technically expert, task-focused leaders sometimes struggle most to acquire this type of interpersonal capability, a problem not helped by the widespread assumption that a leader already has all of the skills that he needs to do the top job, otherwise why has he been selected for it in the first place?

The interrelationship between the personal and interpersonal dimensions underlies the psychology of leadership. This dialectic of self and others is crucial to the whole notion of team leadership, governing the way a leader positions herself in relation to group members, as we'll see in two diametrically opposite examples of leaders trying to get the best out of their teams in Chapter 9. In fact, most of the leader's roles on her interactional map can be gauged along the self–others spectrum. The organization as a whole may be a virtual self-projection of the boss, as is often the case with charismatic leaders; or it may have a more distributed structure, in which the leader plays a low-profile role, working behind the scenes to achieve results.

The time dimension of leadership

The third dimension of interactional psychology is time. This fundamental aspect of human reality plays out through many of the stories and concepts in this book. Yet temporality is an underappreciated dimension, in part, because, it is so hard to analyse, or even represent. As Daniel Gilbert (2007: 128) observes, we tend to represent time in the language of place. The past is always 'behind us' and the future 'in front of us', as though they were physical locations. We talk about 'going places' and 'moving forward' or 'backtracking' and 'revisiting the past'. Time lacks its own grammar and vocabulary. In part, this may be because it is simultaneously objective, the regulated time of the clock and the calendar, and subjective, a lived experience. Time as a subjective reality can stretch 'clock time' out of all recognition; dramatically compressing or extending it, according to the intensity of an individual's interaction with the world.

Leadership time is a similar conundrum. Leaders are well acquainted with objective time with its monthly reviews, quarterly results and annual target setting, to say nothing of the almost minute-by-minute scheduling of their working days. But leadership is also a highly subjective experience, and the leader's reaction to a particular set of possibilities or actual events cannot be fully appreciated from the outside. Being in time implies change and change is an integral part of leadership, one which rewards those who can live with it and unsettles those who cannot. In this sense, choice-focused leadership is always a journey rather than the destination (to use another spatially-based metaphor), a set of situational balances, which constantly needs to be refreshed.

Choosing the future, past and present

The balance between the past, present and future is crucial to the psychology of leadership. As I've already suggested, the leader is in many ways defined by her relationship to the future. In a group, she is often the person who feels least daunted by facing the unknown and most comfortable taking responsibility for choices which may define what is to come. This ability to interact with the future though the power of a 'project' (literally a 'throwing forward') marks out a leader in organizational life, as well as in politics, religion, art, and science. It means being able to work in the province of the unknown, evoking or inventing a future that is sufficiently compelling to make others believe that it worth pursuing. This is an exceptional competence which can take the visionary leader towards a perilous ethical frontier, as well as opening the way for outstanding achievement.

Redefining the future also implies a changed interaction with the past. Radical modernizers like Nelson Mandela not only redefine the future, they simultaneously create a quite different interpretation of the past. What for some in South Africa was seen as a process of civilization, Mandela redefined as a history of total injustice; what some saw as inevitable, and even acceptable, he presented as changeable and unacceptable. Of course, not all leaders reinterpret the past so radically or so negatively. Rather than evolving strategies which create breaks with the past, some leaders seek continuity with what has gone before. A readiness to learn from history can help leaders to see through the frenzy of the market and the ephemerality of the latest fad. Nothing better exemplifies the power of tradition than reviving a cherished commercial brand. Even if this is a partially mythical construct, the corporate leader can often be more successful returning to the past than heading for new, unknown territories. But a psychological attachment to the past can also have negative implications. Distressing experiences can inhibit bold choice-making, causing a leader to adopt safety-first strategies which prevent her from capitalizing on positive opportunities. Even past paradigms of success can be damaging if they lead to complacency and a careless disrespect for the future, although they can also facilitate fast, efficient choice-making.

Whether they look forwards or backwards, all a leader's choices have to be made continuously in a present, which often hurtles towards him at a dizzying pace. The sheer volume of choices a leader has to deal with is huge. This meteor storm of decisions requires a velocity of choice-making which can easily throw a chief executive off balance, leading some to believe that it is better to make any decision than no decision at all. Martin Sorrel, CEO of advertising and marketing giant WPP, goes so far as to say that 'The bad decision on Monday is better than a good one on Friday' (Garten, 2001: 147). This is understandable but as with Allan Leighton's (2012) 70/30 ratio of right and wrong choices, it is still exceptionally dangerous to get the important decisions wrong. Recognizing which choices require a greater allocation of time than others is a crucial constituent of the art of leadership.

The ancient Greeks knew all about time and leadership. They distinguished 'chronos', the time of everyday routine, from 'kairos', the time of opportunity and momentous, now-or-never choices. Kairos choices will often make or break a leader's reputation, casting many of her repetitive, diary-filling decisions into the shade. This opportunity-based time is the 'when' of leadership which sometimes trumps the 'where', 'why', 'who' and 'what' of a strategy. After all, timeliness can be everything. Being too far 'ahead of your time' can be as damaging as being 'behind the times'.

Moments of opportunity eventually give way to longer time horizons and it is against these that the leader will ultimately be judged, although on occasion the short term is all there is, especially in a crisis. The ability to focus on the long term in strategy, resourcing and execution is a factor in building companies that 'pass the test of time', as Jerry Collins' (2001) studies suggests, and is an important consideration for the choice-focused leader. It can militate against illusory achievements, such as rewards built on short-term deals or unsustainable levels of credit, and encourage greater depths of civic responsibility.

Different time horizons also play a part in the cross-cultural interpretation of leadership, which is increasingly important in our globalized economy. The long-term orientation of some Asian and Latin American countries contrasts sharply with the more short-term values of Anglo-Saxon cultures (Hofstede *et al.*, 2010), which can be problematic for some global leaders. In the coming years, this temporal factor may increasingly influence decisions around challenges to human society, which require leaders to choose the future more literally than ever before, as we'll see in our final chapter.

Ubiquitous factors: the ethical dimension of leadership

Throughout the achievement cycle and the interactional self, the ethical implications of choice-making are ever-present. Ethics is about choices and, in this sense, is simply an extension of the basic challenge of leadership choice-making. The leader's task is to take account of the moral dimension of her actions, without unduly distorting her responsibilities to the constituencies on her interactional map. To judge by the apparent deterioration in the ethics of leadership in recent years, and increased levels of corporate wrongdoing, this particular balancing act seems to have become more difficult to achieve. This is a theme which I revisit in Chapters 14 and 15, which also provide a fuller account of the ethical principles outlined here.

From the interactional viewpoint, the quality of a leader's engagement with choice is the key to ethical behaviour. This involves considering the implications of his actions on others and across the other interactions which dominate his situation. Open engagement with choice means treating a situation on its merits, being open to its possibilities, rather than being closed in advance. Engaging with choice implies ambiguity. Significant decisions are rarely black and white. If they consistently appear to be so, it could suggest that something has gone awry in the choice-making process and that it is being driven by biased assumptions, unanalysed emotions or a false consensus. Perceiving the subtle nuances, complex ramifications and sheer slipperiness of a major choice suggests that a real engagement with a real situation is taking place. In fact, ambiguity may be one of the few reliable indicators we have that the full implications of a choice are being considered.

Respecting freedom of choice

Genuine engagement with choice also implies avoiding actions which close down other people's freedom to make choices. This principle of freedom leads to a respect for openness and a rejection of the manipulative, intimidating and violent behaviour which forces people to make choices against their best interests. It opposes discrimination, which involves making choices based on prejudgments about ethnicity, sexuality or gender, which can deprive a person of a fair and free chance to be who he is. This closing down of options even limits the possibilities of the discriminator, because he is deprived of the benefits of a free relationship, as Hegel's (1931) famous philosophical account of the master and slave first demonstrated. States of deception, which ethical impropriety brings about, also deprive people of the freedom to make informed choices, as they distort the information necessary to do so.

Taking responsibility for choices

The outcomes of choices cannot be guaranteed but choices still need to be owned. This is why a leader should try to make her decisions as informed as possible in the first place and prevent choices from being foisted on her. Taking moral responsibility involves a closed attitude, not an opening up to the possibilities of evasion, but acceptance of the consequences of what one has freely chosen. Here the dialectic of the open and the closed, which runs through all human choice-making, switches sides: where it was right to be open now it is wrong. Over the past few years, we have become accustomed to a different pattern, as political and corporate leaders try to disconnect themselves from their choices, blaming their subordinates or pleading ignorance. We've also seen the startling rise of 'the amnesia defence': 'I can't remember' becoming a familiar phrase from leaders unwilling to explain the rationale behind the bad decisions taken on their watch.

Authenticity

An ethical stance to leadership implies what Martin Heidegger (1962) called authenticity. I interpret this as an open attitude to experience which translates into a resolution to act and the courage to take responsibility for one's actions. The interactional leader is authentic in so far as he strives to find the right balance between self and others, standing up for himself but not standing on others, thinking of others but not losing himself. As Sartre (1958) stresses through his notion of 'bad faith', authenticity is not a final state but something to strive for; it is a goal of taking full responsibility for oneself and one's situation which will always be partially elusive.

Authenticity is integrity under conditions of high uncertainty. This is not to say that the choice-focused leader's presence has an easy-to-read consistency or predictability. Leadership theorists who privilege the term 'authenticity' often stress the unexpected side of a leader's personal impact. Goffee and Jones (2006) argue that successful leaders show some of their weaknesses to their followers, as this emphasizes their humanity. Jerry Collins (2001) finds that effective corporate leaders, who achieve long-term growth and above-average profitability, are not necessarily flashily charismatic. On the contrary, they are 'humble' and low-key and you probably have never heard of them.

In other words, authenticity does not imply a simple, undialectical relationship to the truth, as might be implied by the phrase. 'My leader says exactly what he or she means'. To my mind, this item from the Authenticity Leadership Questionnaire (Avolio *et al.*, 2009) is right on the mark if it means explicit promises should be kept. But it is too rigidly simplistic if it implies that a leader never experiences ambiguity nor privately disagrees with measures which he outwardly champions. It condemns to hypocrisy, the leader who, like all of us, must regularly tell 'white lies' in the interests of interpersonal harmony. Authentic leadership is not about escaping into a pure moral world beyond contradiction; it is about living with the conflicting interactions of reality and trying to make the most of them.

Ubiquitous factors: the multirole dimension

Ambiguity is also present in the basic functionality of leadership in that the leader is more than a team leader. She has a multirole dimension to her job, a dense network of relationships which extends well beyond her interactions with her direct reports, important as these are. In fact, leadership is not so much a role as an entire cast of roles, several of which may be in competition with each other. Nor are all a boss's relationships with subordinates or peers. Her interactional map often reveals a surprisingly large number of upward relationships, people to whom she reports, in effect, such as a group chief executive or president, a chairman or a major shareholder. In short, the boss usually has bosses.

Only some of the different functions and responsibilities of a leader's role are likely to be specified in his job description. Many he has to discover for himself. One coachee told me, 'I feel that I'm doing at least four jobs at the same time. Trouble is, I only know how to do one of them.' He was chief executive, acting financial director, managing director of a subsidiary and head of a project making far-reaching decisions on his company's information technology. These functions were in addition to the roles implicit in his CEO job; such as team leader, thought leader, board leader, domestic and global leader, and entrepreneurial leader. Learning how to balance the very different levels of knowledge and responsibility within all these roles became the major theme of our coaching.

The CEO role is like a Chinese cabinet, consisting of boxes within boxes. One of these may be technical leadership, since in many industry sectors specialist expertise is a sine qua non for the top job. But the multirole poses particular hazards for the subject matter expert. Such leaders are often uncomfortable in roles where they lack detailed knowledge and instead of dealing with this challenge openly, they adopt evasive or blustering tactics which frustrate and confuse their technically expert subordinates. This problem appears to account for another of Fred Goodwin's shortcomings – to return to this cautionary tale – his complete inability to manage RBS's highly risky investment banking division, an area he knew little about. As a fellow executive said of him, 'He always has to come top in everything he does. If he's not in complete control and command of something he would rather avoid it' (Martin, 2013: 203).

Communication leadership is another vital role within a role. For the leader of the large organization with tens of thousands of employees, 99 per cent of her staff will probably never have face-time with her. How she communicates with them will significantly influence their impression of her and their willingness to commit themselves to her cause. As a team leader, the boss has an important developmental role, as well as a specific responsibility to select and support the executive who will succeed her (not a role which every leader revels in). In addition, she may have an important role in leading projects within a particular industry or community or on the international stage.

These multiple roles are not components of every leadership role, of course. Not every action leader will be a thought leader, not every domestic leader has a global role or even an entrepreneurial side to his responsibilities. These roles are important varieties of leadership in their own right, as well as serving as significant stepping stones on the way to the top job. That is why I have organized the case studies in this book so that we can examine the plurality of functions involved in a single leadership role in Part 2 and then in Part 3 explore the unique dynamics of more specific roles. There we will also encounter the difficulties of transitioning between roles, which often involves rapidly learning new skills and decisively renouncing old ones. The trickiness of this balancing act can unsettle even the most gifted leader. She has to rely on past roles, to some extent, because these are probably what got her the job in the first place. But the values and skills, which she has learned in different organizations, industries or eras, may turn out to be more of a hindrance than a help in her present role.

The balancing art of the choice-focused leader

Finally, in our exploration of interactional leadership, I want to see how metaphorical thinking can help us to experientially describe this complex equipoise of choices, in which achievement has to be squared with interactional psychology and ethics with multiple roles. There are many metaphors for leadership, as I've already indicated, and they can be useful because they represent what people intuitively value in leaders. Some metaphors stress the visionary, future-oriented aspect of the role, as a guide, a beacon, a lighthouse; others, such as the conductor, the field marshall, or ring master, evoke the multirole and the idea of harmoniously coordinating multiple activities.

The realm of the visionary juggler

Many metaphors emphasize the balancing role of the leader, such as the helmsman, battling with the elements to stay on course. A striking version of this is Homer's Odysseus, steering between Scylla and Charybdis, perhaps the first representation of a secular leader in Western culture; a wily, resourceful, multi-role shape-shifter who never departs from his goal of reaching home, whatever the world throws at him (Hampden-Turner, 1990). The balancing metaphor I have favoured in this book is that of tightrope walker, which implies adventurousness, audacity, and a sense of risk, as embodied by Philippe Petit's (2003) epic high wire crossing of the twin towers of the World Trade Centre in 1974. 'Life is on the wire, the rest is just waiting,' declared another legendary funambulist, Karl Wallenda, and, in spirit, many leaders would surely agree with him. The high wire artist has to negotiate two types of movement: moving forward in order to reach the far side of the wire, and staying upright, which means balancing the gravitational forces which threaten to plunge him into the abyss. This double movement is also captured in the phrase, 'the visionary juggler', which implies finding a way forward amid the constant need to keep many factors in play.

If balance is risky, it also implies an intuitive sense of rightness. 'Getting the balance right' is a consensus-creating statement which can often bring a dispute about extremes to an amicable conclusion. It is not a bad summary of the goal of the choice-focused leader either, indicating his challenge in dealing with a huge range of interactions in many different dimensions, which in the business world, ultimately finds expression in the hard currency of that most demanding measure of equilibrium: the balance sheet.

But balance is more ambiguous, and even paradoxical, than it seems. 'Which is heavier a pound of lead or a pound of feathers?' is a playground teaser which jestingly reminds us that balance is not the static, commonplace state of being which we often take it for. On the contrary, it is dynamic, complex, and often emphatically counter-intuitive, a weighing up of apparently qualitatively different factors which need to be combined to reach a practical state of equilibrium. Balance is a unity of opposites. It does not eliminate the differences between opposing forces but it brings them into a workable relationship, which can be highly productive.

The dialectics of change

In fact, balance is always about change. It is not just about preventing yourself from falling down. At its best, it denotes transformation, as captured by other leadership metaphors, such as the magician or the alchemist, striving to turn base metal into gold. The art of balance can transform negative oppositions into positive outcomes. Whether creating innovations, which transform people's lives, building teams, which bring out hitherto unexpected qualities in its members, or turning around organizations in crisis, the interactional leader is at her best in the dialectics of change. Developed philosophically by Hegel (1931), dialectics can be interpreted as a theory of change, which shows how opposites can be transformed into something new, a subject we delve into a little deeper in the next chapter.

For now, it is enough to remind the reader that the 6D elements which we have reviewed, including the achievement cycle, the interactional self, the ethical and multirole dimensions of leadership and metaphors of balance, all have a single aim. This is to describe the complex process by which a leader endeavours to make the best possible choices for his organization, in order that a coach may better help him to do so.

Chapter 3

The psychology and neuroscience of choice and the philosophy of interactional leadership

What else is necessary to understand the background to the practice of interactional leadership coaching? Before moving on to detailed case studies in Part 2, I believe it will help the reader if I touch on three intellectual disciplines. First, I want to look at some extraordinary neuroscientific and psychological research into human choice-making and see what it reveals about what leaders are up against. Second, I would like to show how interactional philosophers have anticipated many of these empirical findings in their account of reality as an experiential totality, in which contradiction plays a surprisingly positive role. Finally, I move on to the discipline of leadership studies and suggest that interactional leadership's holistic and inclusive stance enables it to bring together some of the competing theories in this important field.

The psychology and neuroscience of choice: what are leaders up against?

Recent research by psychologists and neuroscientists into the way the human brain makes decisions contains much that is startlingly new, although psychologist Barry Schwarz clearly echoes interactional thinkers like Kierkegaard and Sartre, when he says 'Existence, at least human existence, is defined by the choices people make.' (Schwartz, 2004: 42). The existentialist emphasis on importance of the future is also paralleled by neuroscientific studies. As Gilbert (2007: 5) confirms, 'The greatest achievement of the human brain is its ability to imagine objects and episodes that do not exist in the realm of the real, and it is this ability that enables us to think about the future.'

The interaction of reason and emotion in decision-making

The intense interaction between rationality and feeling is one of the most striking findings of recent research into human choice-making. Our prefrontal cortex is the seat of amazing reasoning ability but it is surprisingly limited is some ways. For example, our brains never seem to quite grasp the fact that an article priced at £19.99 is not in any meaningful way cheaper than a £20.00 item (hence the substantial amount of resources retailers spend on pricing goods in this way). We are susceptible to other errors in reasoning, such as the 'availability' heuristic identified by Tversky and Kahneman (1974), which suggests that in framing a choice we are disproportionately influenced by information that is easy to imagine or well-publicized. For example, we tend to rate the chances of death by air crash as much higher than death by domestic accident, although the statistics tell the opposite story.

Emotions can also interfere with our reasoning. For instance, stress can easily distort our judgment. In coaching, it is not uncommon for a coachee who is under pressure or facing a crisis to seem to lose his ability to make simple decisions, as though his IQ score had suddenly dropped dramatically. Anger, inflaming the amgydala area in the brain, can have the same mind-altering effect. Yet emotions are crucial to human decision-making. Extraordinary evidence for this came in the form of Elliot, a patient studied by neuroscientist Antonio Damasio (2006). Elliot had suffered a major injury to part of his emotional brain but his mental faculties were judged to be intact. Undistracted by emotion, some might think Elliot would have been capable of flawless decision-making but, in fact, he was unable to make even simple choices. Every day, he was defeated by decisions which most of us would take for granted, and this made it impossible for him to hold down a job, or, in the end, pursue an independent life.

This kind of case is revolutionary in its implications. As Damasio suggests in his aptly-titled book *Descartes' Error* (1994), Western thinkers and scientists have for centuries overestimated the rational power of the brain. Descartes' (2008) cogito – 'I think therefore I am', first formulated in 1637, has become the cornerstone of Western rationalist thinking. And yet without the emotional brain effective decision-making seems to be impossible. In many cases, our feelings actually enable us to make choices faster and more accurately than rational deliberation, especially when it comes to matters of taste (Wilson and Schooler, 1991). And intuition often leads to better decisions under extreme pressure than painstaking analysis, as Gary Klein (1999) demonstrates in his fascinating studies of firefighters and radar operators.

Interaction of positive and negative aspects of choice

Another interaction we find it difficult to balance is the relationship between the positive and negative interpretations of a choice. Positive emotions can improve choice-making, as under their sway we seem to consider a greater range of possibilities (Schwartz 2004: 132), a finding that has important implications for the possibilizing phase of the choice cycle. But in a positive frame of mind we are also inclined to overemphasize the chances of success. A negative outlook also creates distortions. In one experiment, most respondents answered affirmatively when asked if they would opt for a (hypothetical) surgical operation in which they had an 80 per cent chance of surviving but far fewer said 'yes' when asked if they would decide to have the same operation, if it entailed a 20 per cent chance of dying (McNeil *et al.*, 1982). For many people, seeing the identical situation from both sides produces quite different conclusions. Like the ambiguous figures of Gestalt psychology, where a vase turns into a face and back again, these subtle reversals show just how slippery choice can be.

Another negative phenomenon is 'loss aversion' (Kahneman, 2011), which can make us cautious and excessively risk-averse in our decision-making. In choice cycle terms, it seems to induce probabilizing before we have fully possibilized a set of options. Our dread of loss also shows up in relation to 'sunk costs'. One study found that equity investors consistently opt to sell stocks that have risen in value rather than ones that have lost money, potentially resulting in a portfolio entirely made up of depreciating shares (Odean, 1998). This reluctance to confirm a loss perhaps explains why failing projects in business and the public sector are often allowed to run up huge costs before anyone has the courage to terminate them.

Reversible decisions seem to be another source of dissatisfaction. Maybe because they are too easy to go back on, they feel like a cop out. Bold choices seem to give more satisfaction, although of course they are riskier. In fact, the choices we appear to regret most are ones we don't make, a phenomenon called 'omission bias' (Schwartz, 2004: 148). Yet, in findings which have a huge significance for leaders, it seems that we adopt quite different rules for macro-choices than for micro-choices. Simple guidelines learned from experience often fly out of the window when we are presented with major decisions. In these circumstances, we seem to search for a much higher level of evidence than usual which, paradoxically, can lead us to ignore obvious cues. This fallibility has clear relevance for leadership choices – and for the role of coaching in helping to improve them. For instance, it may explain why when it comes to game-changing mergers and acquisitions, leaders sometimes forgo the strict due diligence their organizations would routinely use when making relatively trivial decisions and as a result end up losing vast amounts of value for their companies.

Choice avoidance

Given these challenges, it is not surprising that humans should be prone to avoiding choice-making altogether. 'The tyranny of choice' (Salecl, 2010) has become a recognized feature of consumer society. After all, how can you make the best possible selection between 100 breakfast cereals in a supermarket? Against the expectations of rational choice economists, who argue that the more options we have the better, too many alternatives can in fact lead to a psychological reduction of choice. In this 'inversion of choice', as Edward Rosenthal (2005: 40) calls it, 'too much choice can equal none at all'. Offered a dazzling array of options, we may decide to act arbitrarily or impulsively, without thinking. Or we may make 'prechoices', where we mechanically rely on habitual patterns, which prevent us from considering the real merits of the options on offer.

The tyranny of choice has obvious implications for strategizing, explaining why some leaders prefer to stick with imperfect strategies rather than open up a Pandora's Box of new options. Conflicting choices can lead to indecision. I remember one coaching client who would become very distracted if presented with too many alternatives and only gradually learned to deal with a full range of options. Political leaders can also be affected by an abundance of choice. US president Ronald Reagan was said to become 'angry and depressed' if presented with conflicting options (Schafer and Crichlow, 2010: 20). Part of the conflict is in the conditional tense, as 'what if' choices can make it harder to focus on real choices. Opportunity costs – what you have to give up in order to accept something else – can also enormously complicate choice-making, yet another confirmation, if one were needed, that arriving at the best possible decision is no easy task for a leader.

Methods of choice-making

What strategies do choice scientists recommend? Needless to say, there is no magic formula for getting your decisions right. Weighing-up the pros and cons of a choice is one of the most popular, a balancing act which many people try to employ. This 'decisional balance sheet' (Janis and Mann, 1977: 135) can become very sophisticated but techniques which take too literally Benjamin Franklin's description of it as 'moral or prudential algebra' run the risk of shifting responsibility away from the chooser.

Barry Schwartz (2004) recommends avoiding 'maximizing' or trying too hard to get every choice right. Choosing what to choose and what not to choose is preferable, in his eyes, which takes us back to the meta-level of choice I've described as an aspect of choice virtuosity. Knowing when to go with gut feeling is another facet of optative awareness, which often involves the use of time, deciding when a choice needs to be given a generous amount of analysis, and when a more instantaneous decision is called for. Involving the group in decision-making offers an even wider-range of strategies and is clearly relevant for leaders operating within multiple group contexts. Democratic voting or consensus-hunting (trying to get the agreement of the entire group) are two options. Another is consultative decision-making in which group members reflect on and record their thinking about a choice before engaging in a group debate, so as to minimize the influence of personal inhibition and dominating individuals.

Varieties of choice

The most celebrated types of leadership choice tend to be bold, adventurous forays into the unknown against a horizon of endless possibilities. But in reality many decisions are narrow and even vice-like in their restrictions. These choices resemble straitjackets, which require the skills of an escapologist to get out of, to add another image to our metaphors of leadership balance. The lesser of two evils is frequently the real choice facing a leader, a matter of settling for the least bad option, which may involve identifying the constituencies on your interactional map you can least afford to displease. The 'mirage choice' often hovers on the leader's horizon, as a seemingly free play of options turn out to be nothing of the sort, as in Hobson's choice, which boils down to just one set of alternatives: take it or leave it! Morton's fork is another long-standing mirage choice, similar to Catch-22, in which two seeming alternatives result in the same conclusion. Another difficult dilemma is the U-turn, which implies a high degree of inconsistency with a past policy, and is a variation on the cut-your-losses choice in that it gets more difficult as the stakes get higher.

Avoiding choice and evading it

All of this provides further explanation why leaders sometimes seek to release themselves from the crushing grip of difficult choices by irresponsibly delegating decision-making to others or making easily reversible choices. Some leaders engage in complex, multilayered 'parallel choices'. These may be legitimate methods for hedging a bet and providing effective insurance for wrong outcomes, or they may be examples of bad faith, ways in which a leader seeks to absolve himself of the responsibility for his choices. This is not to say that choice avoidance is never justified, as often a chief executive may genuinely need to buy herself more time. But choice evasion is another matter. Postponement tactics, which amount to 'kicking the can down the road' or the practice of employing external consultants for the sole purpose of pinning responsibility for a decision on somebody else, fall into the category of evasion. In truth, these deliberately prevaricated decisions are often non-choices and these can be the most influential leadership choices of all. Non-choices provide the clearest distinction of all between the choice-focused leader, who fully engages with the choices in his world, and ineffective leader, who tries to evade them.

The philosophical background of interactional leadership

The picture of human choice-making which emerges from this psychological and neuroscientific review suggests a dynamic, holistic, interactional process, which sometimes can be so challenging that we try to resist engaging in it at all. The brain, it seems, is in a constant state of dialogue with itself, engaging in an often raucous debate between competing voices, which somehow has to be managed. These findings carry an important philosophical message, namely that the excessive respect for rationality which has dominated Western thinking since Descartes has produced a seriously unbalanced view of reality. Philosophically, precisely this point has been made since the beginning of the nineteenth century by existential, phenomenological and dialectical philosophers such as Hegel, Kierkegaard, Heidegger and Sartre. This tradition of interactional thinking, which should be seen as a way of making sense of the world rather than a formal system, can provides an invaluable conceptual framework for understanding the multidimensional world of leadership.

I am not a philosopher, so I must precede cautiously here but, as I see it, interactional thinkers put forward a model of reality which conceives it as a dynamic process in which apparent opposites, such as subjectivity and objectivity, reason and emotion, the individual and society, are constantly interacting. The art of balance was first explored philosophically by Hegel, who insisted that there must be an interaction, or dialectical relationship, between the subject and object of thought. This may sound abstruse but it was his response to Kant's (1997) immensely influential, rationalist assertion that there is an insuperable barrier between human subjectivity and the objective world. According to Kant, we can learn about the phenomenal world and the categories of human mind, such as space and time and causality, but noumena, or things-in-themselves, can only be inferred. Now one thing we know about balance is that it is impossible to balance something on its own. Likewise, the subject presupposes an object which shapes and defines it, even if it cannot be fully known. The human mind cannot be staring into empty space. Or, as Sartre (1947: 33) says in characterizing the contribution of phenomenologist Edmund Husserl, 'all consciousness is consciousness of something'.

How does interactional thinking seek to come up with insights which elude the rationalist model? Instead of taking pure thought as the starting point for their investigations (aided by traditional logic or mathematics), existential thinkers start by examining their own experience of the world and draw conclusions from this. As Sartre (1948) famously said, 'existence precedes essence', implying that our experience of the world needs to take precedence over dogmatic, 'essentialist' interpretations of reality, which try to preordain what it is. For interactional thinkers, personal experience is not a poor substitute for scientific observation or rational calculation but a fundamental resource for understanding reality. If this reality turns out to be ambiguous and changeable, so be it: the hard-to-categorize stuff of human life is what interactional thinkers take as their subject matter.

Experiential analysis reveals, for example, the way our point of view changes the meaning of the external world. For example, the office which is entered by a young employee in her first day at work, an interior designer with a new commission and a chief executive with cost-cutting plans will look quite different to each, although objectively, in every detail, it is identical. Focusing on subjective experience leads us to grasp the importance of time, especially our projection towards the future. And it produces a very a different attitude to the concept of contradiction, which lies at the heart of conventional, rationalist thinking.

The law of non-contradiction

The basic law of non-contradiction was summed-up by the seventeenth-century philosopher John Locke (1997: 60) when he said, 'it is impossible for the same thing to be, and not to be'. In other words, A excludes B. Either A is true or B is true but both cannot be. For example, the statement 'it is light now' cannot be true if the statement 'it is dark now' is also correct. At one level, this is plainly true, but how does this rationalist proposition stand up to the litmus test of experience? Both statements can be simultaneously true if we see one as a description of objective light conditions and the other as expression of a person's sombre mood or anticipation of a negative event. If we add the time factor, we might read these statements as describing the transition from day to night or as a movement through a partially shuttered room. What seems certain is that these terms are relative to each other. We cannot understand what we mean by 'light' in this context unless we know the significance of 'dark'.

If A and B depend on each other for their meaning, neither can be totally excluded from the truth. Hegel (1975) demonstrates this neatly when he opposes Being and Nothing. According to the laws of non-contradiction, 'Nothing' has no value here; its 'claim to truth' is non-existent. But how can we really understand 'being' without reference to what it is not, 'non-being'? For example, as Heidegger (1962) pointed out, it is the permanent possibility of our death that frames, and gives meaning to, life. To dismiss as meaningless one term in a pair of opposites is like eliminating zero from the endless sequence of interacting zeros and ones, which forms the basis of our digital world. Hegel, of course, puts it slightly differently: 'The truth of Being and Nothing is the unity of the two: and this unity is Becoming' (1975: 128). In short, by seeing opposites as mutually inclusive realities we can experientially bring them to life, as it were, and this animation enables us to move towards a possible resolution.

Oppositional logic

This idea that truth is to be found in the totality of experience and the dynamic relationships this discloses, I refer to as oppositional logic. It implies that contradiction is not the enemy of truth but its ally, which is why Hegel (1975: 174) says 'everything is opposite' and 'contradiction is the very moving principle of the world'. Similarly, against the conventional view that 'it is impossible for the same thing to be and not to be', Sartre (1958) defines the human being as precisely that, the being who is and who is not. This is not a play on words but an expression of the fact that we can only truly define a person by reference to the combination of differences he embodies, for instance, his different moods, traits, talents and relationships. He is both his past, which he carries with him at all times, but he is also his future; what he is aiming to be. He is both a unique individual and a representative of something else, a family perhaps, a profession, an organization, a culture, a nation, a historical epoch, and so on. In short, he is what he is not.

What this revelation about the value of negativity enables us to do, paradoxically, is to appreciate both the positive and negative aspects of any situation, rather than completely dismissing one aspect of it. This opens up the possibility of dramatic reconciliation, breakthrough and synthesis. So whereas Karl Popper (1963) uses his criterion of falsifiablity to dismiss psychoanalysis as a 'pseudoscience', incapable of making any truth claims, Sartre (1958) seeks to recuperate Freud's startling insights into human behaviour by placing them in a constructive, conceptual framework, which moves beyond Freud's rigid, dualistic barrier between conscious and unconscious thoughts.

Oppositional logic is inclusive rather than exclusionary, inquiring rather than dismissive, and so can capture the multi-faceted nature of reality in surprising ways. Take the notion of anxiety, which conventional, 'abnormal' psychology sees as a negative state, the symptoms of which need to be eliminated as far as possible. For an interactional thinker like Kierkegaard (1980), anxiety may have negative aspects but it also has a positive side, alerting us to our responsibilities for making choices without guarantees and our ability to imagine possible futures – some of our strongest human qualities. Or think back to my metaphor of the high-wire walker: he doesn't ignore the dynamics that pull him this way and that, as he sways above the abyss; if he did he would crash to the ground. Instead, he cunningly uses his balancing pole to play off one gravitational force against the other.

The implications for choice-making

Of course, when it comes to finalizing a choice we have to exclude one or other option. But from the interactional point of view, this is only a temporary release from the world of contradiction and ambiguity. When the next choice comes, as come it will, it is back to dealing with the relentless play of opposites, taking all on their merits, and trying to achieve the right balance for a unique situation. One of the problems with rationalist thinking is that it produces dualisms, in which one oppositional term is always superior to another. So 'reason' becomes permanently superior to 'emotion' or 'the individual' to 'society'. This distorts the open-minded information search which precedes good choice-making and biases the final outcome. It also tends to sever the part from the whole, which is why interactional thinking insists that the totality of a situation can only be found in the pattern of interconnections which leads from one part to another. In this way reality is seen holistically, as a process of change, existing in time, and always moving towards new sets of interactions. In the end, this is the true meaning of the term 'interactional'.

The certainty snare

A final danger for rationalist thinking lies in overestimating the degree of certainty available in human affairs. Kant's ethics (2012) is explicitly based on a claim to have devised moral imperatives which are non-contradictory, absolute and universalisable, i.e. good for all situations. Of course, adrift in a sea of ambiguous values, we all long for the life raft of certainty. Indeed, the ability to convey reassurance in unsure circumstances is a prime asset of leaders. However, it is one which they themselves can be deceived by. It is easy to get trapped in

36   What is interactional leadership?

what I call 'the certainty snare', an uncritical belief in one's capacity to definitively interpret situations and to forecast the future with absolute precision. Winston Churchill once ironically defined this as the politician's main gift, namely, 'The ability to foretell what is going to happen tomorrow, next week, next month, and next year – and to have the ability afterwards to explain why it didn't happen.'(quoted in Langworth, 2008: 489). Many political, corporate and thought leaders were caught in the certainty snare before 2008, failing to notice the stealthy approach of one of the worst economic downturns in history.

A new synthesis between leadership theories?

Finally, let's briefly consider the implications of interactional thinking for other leadership theories. As it is based on a philosophically-informed psychology, which focuses on the central human activity of choice-making, I believe the interactional model may be able to form a useful bridge between some of the theories, which have dominated the discipline of leadership studies since 1945.

For example, the interactional approach can provide a link between rationalist models, which see decision-making as the principle function of a leader, and emotional intelligence models of leadership. Once we view emotion and reason, not as irreconcilable opposites, but as elements in the same experiential continuum, we can add an emotional dimension to an approach such as Vroom and Jago's (1988) normative model of leadership. This heroic study of choice-making attempts to classify all the situations in which a leader takes decisions but it is ultimately too abstract, complicated and mechanistic to be useful. In fact, it exemplifies the type of dry rationalism that in the 1990s provoked a movement to the opposite theoretical extreme, which focuses on the leader's emotional self-management and empathetic interpersonal skills (e.g. Goleman *et al.*, 2002). The interactional model could make it possible to appreciate the immense value of a leader's emotional brain, without obliging us to see this as a self-sufficient alternative to the pre-frontal cortex, the seat of human problem-solving ability and perception of the future. A new balance between IQ and 'EQ' is certainly needed.

Interactional leadership also aims to break down the barriers which separate business and psychological approaches to leadership. For instance, the interactional approach has much in common with whole-cycle leadership theories, such as Dotlich, Cairo and Rhinesmith's (2006) 'Head, Heart and Guts' model of 'complete leadership' and Bossidy and Charan's (2009) execution-focused account of the all-round leader. These theories emerge from real business experience and practical analysis. They recognize the multirole character of the leader and provide perceptive analysis of the interaction between different stages of the achievement cycle. In the same category, we can place empirical studies of 'what leaders actually do', such as Henry Mintzberg's (1990) account, or John Cotter's (1996) examination of the practical difficulties of leading change. However, insightful as they are, none of these approaches does full justice to the psychological dimensions of leadership, in my view. I would also argue that the philosophical basis of the interactional focus on multidimensional choice-making as the core leadership activity offers potentially richer and more explanatory interconnections than are available to self-contained empirical approaches.

A third area of possible constructive synthesis relates to the model of the leader as an agent of change. Burns's (1978) brilliant construct of the 'transformational leader', highlights the fundamental change which some leaders can bring about and has inspired many theories. But as Gary Yukl (2002: 262) points out this concept ignores too many other factors about the leader's interactions, such as group process and her relationship with the outside world. For me, the model also creates an over-simplistic, dualistic, opposition between the transformational leader who appeals to his followers' higher interests and the transactional leaders who only engages his followers' self-interest. Once we understand the realties of the resourcing phase of the achievement cycle, and the complexity of the self–others dialectic, I think we can see that many types of influencing are necessary for a leader to actualize his vision.

The interactional focus on choice may also make it easier to integrate an ethical perspective into mainstream leadership theory. Some specialized ethical models, such as 'servant leadership' (Greenleaf, 1977), in my opinion, go too far in separating the leader's ethical role from his achievement responsibilities. As laudable as this focus may be, it potentially sets the bar too high for many leaders and makes it easier for some of them to reject ethics altogether. The multirole perspective enables us to see that the leader has many constituents to serve and that focusing exclusively on his 'dyadic' relationship with his followers runs the risk of confusing the part with the whole.

Finally, an approach which prioritizes the principle of interaction in our understanding of the world can help us to balance objective and subjective approaches to leadership. Although the 'great man' theory of leadership has long been debunked, as have other attempts to argue that one form of leadership is superior to all others, this need not leave us with a myriad of purely contingent models. The achievement cycle can offer a measure of objectivity, by providing a framework for judging a leader in terms of his ability to put his strategy into practice. This, however, needs to be integrated with the subjective element in our evaluation of leadership, as our interpretation of a leader's intentions is always likely to colour our assessment of his performance. In some cases, it may even cause us to prefer the heroic failure to the villainous success. In the end, the subjective point of view of the observer is ineradicable in matters of leadership, not least because the observer is a potential follower, without whom no leader can exist. In organizations, as in democracies, this mutually-defining relationship should not be forgotten. With this in mind, we can now come down from the airy heights of theory to the terra firma of practical leadership coaching and a particularly challenging assignment.

Part 2

Coaching the choice-focused leader

Interactional leadership coaching in practice

Chapter 4

Coaching the non-resourcing leader

'Dracula' in the boardroom: the case of Blake S.

In Part 2, we shift from theory to practice, examining in depth three leaders who are challenged in different phases of the achievement cycle, as well as by various psychological issues. In Chapter 6, we encounter Arjun, who lacks a strategy to guide himself out of his increasingly compromised position in his bank. In Chapter 7, we'll meet Deborah, whose poor actualizing skills mean that she is failing to deliver the results desperately needed by her organization. In the next chapter, I'll say something more about the coaching techniques which are used in these cases – and which underlie the practical examples presented throughout this book. But let's start our exploration of interactional leadership coaching practice with the dramatic case of a leader with a strong vision, whose inability to master the resourcing stage of the achievement cycle is causing chaos.

Introduction

> They call him Dracula. That's because of the staff he's sacked and the way he strides around the place, never looking at you. His management team are going down like nine pins. It can't carry on like this.

'You said it was urgent,' said Blake S., the chief executive of Entertain TV, drumming a long forefinger on the wide desk that separated us.

'Yes, I feel you have a crisis here,' I said. 'Your staff seem to have levels of stress that are really problematic.'

'I understand that's what we got you in here to fix,' he replied tersely.

A month earlier I had been called into Entertain by the company's human resources director. She had given me the description of Blake quoted above but when I arrived at the company's ultra-modern offices in Soho, I was somewhat alarmed to find that she had quit her job, herself apparently a victim of stress. This did not bode well and I felt a general air of tension among the blaring TV monitors and funky furniture on the company's open-plan floors. Interviews with the heads of the two main channels and some of their staff followed and I started listening to their stories. The channel heads seemed personable, intelligent and dedicated to improving their programmes but they were unable to find their own styles or strategies. Everything was being controlled by their boss.

Janie, who was in charge of Channel 1, had consulted her doctor over some of her symptoms of stress. And she was not alone. Rarely in my coaching experience has such a strong, unequivocal image emerged from a series of disparate conversations. It is a phenomenon familiar to coaches how a particularly powerful and 'difficult' individual can come to dominate the coachee's conversation, especially if that individual is the coachee's boss.

So, now sitting in Blake's spacious corner office, which looked out on the dark walls of the adjacent building, I felt that I already knew the man, although this turned out to be a deceptive impression. One suspicion had been removed immediately: he didn't look like Dracula. Heavily built, tanned, and ruggedly good looking, he was wearing a well-cut suit and brilliantly white shirt. I couldn't help noticing the contrast with the dress code of his staff, who mainly wore jeans, wool tops and T-shirts, all soft and loose, whereas Blake's look was crisp and hard; trainers versus sharp Italian shoes.

The vision

I asked Blake what he was trying to achieve at Entertain because that might help me to understand the mood of the staff. 'Since you ask,' he replied, 'I want to make Entertain the most innovative and profitable TV network of its kind in the UK.' He went on to outline how he intended to use the huge financial and programming resources of the company's American parent company to carve out a unique niche in the UK. I felt immediately how centred this strategy was and yet how at odds it was with the troubled, confused chaos that I had experienced at Entertain. Blake's ambitions were on a grand scale. Indeed, he confidently communicated to me one of the most impressive visions for a company that I have ever come across.

And yet, I wondered, was this a vision or an ambition? It said a good deal about the strength of Blake's desire to choose the future but nothing about the resources needed to do so. A viable vision needs a 'how' as well as a 'where' and that was totally missing. As it turned out in later sessions, Blake had many ideas about new programmes, channels and platforms, but when I asked him how he intended to actualize his strategy, he just replied curtly, 'by hiring the right people'.

I said, 'I'm sure that will help, but there's another problem you need to address. It's the reason why you're causing so much stress here.' At this, Blake first looked surprised and then his expression changed. I now encountered a look that would become familiar to me: piercing blue eyes narrowed in anger, eyebrows clenched, mouth tensed, an expression that could intimidate the most confident executive. 'Explain.' is all he said. So I started to explain.

I said that in my opinion there was a crisis of decision-making at Entertain TV. Blake's leadership team didn't know what his strategy was. They felt he interfered with their plans, micro-managing every aspect of their operations. He was making choices left, right, and centre; hiring, firing, making programming choices, systems choices and choices about what to communicate and with whom. But what were those choices based on? In terms of technical expertise, he had no practical experience of running a television company, which made his an unusual appointment in the industry. Few of his direct reports could be described as seasoned broadcasting professionals but they all had more experience in this area than Blake, who had made his name in sales. Team meetings were tense and one-to-one conversations were sometimes so painfully inquisitorial that one of Blake's direct reports had been physically sick before meeting him. Lower down the organization, people complained that they did not know who Blake was. They were aware of his sinister reputation but they hardly ever saw him in person, shut away as he was in his fortress of an office. He had never addressed his whole staff on any subject.

Blake, to give him credit, listened without interruption. It was hard to interpret his reaction but it was not simply anger. 'I don't accept a lot of that,' he said defensively. 'But what are you proposing? What's your solution?' I suggested we might start with some coaching for him to work out a strategy for interacting with his team and his staff. He shook his head. 'We need action here, not more talk. And I don't need a shrink. If that's what you're selling, I'm not buying.'

'So nothing stresses you at the moment?' I asked. 'Having people I can't trust because they don't have the right experience is stressful,' he replied. 'I don't even trust them to run our systems let alone upscale our creativity.' 'What else?' I went on. He looked irritated at the question and tapped the desk once more. I had the distinct feeling that my association with Entertain TV was about to be terminated.

Then he suddenly leant forward, lowering his voice. 'Public speaking stresses me. It weirds me out.' He said that he had stopped giving presentations two years before, after giving a series of speeches in Scandinavia. 'I was so jittery before presentations that I went on medication,' he explained. 'These days I only present to those who really matter.'

Here was the reason he had never presented to the company. This was why hundreds of employees in the offices and broadcasting suites across town had never seen him. 'That's something we could work on,' I said. There was another long pause, as he toyed with a faded baseball on his desk, and then, somewhat to my surprise, he said flatly, 'why not?'

The paradox of leadership coaching

In coaching, it is important to start where you can. It is a sad but true paradox that it is often the executives who need coaching most who want it least. In some organizations, leaders with problematic management styles remain stubbornly impervious to any attempt to persuade them to change their ways. Perhaps their financial results buy them immunity or the fear that they engender puts off well-meaning colleagues. Either way, they remain a problem everyone talks about but no one can change. Had I from the start insisted on leadership coaching with Blake, the relationship would almost certainly have ended there and then. It seemed easier for him to engage with me on the basis of stress rather than his leadership style but when we concluded a formal coaching contract, as we soon did, it was predominantly focused on helping him achieving his extraordinary leadership strategy for his company.

Interactional mapping

Since I already had a sense of where Blake was psychologically – though much more exploration was to follow – I began our first proper coaching session by taking him through his interactional map. This produced a strikingly different image from the one that emerged from talking to his staff. It was not an image of an angel, to be sure, but it put 'Dracula' into context. Whereas Blake's direct reports tended to see him as the ceiling of their reporting structure, for him this structure seemed to reach up to the stars – or at least to Los Angeles— where the media conglomerate which owned Entertain was headquartered. Blake dealt directly with some of the most senior US managers in the group and was also part of the European, Middle East and African management team, presided over by EMEA chief executive, Les. There was also an international network to which the European team belonged, as this ambitious enterprise covered the entire globe.

In this fearsomely intense and political world, executives seemed to compete with each other almost as much as with other broadcasting outlets. Blake's role in the UK, perhaps the most sophisticated TV market in the world at this time, meant he was under pressure from all sides. Taking unannounced telephone calls at 2.00 am from executives based in L.A., who wanted him to justify his audience ratings, was a routine part of the job. And the annual allocation of financial resources within the group was a bitter budgetary struggle which seemed to go on for most of the year.

As if this wasn't enough, another of Blake's key interactions was with one of the world's largest satellite TV distributors, a company with a notorious reputation for tough business tactics and merciless negotiating. Blake was Entertain's chief negotiator and during the period that I worked with him he was invariably in the thick of these long-drawn out negotiations – or recovering from them. As one of his management team observed, 'I can look after myself in business but I wouldn't want to do battle in that bloody arena that Blake has to enter.' Blake paid a price for his encounters with wills of iron as resolute as his own in various symptoms of stress, such as headaches and insomnia.

Les tended to step aside to allow Blake to conduct these negotiations directly. As Blake's line manager, he had a genial but rather remote approach. He gave Blake a good deal of autonomy – 'just enough rope to hang myself with', as Blake once wryly commented – but not much support or development. Cynics said he had promoted Blake in order to lead a downsizing process ordered by L.A., for which Les himself had no appetite. Certainly he seemed to do little about the rising chorus of discontent with Blake's leadership.

So this was the interactional context in which Blake's attitude to his direct reports developed. In one sense, I could see how he simply regarded them in the same light as his other interactions, as just one more theatre of competitive negotiation. His team didn't appreciate Blake's other responsibilities, largely because he made no attempt to communicate them. His interactional map revealed that he had a really good relationship with only one of his ten direct reports, Eamon, the finance director. The other members of his management team were fast losing Blake's trust or had already lost it, in which case he was planning to replace them.

Trust is a complex notion, which illustrates the oppositional logic underlying human interactions. It implies the mutual respect that enables two people to rely on each other to consistently make the right choices. This is easy enough as long as they make the same choices but more problematic when their choices clash. This toleration of difference is where trust comes in. Without it the relationship is not authentically free, it is simply dull servitude. To my mind, this was just one of the many new balances which Blake would have to learn, if he was to become a choice-focused leader.

Coaching objectives

The plan that emerged after our initial coaching sessions aimed at making dramatic changes to Blake's choice-making as a leader. If he was to achieve his vision with Entertain, we agreed that he needed a practical action plan, which was likely to involve new channels and platforms and a host of new programmes. This would require new funding which meant that Blake had to have a powerful justification to win over Les and his senior managers in L.A.. Blake initiated a series of strategy reviews to develop his ideas. He also agreed to work on his interpersonal skills, especially his presentation skills. This was obvious development territory for a non-resourcing leader. In Blake's case, however, he also required some in-depth exploration of his psychology. Without progress in this area, his explosive mixture of impulsive decision-making and angry disrespect for his management team would continue to sabotage any strategy he came up with.

In summary, Blake's coaching goals were as follows:

1 Invest in himself psychologically and develop his interactional skills
2 Turn his leadership group into a real team
3 Get his key hires right, especially around Entertain's creative talent and advertising managers
4 Develop the creativity of the staff and communicate with them
5 Invest in new channels and pioneer online platforms
6 Build his leadership profile within the industry.

In one way or another, these ambitious objectives touched on all six dimensions of the interactional leadership model.

Leadership psychology

Why did Blake interact so aggressively with others? Why did he make choices by acting first and thinking later? To my surprise, Blake started opening up to me very quickly about these issues, discussing aspects of his life which he had never spoken about before. His self-knowledge seemed fairly limited. At times I felt that we were shining a torch into a dark cellar and he was glimpsing facets of himself for the first time. That is not to say that there was anything shadowy about Blake's personal style. Behind the mask of 'Dracula', there was a complex, wide-ranging and talented individual who was an extremist in personality terms. Although he was a moderate extrovert, all of his other personality characteristics on the Interactional Styles Outliner were towards one pole or the other. He was emphatically competitive then supportive, strongly rational as opposed to emotional, originating rather than accommodating and confident rather than doubting. These pronounced personal biases drove his decision-making and his leadership style.

Blake's competitive, dominant power style was perhaps his most striking characteristic. A key set of values in his worldview was around the notion of aggression. 'Aggressive' was his favourite word of approbation and 'not aggressive enough' was one of his most damning criticisms. He associated being supportive of others at work with 'not being in control'. He immediately recognized this competitiveness in himself. 'I've always wanted to be on top. I'm not interested in second place'. Exploring this characteristic soon revealed the major event of Blake's early life, his mother's death from cancer when he was eleven. This sad loss exposed him very directly to the influence of his father, a distinguished lawyer and judge in Chicago. A man of stern intellect and fierce ambition, he seemed to have left Blake and his two younger brothers to the care of nannies, encouraging them to compete fiercely with each other and giving them little emotional support.

Emotional patterns

Emotionally, Blake described himself as 'cold'. 'I tend to calculate,' he said, 'I can be almost without feeling at times'. This he related to his mother's death. 'Are you always in this state?' I asked him. 'Hell, no,' he said forcefully, 'do I look like that to you? I feel excitement and joy at times. I just control those feelings at work.' 'Why?' I asked. 'Because it sends the wrong message. I'm much more likely to express anger – because it works.' He described a recent incident when he had publicly shouted at his marketing director, prompting his resignation. 'It cut a long story short,' he said in a rather chilling tone. 'He's not up to the job. I can now get someone who is.'

'So anger makes decisions for you?' I suggested. He shrugged his burly shoulders. 'When I feel totally uncertain about something,' he admitted, 'I just let rip. I guess it solves things one way or another.' As we dug deeper, it became clear that fear of uncertainty was driving much of this anger. The aura of certainty he prided himself on was actually a much thinner veneer than he was prepared to admit. In fact, anger led him into the certainty snare. It gave him an illusion of sureness in a deeply unsure environment. But, of course, it only added to the real uncertainty of everyone around him. Over time, he became aware of the destructive effects of that anger, although it never entirely disappeared from his emotional repertoire. Some of Blake's angry outbursts made me question whether the coaching could ever succeed, and more than once I left the Entertain office wondering whether I was actually making things worse. But gradually, his self-restraint improved and his ability to tolerate opposition without losing his temper increased appreciably.

Another breakthrough came in his emotional world. He cited getting married as one of the primary choices of his life. After many years of single life – 'heaps of relationships, some serious, most not' was all he chose to say on the subject – he had 'fallen in love with the right woman'. As the sessions developed, he revealed more about his personal life, which was centred on his family. He worked long hours in the office and went to bed soon after he returned home, in order to get up early in the morning and spend time with his two young daughters. His wife, who was French, had given up her academic career to bring up the children and the family seemed to be very close. Blake was surprisingly touching in his descriptions of his daughters and seemed to delight in their company, patiently helping them with their homework. This was all in marked contrast to the tense, utilitarian relationships Blake had with his work colleagues. In his almost idyllic family group, I thought I saw another sharp contrast – with Blake's bleak life in his original family after his mother's death.

As vivid as Blake's account of his children was, I didn't realise just how radically compartmentalized this experience was until I asked him to compare being a parent to being a leader. He looked genuinely taken aback by this. 'What the hell do you mean?' he asked coldly, with the beginnings of an icy stare that I was coming to know very well. It was as though I had insulted his children. For him, his family was a cooperative realm, which was completely shut off from the competitive world of work. But I returned to this subject on several other occasions, risking Blake's glacial look, and he eventually began to ask himself why the kind of care and concern he felt for his children should be so utterly different to what he felt for his staff. And so the Berlin wall that separated the zones of Blake's interior life started to come down and he set out on the long journey towards trusting his emotions.

Building the leadership team

At the same time as working on his own psychological development, Blake had to confront his own way of interacting with others at work. His lack of resourcing skills was at the heart of the problem with Entertain. Blake had little knowledge of, or respect for, the whole cycle of TV programme development or indeed the craft of television production. His management team meetings were typical of his approach. They were dominated by a manipulative, overtly aggressive management style, which Blake himself would later come to characterize as 'brutal'. He was constantly late for meetings, while severely reprimanding the same behaviour in others. He tended to talk over people, changing the subject at will, and publicly dressing down anyone who he felt was not delivering what was expected. As far as creativity was concerned, his view was that 'the best idea wins' but this contest didn't take place on a level playing field. Other people's suggestions and proposals were often crushed by Blake's sarcastic comments and insistence on keeping a very tight rein on costs. It was no wonder that very few new programme or marketing ideas were actually being developed at Entertain.

Listening

Among the range of interactional resources Blake needed to develop, listening expertise was central. I noticed early on in our coaching that Blake often seemed to find it very difficult to listen to me for any length of time. Within a very short period of time, his eyes would move away from mine and it was clear he was pursuing his own thoughts. I pointed this out to him and he admitted it was not one of his strengths. 'I get bored quickly,' he said, 'and there's always so much going on in my head'. I asked him what happened when he made an effort to listen to people. 'You can lose the initiative and that can make you vulnerable,' he replied. As we expanded this idea, it became clear that for Blake listening to others somehow conceded them a competitive advantage. 'Does someone else's good idea mean a defeat for you?' I asked. In the zero-sum game, which Blake was playing, it seemed a reasonable inference, although no doubt it went too far. But Blake was intrigued by it and it seemed to start him thinking about listening in a different way.

In fact, Blake's listening style mirrored many of his leadership choice-making habits. This became apparent when we analysed a recent conversation with Janie about Channel 1's falling ratings. He constantly seemed to anticipate what Janie was going to say, delineating problems before she had even started describing them. He hurtled to conclusions ('jumped' would be too tame a description) to a point where unconsciously he was more or less eliminating Janie from the conversation. If she reacted to this with any emotion, such as embarrassment or anger, he stopped listening completely. 'I turn off then,' he said. 'It's for her own good. I can see that she's not at her best and is probably going to say something she regrets.' Having examined the ingenuous ways in which Blake failed to listen to Janie, I ventured to suggest that his dialogue with her was largely a conversation with himself. 'Yeah, good point,' he said rather ruefully.

The first signs of a breakthrough for Blake came not in conversation with Janie but in a job interview with a candidate for the post of director of strategy.

'I was getting impatient,' he said. 'When I asked him for his ideas for Channel 2, he went way off at a tangent. I was about to say something pretty cutting and then I thought, "Hey, give it the Michael Harvey play!" And man, did I listen. I could practically hear his brain whirring and, you know what, I began to pick up something. His ideas were shit, frankly, you know, obvious stuff we've tried before. But there was something else that was exciting – the way he put ideas together and connected audiences with brands. Well, he got the job anyway!'

This turned out to be an inspired piece of recruitment and it encouraged Blake to start making a concerted effort to listen to others. This appeared to have an immediate effect on Janie for one. According to Blake, she started outlining some of her best creative plans, which she had been withholding from him because of frustration and uncertainty about her future. Blake also began to apply this new approach to his team meetings, trying to listen in order to learn, and offer his direct reports encouragement and creative stimulation rather than carping criticism and belittlement. He even began to make an effort to arrive at team meetings on time – or at least to apologize if he was late.

'The fantasy hire': getting the recruitment right

Recognizing the creative power of listening helped Blake to adopt a more productive attitude to the recruitment of his staff, another balancing act that he urgently needed to master. A leader needs to bring in the right new team members but he also must be able to work with and develop those he already has. Blake was in thrall to what I called 'the fantasy hire', a belief that there were executives in the job market who could simply walk into Entertain and do a perfect job, without any assistance from Blake. True, Entertain was a glamorous company and there was never any shortage of talented people wanting to join it but Blake's attitude to recruitment was definitely misguided, a typical non-resourcer's fantasy in fact. Ironically, it meant that Blake spent a disproportionately large amount of his valuable leadership time in interviewing job candidates and in discussing the legalities of firing existing employees. He could also be extremely erratic in his recruitment choices, once hiring an advertising manager with woefully inadequate experience simply because he had the nerve to pitch himself to Blake face-to-face.

Blake's assumptions about the human resources department were part of the problem. At the start of the coaching series, he took a sly pleasure in using the term 'human remains' to refer to what was left of the HR function. Gradually, he began to change his attitude to staff development (as to his own) and started investing in the human resources and training departments. He promoted Rowena, his resilient, resourceful new HR director to his management team and together they worked on hiring some of the brightest, up-and-coming talents in the business and providing them with the development they needed to excel at Entertain.

A revolution in creativity and communication

A new phase of creativity now opened up at Entertain. Blake committed himself to getting to know his staff, holding lunches and open meetings to get new ideas from his employees and feedback on the direction of the station. He became convinced that he needed to set up regular get-togethers of the entire company in order to build solidarity and cross-fertilize ideas. This meant working on his presentation skills in coaching. We began focusing on clear leadership messages and developing Blake's confidence in public speaking. In spite of his stressful experiences, it was clear from the outset that Blake had the capacity to become an outstanding pubic speaker. He had an ability to project himself to an audience in a charismatic way, which it is hard, if not impossible, to teach. Once he became convinced of this talent – partially though my feedback and the evidence of the video playback – he built up his confidence in his public speaking, although actual presentations were always preceded by some nervousness.

Cross-functional creative teams became a theme of the regular new company awaydays and these were continued in everyday work. These teams lowered some of the barriers which existed between different areas of the company, particularly the creative and commercial areas. Working on ideas in groups which mixed producers and advertising executives meant that programme ideas could develop in a way that respected both sets of interests. It gave the creatives the possibility of securing the finances they needed to develop their ambitious ideas, while assuring the sales people that they had a viable product to sell to advertisers. The antagonism between these two departments, which at times had been bitter, now began to turn into a positive interaction, a clear case of dialectical change. People in other areas of the company who had never talked to each other now started to dedicate themselves to the same programme ideas. Another thing Blake worked hard to change was his tendency to blame others for failure. Getting rid of 'the blame culture' was fundamental to turning around creativity at Entertain TV. It raised the morale of the production staff and improved communication within the management team and the wider company.

New channels and platforms

With bright ideas flowing within the company, it was time for Blake to launch new channels and invest in online platforms, strategies which had been reinforced by strategic reviews and staff feedback. Selecting the channels to launch across a range of entertainment areas, with defined demographic targets, involved another new balancing act for Blake. He had been inclined to make market research the basis of his programming strategy, using a mass of data about audience preferences and actual viewing habits. He now started balancing research with the intuition of his production staff and the expertise of his brilliant programme schedulers.

He also began to change his orientation to time, as far as programme development was concerned. One of his biggest successes was holding out against pressure from above – and indeed pressure from his own self-doubt – to renew a reality TV series which had done badly in the ratings during its first season. Blake courageously rejected a short-term response and allowed the show's enthusiastic producers to convince him that it needed another chance to succeed. He successfully fought for the funding for a second series. The show turned out to be one of Entertain's most notable success stories, producing high ratings and stellar publicity, as well as several spin-offs on other platforms.

The need to balance creativity and audience size was also a powerful impulse behind Blake's investment in online platforms, at a time when the commercial logic of this was still unproven. He moved beyond his belief that market research can tell you what an audience will want in the future (it is better at saying what they want in the present) and boldly staked his reputation on the future of online audience engagement. Operating in this unknown realm, rather than clinging to spurious certainties, led to huge creative advances, which were later recognized by the TV and film industry in a number of high-profile awards for digital innovation. In time, this also produced sufficient online advertising revenue to offset the trend towards falling income from TV advertising.

Building a leadership profile

Towards the end of the coaching series, we focused on raising Blake's leadership to a higher corporate and industry level. This required some changes to Blake's interactional map. It was now a matter of working on a bigger stage within the Entertain parent company, building a reputation inside a multinational media corporation with tens of thousands of employees around the world. Blake also worked on developing his influence within the UK TV industry, moving from his hostile attitude to competing channels to a whole-industry perspective, from 'them versus us' to a focus on 'we'. Making speeches to industry experts at a major TV conference was a far cry from the deep anxiety he had experienced in contemplating addressing his own staff. He was now able to juggle several leadership roles simultaneously and see beyond the immediate delivery of his strategy, which was increasingly overseen by his excellent direct reports. His corporate commitments also involved him in taking the lead on diversity issues and an anti-drug campaign for young audiences, signs of a striking transformation from a 'brutal' hirer and firer to a leader who was increasingly ethically conscious in his choices.

Conclusion: an interactional leader?

At the end of the second year of coaching Blake, I bumped into the HR director, who had originally hired me. She had just met Blake for the first time since she left Entertain and was astounded by the change she observed in him. 'It's amazing,' she said. 'He seems like a completely different person.'

In many ways, she was right, but this change, to which many people at Entertain had contributed, was not total. Blake still had relapses. He could be obstinate, difficult to work with and, on occasion, aggressively outspoken. Nevertheless, the psychological and interpersonal work he had done had definitely helped him to overcome many of his resourcing deficiencies and this enabled his vision and action-orientation to flourish. With greater self-knowledge, Blake was now able to make effective choices throughout the achievement cycle. He had achieved many of his initial goals and Entertain was in the process of becoming one of the most successful and innovative TV companies in its field. Presiding over an organizational culture which balanced creative autonomy with multi-media commercial success, Blake now possessed many of the attributes of a genuine interactional leader.

In my last session with Blake, I could not help reflecting on how different things were now. We sat in his new, open office area, on a sofa frequently occupied by members of staff who could drop in quite freely. We looked out on a company which was several times larger than the organization I had first started working with. And yet it now seemed smaller and more intimate than before. There was more light in this office and fewer closed doors, both literally and metaphorically. Somehow you could feel that the choices at Entertain were now being made in the right way.

My attention was drawn to a glass case above Blake's desk. It contained a Dracula mask, luridly gory with bloody fangs and strangely comical hair, which had recently been given to Blake by two of his direct reports. This pointed allusion to Blake's previous leadership style seemed to be a good indication of how relaxed his leadership team now felt about him, in spite of his occasional setbacks. It also showed how confident Blake himself was about fielding the questions the mask inevitably raised. To me, this confirmed how determined he was to continue his development as a choice-focused leader throughout his career. It was a good thought on which to conclude our coaching relationship.

'Many, many thanks, man,' Blake said, as we stood up and shook hands for the last time. 'It's been quite a ride.'

It had indeed.

Chapter 5

The practical techniques of interactional leadership coaching

The Blake S. case study gives one example of how a coach can help a leader to develop the art of balancing choices. The relationship between the achievement cycle and the interactional self was particularly important in his case. Without a strictly business approach it was unlikely that he would have committed himself to coaching and he responded positively to the idea that his main challenge was matching his strategy with his resources. Yet it turned out that a significant psychological rebalancing was necessary for Blake to have any chance of achieving real business success.

Some of the techniques used in this assignment were obvious, some played out more subtly, between the lines of the thousands of sentences exchanged in a typical coaching dialogue. Before moving on to other case studies, I now want to bring these methods to the surface and show how they relate to the overarching theoretical model of interactional leadership. In this chapter, I would also like to indicate how the techniques of oppositional enquiry can help to neutralize some of the threats to effective leadership choice-making which I outlined in earlier chapters.

In practice, leadership coaching often turns on the coach's ability to listen to the client. Through 'expert listening', the coach tries to suspend his own choices in order to stay open to the possibilities which define a leader's situation. This often helps the coachee to disclose her hopes and doubts and reveal where she wants to go and perhaps what prevents her from getting there. Listening and responsive questioning may also identify the choice-focused competences a leader needs to develop around strategy, self-knowledge, interpersonal and communication skills and creativity, as I described in detail in *Interactional Coaching: Choice-focused learning at work* (Harvey, 2012). Other elements such as confidentiality, feedback and commitment to the coaching relationship, all contribute to building a relationship which enables the coachee to understand what he really needs to do in his situation.

Interactional coaching usually involves a movement through the six dimensions of the interactional leadership model, although this does not necessarily occur in a specific form or order. It is important for the coach not to sacrifice spontaneous, organic relationship-building for anything that smacks of a formal coaching programme, except where this appeals to, and is chosen by, the coachee. Nevertheless, sooner or later, by whatever route seems most fitting, the coaching journey will probably visit most of the 6D leadership destinations.

Developing choice expertise

The best way of developing a coachee's choice consciousness is by identifying the key interactions which are present in her situation or life history. These may include significant career turning points, for example, or the reasons for her choosing a particular strategy. Sometimes, it can be useful to approach this area more abstractly. For example, I might ask about her prioritizing. Does she have a formal technique for this or does it evolve pragmatically? How does she make major decisions, in a group or individually? Does she make decisions in advance of an event or at the last minute? What choices does she feel she is avoiding? Or perhaps I ask her to name a choice which, with hindsight, she realised that she had made without conscious reflection. Through questions of this kind, it is possible to develop the leader's awareness of her choice-making, as well as to get a real sense of her unique personality and working style. 'You know, I've never really thought about how I make decisions', is a common response in this context, which may mean that the coachee is in line for a rapid increase in her optative awareness.

Coaching the achievement cycle

1. Strategizing

Often the most effective way of beginning a coaching assignment is to focus on the leader's strategy. This can immediately reveal the strength of his forward-facing trajectory, as we saw with Blake S.. Or it may suggest that strategic formulation will be the initial task of the coaching series (or in some assignments its entire remit). Identifying a workable vision may involve refining an existing idea or brainstorming new ideas. It may involve challenging or testing out a seemingly robust strategy to see how it holds up in various hypothetical situations. If the strategy is too vague, scenario construction may help to join up the dots. In some situations, it may be appropriate to go back to the drawing board and consider the best collective means to develop a strategy using internal or external resources.

Strategy can emerge in all sorts of ways – 'it just seems to happen' was the modest but probably accurate view of one CEO I worked with. But emerge it must, because a vague strategy will affect the whole cycle of achievement. If a leader's goals are not clear – or there is not a viable way of clarifying them as a project develops – a project struggles for definition and may collapse under the weight of conflicting aims. For some leaders, it is important to make an emotional connection with a strategy, rooting his vision in personal experience rather professional expediency.

The possibilizing skills of imaginative speculation and problem-solving are central to the strategizing process, as is the ability to conduct rigorous information searches and seek out alternative plans. But leaders who are not natural possibilizers should not be put off, as these skills can be learned. Nor do all strategies need to be new. Some leaders are right to stick with successful formulas, as long as they constantly review them and test them against alternatives. Others develop positional strategies, as we've seen, and trust to the cairos dimension of time to enable them to seize an opportunity when it presents itself.

2. Resourcing

If the strategy is clear, the coach may ask, 'How many of the resources which you need to implement it do you have?' This is a wide-ranging field of enquiry. It can involve finance, stakeholder commitment, tactical planning, logistics, hiring decisions, training and development, and so on. It may be the resources already exist or they may have to be built from scratch. In working towards an equipoise between strategy and resources it may become apparent that the strategy is too ambitious and needs to be trimmed or, more rarely, that the plan falls short of the full potential of the resources to hand.

Examining available resources is another way to develop a vision. The coachee is asked to think about the strength of her organization in terms of personnel, brand, customer base or market position. From these resources, the strategy may emerge. 'I've got great people, I just need to find a project which fully extends them,' was one leader's strategic starting point. The coach may also draw attention to the leader's own resources and help her decide what skills she needs to develop, in order to provide the right blend of competences necessary for the task ahead.

3. Delivering

If the fit between strategy and resources is good enough, coaching the delivery stage of the achievement cycle may involve no more than monitoring progress and dealing with any snags which might emerge. At this stage, leaders who are most comfortable in the strategic or resourcing phase of achievement may start to lose interest in the finer details of actualizing a policy. 'Going over yet another field report makes me lose the will to live', complained one strategically gifted leader. But sometimes there is no alternative to repetition and an unrelenting insistence on the implementation of a policy, if real success is to accrue.

But what if there is an intractable problem at the implementation stage? Diagnosing its cause is the first task for coaching. Perhaps the leader has failed to inspire others or lacks calmness under pressure. Sometimes what is missing is the will-power to throw oneself into the heart of the action. In the delicate web of judgments that surrounds a plan, paralysis by analysis can easily set in. I remember a colleague telling me, as I hesitated endlessly on a career move, 'you can only look for so long – sometimes you just have to leap'. Leap I did, successfully, as it turned out, and many leaders have done the same.

Focusing on the achievement cycle helps to develop funnelling skills, the ability to drill down from ideas to reality. The coachee needs to identify what is happening – and not happening – in the implementation process and, if necessary, find ways to gather more accurate information. This can help to restore her confidence in her ability to achieve results. If everything seems to be in place for achievement except achievement itself, it may be time for the coach to help the coachee to reappraise the balance between strategy and resources and assign a new weighting to each of them.

Coaching the interactional self

4. The self

Closely related to questions about strategy is a more personal emphasis on the leader's desires. The first cardinal question, 'What do you want to achieve?' is one of the most powerful of all human enquiries, which helps the coach in the vital task of understanding the coachee psychologically. Others may assume that the leader's track record and the exhaustive selection process that usually accompanies a top job are enough to ensure that he has the self-knowledge and psychological poise to deal with the manifold demands of leadership. But, as we saw clearly in Blake S.'s story, this is not always the case.

In coaching, illuminating a leader's emotional self and personal values is often essential, because the failure to connect professional goals with personal experience can be destabilizing. One head of a public sector organization told me that he became so 'carried away' with promoting his leadership vision that he no longer knew how it related to the creative self, which he felt was at the heart of who he was. A leader's values can have major implications for what he feels comfortable doing or not doing, as can his emotional patterns. It may be revealing to ask him when he experiences joy and fear in his work and to describe the relationship between these two states. Often a leader feels fear much more often than he would care to admit to others, so it is important that he uses the coaching relationship at least to admit it to himself.

Personality balancing can also help the coachee to find her personal dialectic, the ideal meeting point between the key factors in her personality. The Interactional Styles Outliner (ISO) identifies the polarities of confident/supportive, extravert/introvert, dominant/supportive, accommodating/ originating and rational/emotional, which illuminates the spectrum along which the coachee's personal biases operate. More spontaneous questioning can often achieve the same goal, identifying the personal equilibrium which is most effective for a leader's situation.

5. Others

'Who do you need to interact with in order to achieve it?' The second cardinal question often opens up the leader's interpersonal world and leads to interactional mapping. This will identify the principal stakeholders he needs to target inside and outside the organization and the skills he needs to use – or to develop – in order to win them over. Not all of these interpersonal relationships are overt. There are many subterranean, prereflective ways in which a leader can be influenced into acting in the interests of others. The presence of what Heidegger (1962: 165) calls the 'they' (Das Man), in which 'everyone is the other, and no one is himself', can be deeply disturbing. It may take the form of a herd mentality, a headlong rush to achievement, in which passion takes over from measured judgment. Helping a leader to separate his thoughts and feelings on a subject from the intoxicating swirl of group consciousness can be vital. Moving the focus from the others to the self can help, especially if it becomes clear that the ultimate responsibility for choices lies with the leader. Faddish enthusiasm often evaporates once this hard fact comes into view

The unconscious influence of others can manifest itself in many ways. One exceptionally talented potential leader I worked with was held back by an undue degree of deference to the most senior leaders in her organization. Only when we fully explored this tendency, tracing it back to her school years, was it possible for her to express the constructive criticism of her senior managers which was required of her in her new role.

6. The time dimension

Part of the coach's task is to create a varied temporal environment. Often this is about giving the coachee more time to develop his thoughts and unpack the implications of a situation, away from the hustle and bustle of the job. But it may also involve restricting time. As Gerd Gigerenzer (2008: 33) shows 'less can be more' when it comes to the time of decision-making, citing experiments that demonstrate too much time can confuse and even paralyze the choice-making of experts. So gently pressurizing the coachee for a decision or inviting her to pick the first option that comes into her head can also be extremely helpful tactics for the coach.

Interpreting time is always central to a leader's success. This often involves helping her balance the claims of the future, past and present. The power of the future is fundamental to the leader, as we know, but the way we look forward is influenced by the way we look back. The past can be source of inspiration and insight or an inhibition preventing a leader from fully facing up to the possibilities of what lies ahead. Of course, the past and future both express themselves through the present and it is this temporal mode which most obviously occupies a leader's time. Many chief executives require the services of a personal assistant (sometimes more than one!) to maintain their diaries. During the scores of meetings which fill this ever-changing chronicle of a leader's day-to-day commitments, many choices are made – some momentous, some trivial. Indeed, in this apparently banal space, leadership achievement is often forged or destroyed, which is why it can be useful for the coach to examine it. At this granular level of leadership, imbalances often appear which can skew a leader's choice-making, such as too many strategic meetings and too few performance reviews, or excessive amounts of time spent on pet projects and too little on impending problems.

The ethical dimension

When it comes to the ethical dimension of interactional coaching, this is not a matter of preaching or proselytizing. As often as not, it's a simple matter of drawing out the implications of a leadership choice. This may involve clarifying the language surrounding potentially problematic issues, such as redundancies, in order to ensure that the coachee is aware of his responsibilities – a theme we return to in Chapter 14. This may be enough to ensure a sufficient intensity of engagement with a choice, which can often be measured by the amount of perceived ambiguity it raises.

Sometimes the ethical frame emerges through exploring how an actual, or contemplated, decision impacts on the freedom of choice of the other people concerned in it. Ethical choices often rest on the balance between the interests of the self and those of others. Where the coach feels that a leader is raising his own interests far above those of others, it is worth drawing her attention to this, in order to establish how she justifies this, as well she may. Weighting the scales on the side of other people is probably the most likely route to admirable ethical behaviour but altruism needs to be authentic. A leader must be able to live with a potentially unbalanced relationship between himself and others. There is little point in sacrificing financial rewards in order to encourage your team, if you end up feeling bitterly resentful because your peers are not doing the same, as was the case with one senior manager I coached.

The leadership multirole

Coaching the multirole aspect of leadership involves identifying the leader's different functions and responsibilities, because it is far too easy for him to assume that one way of behaving will work for all of these. Establishing the possible differences between his role as a strategist, for example, and a team leader can come as a revelation. Recall how Blake S. had to take a very different stance in leading his management team than to negotiating contracts with his channels' notoriously aggressive distributors. The challenge in accepting multiple roles is often psychological, in that it implies renouncing strength in one role and accepting weakness in another. Moving out of the comfort zone of your specialism, with its accompanying high status and self-confidence, is always testing.

To some, it may seem paradoxical – to put it no more harshly than that – if a leader knows very little about a situation, which he is in charge of. Yet it happens all the time. One chief executive, taking over a major international research programme at the last minute, admitted to me that his 19-year-old intern was 'infinitely more knowledgeable' about the project than he was. The prospect of staring at 'a sea of strange faces' around his boardroom table, many of whom were flying in from different continents, 'scared the living daylights' out of him, he said. But in coaching he resolved to get a solid, entry-level briefing to the programme from his colleagues (especially his intern) and this willingness to learn, combined with his transparency in acknowledging his status as a novice, held him in good stead throughout the project.

The leader's ability to learn new roles quickly, in the face of many other demands on her time, is a much underestimated aspect of her role. Sustained leadership performance depends on managing multiple interactions and finding the right balance from role to role, as well as coping with the changes in the 'same' situation. Learning how to learn is never easy. In leadership workshops, it may be possible to use physical exercises to help develop balancing skills, such as juggling or slacklining, but these can never have more than a metaphorical relationship to real leadership. In coaching, the most effective way of helping the leader to achieve a better sense of balance is through increased awareness of the choice dimensions of his situation and the relationship between them. This dialectical process is reinforced by the broad coaching approach which I call oppositional enquiry.

Oppositional enquiry: tipping the scales of the psychology of choice

Oppositional enquiry is a series of techniques which are intended to tip the scales in favour of effective leadership choice-making. It addresses some of the imbalances which can prevent sound decisions from being made. It also puts into practice the goal of interactional thinking to treat opposites not as permanently conflictive but as mutually defining elements, which in the right circumstances can be resolved into a higher unity. Let me you give a brief impression of what this can entail.

Rationalizing

This technique helps to disclose the distorting bias of emotions by clarifying the coachee's thought processes, away from the turbulence of her everyday working life. Disembedding the assumptions and prejudices that underlie the coachee's ideas helps to prevent pre-choices and biases of which the coachee is unconscious. All of this can have the effect of bringing pre-reflective ideas and images into reflective consciousness. In the process, myths may be debunked, stereotypes unravelled and some of a leader's working hypotheses revealed to be nothing more than outdated habits.

Emotionalizing

The coach may also try to bring out the emotional reality underlying choices. An excessive reliance on rational problem-solving, or a fear of being seen as impulsive, can obscure a leader's real feelings. The coach's ability to help the coachee to contact his emotional self can have a liberating effect, encouraging effective, intuitive choices or emboldening the leader to take a stand on something she feels strongly about. Emotions can also help the coachee to realise what others may be going through or make insightful connections with previously hidden or compartmentalized personal experiences.

Balancing positivity and negativity

The balancing of support and challenge is one of the key tools of the coach's craft. Support may provide positive encouragement for elements the coachee has never considered favourably. It is extraordinary how even the most successful people can be tormented by doubts, which lead them to pay much more attention to their perceived liabilities rather to their assets. 'Problems are what matter,' one leader said to me, 'why waste my time on flattery?' The answer to this, in my view, is that a positive appreciation of yourself or your situation can change your point of view and prompt actions which a negative state of mind rules out. As we've seen, dwelling too much on the negative can encourage loss aversion and a flight from risk-taking.

At the same time, the effects of an over-confident, exclusively positive attitude can be equally unbalancing. Some leaders are extremely sure of their own abilities – perhaps this is what enabled them to rise to the top – and can easily be led astray by their own enthusiasm. That is why it is important to look at the negative aspects of a situation, perhaps constructing worst case scenarios to fully test a possible course of action. If this tactic punctures the coachee's ebullient mood, this is unfortunate, but it may be a useful sign of the fragility of his approach to a subject.

Challenging is a crucial dynamic in the coaching relationship. It is part of the distinctive, 'equalizing' role of leadership coaching. As we know, CEOs and other powerful executives often work in the steeply banked hierarchies of today's large organizations, where they may enjoy virtual immunity from being challenged by others. The coach may be alone in being able 'to say the unsayable' and question aspects of a leader's style which his colleagues, mindful of their job security and career progression, are reluctant to voice. This 'democratizing' effect of coaching can productively break down the isolation – even estrangement – of life at the top, which if unchecked can easily lead to distorted choice-making of the kind that characterized the run up to the Great Recession.

Ambiguating and disambiguating: springing the certainty snare

The more a leader flees uncertainty the more she can be snared by certainty. The more she tries to prove that she knows everything, the greater the chance that she overlooks what can be known or is tripped up by what cannot be known. That means both the known and unknown need to be interrogated. Coaching sweeps across both opposites, by ambiguating and disambiguating. Conventionally, the latter term, indicating clarifying the meaning of a phrase by deconstructing its possible references, is said to be the only positive in this opposition. But the value of ambiguating should not be dismissed out of hand. Sometimes, drawing out the true complexity of a proposition is the only way to grasp its true meaning. This to-and-fro movement is similar to what Kurt Lewin (1947) referred to as the tension between the 'freezing' and 'unfreezing' phases of decision-making. Sometimes we need to tighten the process, funnelling towards an unambiguous, actionable collusion; sometimes we need to loosen it, opening up to the (potentially infinite) possibilities of a situation. As always, getting the balance right is the key to the art of successful choice-making.

Empathizing

Finally, empathizing (or othering) is a technique that involves helping the coachee to move towards understanding the perspective of others in order to see how this affects his own position. The dialectic of self and other enables us to understand a process, which is too often described as being predominantly emotional. In fact, it is a holistic process, involving all aspects of human experience, from the emotional to the rational and the imaginative to the factual. It also has emphatic ethical implications, in that it helps a leader to understand the possible impact of his actions on others.

This movement from the self to the other (and back again) also has relevance to the role of the coach, as he constantly commutes between the coachee's world and his own. The choices the coach makes in suggesting options, staying silent or disclosing personal experience are all part of her own balancing process, aimed at helping the leader find the right point for his own choice-making.

If the coach herself falls from the high wire, as she will from time to time, her best safety net comes in the form of the trust built up in the coaching relationship. This trust may persuade the coachee to interpret these slips in the helpful spirit in which they were intended. The interaction between the technical and the relationship-based aspects of coaching is very important and can often make the difference between success and failure in an assignment, as we'll see in our next case study of a leader struggling to find his way towards choice-focused leadership.

Chapter 6

Coaching the non-strategizing leader

'Zombie leadership': the case of Arjun J.

I'm not a leader. Jesus, Ghandi, they are leaders, I'm a follower. I go to meetings and sign off what other people do. I feel like a zombie these days.

Arjun J.'s first words to me, in our initial session were not the most promising start to a leadership coaching assignment. On the surface, he was a competent leader, very orientated to others, and with great probalizing ability. But unlike Blake S., Arjun seemed to have lost any ability to enter into the world of possibilities with any excitement or verve. He had become a non-strategist, capable of using the resources around him but unable to access that most precious skill, the ability to imagine something different to the status quo.

Leaders make the possible happen, whereas managers often trade in the probable – and Arjun was now definitely in the latter camp.

The effect on him was psychologically devastating. He admitted that he had become 'a zombie leader', doing the same routines, unable to learn his mistakes but fearful of making errors. He was in danger of turning choice-avoidance into an art form. His strong interpersonal orientation meant he could function as part of team, which can be an effective leadership style. But not if a leader lacks a sense of direction. Without a strategy, he can get lost in the group, worn down by others and robbed of his self-confidence. Arjun was like a painting whose vivid colours have become blurred and dull under a film of dust.

Of course, this opinion only formed in time. To begin with, as we started our coaching in Arjun's large, comfortable office among the labyrinthine streets of an ancient part of the City of London, I simply listened to his story. Arjun was chief operating officer (COO) for a UK-based bank, let's call it Hoskins Bank. In his mid-forties, with black wavy hair and a slow smile, he had been an outstanding cricketer in his youth, not something that was readily apparent from his present, rather portly, appearance. Born of Indian parentage, and raised in West London, he had worked hard and done well at school, going on to study chemistry at Imperial College, but had abandoned his degree after a year because his mother fell ill and his father lost his job. 'Did they pressurize you to make this choice?', I asked him 'No, on the contrary,' he replied, 'they wanted me to keep going. It was a decision I made myself. It was the right thing to do.'

This kind of integrity and care for others, I came to learn, was characteristic of Arjun. Immensely polite, considerate and diligent, he rose through the bank's branch system from teller to assistant manager, becoming one of the banks youngest ever bank managers, before moving on to senior roles in Hoskins' group operations. He had occupied his current positions as chief operating officer for almost five years. Although not yet on the critical list as far as his performance at the bank was concerned, Arjun felt that the shine had gone off his career. As he put with typical verbal dexterity, 'I used to be in a groove, now I'm in a rut.' His HR director agreed. 'Arjun has lost a lot of his drive and dash', he told me. 'It's hard to say why.'

The 'collapsed vision'

Arjun's own sense of the problem was more tortured. It poured out in our first session: 'I tend to doubt my abilities for no good reason. I see myself surrounded by people who are brighter and more go-ahead than I am.' He said that at the end of the day, he would go home exhausted 'with my head down'. The concern for him felt by his wife and two teenage sons only depressed him further, a negative spiral from which it was hard to escape. In the mornings, he often wondered if he should go to work at all. 'At 6.00 a.m. that's not a great thought, especially this time of year', he said, nodding in the direction of the streets outside, which were threatened by snow, not for the first time that winter.

He said he had considered moving to another bank. 'But if I think of changing jobs I just get scared. I'm just clinging on because I don't know what else to do.'

'Is "clinging on to where you are" your vision of the future?' I asked, genuinely interested. A positional strategy may take many shapes and forms. Arjun seemed to be in 'survival mode', which can be a classic positional tactic, hanging on until something better makes an appearance.

'Sounds exciting, doesn't it?' Arjun said with a dry smile. 'My only "plan" is to keep going until I get sacked or can pick up my pension. I'm sorry if it sounds dull but there it is.' He added that several of his slightly older colleagues, whom he had worked with for many years, had retired recently.

When I asked him what he really wanted to achieve, Arjun simply shook his head. I asked him to imagine a time in the future when he would feel proud about what he had done, but he was unable to. I persisted, questioning him about what had motivated him in the past, a way of going backwards to move forward which sometimes produces positive results. For a moment, this seemed to jolt Arjun into a livelier mood. He placed his elbows on his desk:

> You know, I used to think honesty and integrity, dealing with the customers – and with your own staff – was absolutely essential. We seem to have lost that now. I don't know where that leaves Hoskins.

There was the outline of a vision here but really it was still empty, lacking in vitality and belief. And as Arjun slumped back in his chair, I had the sense that his situation had sucked the life out of him.

Interactional mapping

If Arjun's sense of forward time was blurred, his perceptions of his colleagues were razor-sharp. Talking through his interactional map released something in him, a certain authority and ease, as if he was in his natural element. His operations team was mixture of senior, long-term employees ('lifers like me', Arjun joked) and younger, highly educated executives hired within the past few years. This latter group was typified by Ken, an ambitious former accountant, in charge of a large processing team, who seemed to have his eyes on Arjun's job. Arjun seemed relaxed about this. As he described the relationship, it became clear to me that Ken's competitiveness did not nonplus Arjun, simply because he had such an intuitive grasp of Ken's strengths and weaknesses that he felt he could easily neutralize him. But when it came to stretching the team – either the new or the old hires – Arjun seemed weary and uninterested. In a deadpan voice, he explained:

> I quarrel with them over their balanced score cards at the start of the year, give them a pat on the back every now and again and then wrangle with them over their bonuses at the year end. Frankly, that's all that really motivates them.

His relationships with members of Hoskins' main board were equally uninspired. He liked the bank's chairman, Sir Philip, but did not entirely trust him. He was a rather distant, patrician figure, who tried to duck out of difficult choices and broadly supported Renton, the bank's CEO. Arjun's relationships with members of Renton's executive committee seemed to be moderately good but nothing like as close as in the past. Much of the mapping conversation was dominated by Renton, an Australian of Scottish origin, who three years before had left a successful career in investment banking to take charge of Hoskins. I wondered how much of Arjun's decline could be attributed to Renton's arrival? 'That's a thought,' Arjun replied with a wan smile. 'It's certainly been a battle: he's very combative, not like our previous boss. Renton's not into consensus!'

What did Renton think of Arjun? I asked him. 'Not much, I suspect,' he replied:

> I never get any clear feedback. He's not a people person. Any conversation we have is strictly operational. He'd probably like to get rid of me but he still thinks that I know how this bank works. And I'm definitely cheaper than an alternative!

The substantive issues between the two leaders had to do with the direction of the bank. A medium-sized player in the UK retail market, Hoskins also had a profitable private bank and a good book of corporate customers. Renton was all for expanding the investment banking side of the bank's operations and fully exploiting its existing business customers. Arjun was not opposed to this policy. At any rate, he realised that the kind of profits available from these transactions meant that resistance was futile. But he wanted to make sure that the complexity of some of these derivatives and hedging instruments did not taint the banks longstanding reputation for dedicated customer service. 'Take that away and what have we got?' Arjun said. "A highly profitable business', Renton would say but I disagree.' Did Arjun express that disagreement?, I asked. 'Rarely,' he replied, shrugging his shoulders, 'it would cause ructions. And as my dad used to say, "if you live in the water don't make an enemy of the crocodile!"'

Arjun's choice-making style in relation to Renton and the executive board of Hoskins was intriguing. He graded his fellow directors and non-executive directors along a spectrum of affiliation to Renton, from 'gung ho support' to 'outward compliance but inward reservations'. In the past, Arjun seemed to have used a rather sophisticated interactional strategy to win over members of the board to his point of view by rewarding them according to what he knew they wanted from their jobs. As time went on, however, his role increasingly became a matter of 'kow-towing' to the CEO and following the course of action that most easily enabled him 'to tick whatever box needs to be ticked'.

In fact, Arjun's attempts to influence his peers had dried up. He said it was probably two years since he had taken a stand on any issue. In that time the bank had become increasingly aggressive in its propriety trading and sales of derivatives products. Arjun had given up making protests; the board's decision-making had become a meaningless game for him. He also realised that he had become isolated from others in his industry. This realisation produced a resolution to start attending industry networking forums again, a choice which he put into practice almost immediately. To me, this was a useful reminder that Arjun was still capable of decisive action.

Rebuilding self-confidence and regaining a sense of self

In order to get more of a sense of Arjun's interaction with himself, I used the personality balancing aspects of oppositional enquiry. He said he was someone who was rational but unable to express emotions spontaneously. 'I keep a close guard on myself,' he said, 'I think I come across as uptight to my team.' I wondered whether he ever let his feelings dominate his choices but he was completely unable to answer this question. For a moment I was reminded of the case of Elliot, the patient I referred to in Chapter 3, who was deprived of the emotions which are necessary for ordinary decision-making.

Arjun did not see himself as an extrovert, and, if anything, was becoming more introverted. 'I can still be outgoing when I'm with friends,' he said, 'but rarely at work.' He was becoming increasingly negative in his outlook – that was also clear. His first thought was for what could go wrong rather than for what could go right.

The main problem, he felt, was that he was 'prey to constant self-doubt'. And yet – to run ahead of ourselves for a moment – it was the power of doubt, directed at Renton's profit-driven strategy that proved to be the making of Arjun as a leader.

Exploring the polarities of his creativity – the opposition between his originating and accommodating tendencies – produced the biggest surprise for Arjun. This suggested that he was much more innovative than he thought himself to be. He was pleasantly surprised by this – and indeed, in the next session, for the first time expressed something close to joy: 'I never thought of myself as having ideas, just solutions to problems, but I suppose that's the same thing really.'

Another breakthrough was his recognition of his deep sense of other people's needs. The coaching itself seemed to inspire him because it showed him a new way of working, which in effect reinforced his basic management style. He saw a value in his desire to support others and over the next few sessions, I got a sense that he was beginning to flex his people skills on his team. He also began to recognize his long-term time orientation, a sense of needing to build slowly for the future, which he in part related to his Asian cultural background. This temporality was in stark juxtaposition to what he saw as the bank's increasingly short-term, bonus-obsessed culture.

Crossing the Rubicon: the vision emerges

Still, Arjun lacked a real vision. He had some new, fringe projects to finesse but nothing that resembled a real purpose, a cause that would reinvigorate him and direct his day to day work. The breakthrough came in the form of an apparently minor choice. Arjun causally mentioned to me that one of his direct reports, who was in charge of confirming sales contracts, had proposed a training course because he was concerned that the sales team failed to understand the impact of their derivates deals on some of their customers. Arjun had proposed the training course during an executive committee meeting, but without enthusiasm or conviction. As he expected, the proposal was more or less ignored by Renton. 'What were his reasons?', I asked Arjun. He replied that none had been offered. I decided to delve a little deeper:

Michael: Do you believe it's a good project?
Arjun: Of course, but it won't happen.
Michael: Why not?
Arjun: It would fall into Renton's category of 'business-blocking activities'. Others are concerned about the high level of complaints but they aren't prepared to take a stand.
Michael: Are you?
Arjun: It's not something you do lightly. You take on Renton and he can hold it against you forever.
Michael: You feel you've got too much to lose?
Arjun: Yes. (Long pause) But then again, maybe I've lost a lot already...

We went through the pros and cons of presenting the training proposal to Renton again. As we did so, Arjun seemed to gain energy and liveliness. He was clear about the members of the leadership team he could co-opt into the project. He put forward some clever suggestions about covert quid pro quos, as well as overt negotiating tactics, which surprised me with their mixture of psychological insight and almost Machiavellian political bargaining. But in the end, we left the session with no resolution and no great sense on my part that anything would come of the discussion.

As so often happens in coaching, it is the time between sessions which produces the most startling results. At the start of our next session, a fortnight later, Arjun could not wait to tell me the results of the latest leadership team meeting. He had re-presented the proposal, using some of the tactics we had discussed and, to his great surprise, Renton had accepted it. Perhaps there had been something about Arjun's persistent, quietly passionate tone, backed up by implicit support from his peers, which had taken the chief executive aback and even impressed him. Who knew what he really thought about his COO? Might he not have actually preferred someone who challenged him from time to time?

In any case, the result was that Arjun was beginning to think of other measures and proposals, preparing for a more sustained battle. The distinct outlines of a powerful vision were emerging. 'I need to make sure that we don't fall over the cliff with our mad rush to profits,' he said firmly. 'We need to maintain our transparency or we'll suffer with our customers.' In the context of the problems which only emerged into the full light of the day after the credit crunch in 2008, this realisation was remarkable in its prescience. Arjun outlined a strategy for regulating the bank's exposure to risky transactions, which went well beyond what was required at that time by the industry regulators.

It seemed that overnight, a strategy had appeared and yet all the materials for it were already to hand in Arjun's values and beliefs: it just took the spark of a positive choice to ignite them. In searching for a vision, it is easy to get misled into thinking that the goal is always 'a big idea', something 'out there', which has never been thought of before. But often it is already 'in here', so to speak, deeply rooted in a coachee's present reality, just waiting to be uncovered.

Later, I remembered our first coaching session, when – perhaps as a deliberate test – I had asked Arjun how much he earned. He looked surprised and even affronted – in the bank it was technically a dismissible offence to discuss your remuneration. But after a pause, and with a slightly amused smile, he told me what he earned. This incident gave me a sense of a man of exceptional honesty who was fully prepared to place his trust in the coaching process. Now a few months later, Arjun's deep commitment to integrity and care had finally come to the surface, informing his choices for the future. He shook my hand at the end of the session with a new sense of vigour, and added, 'You know, I feel I'm getting back into the groove.'

Achievement choices: putting the vision to work

A committed vision can work wonders. Arjun now began to make bold choices throughout the achievement cycle, as he put his new strategy into practice. He started to build a coalition among his peers to introduce better documentation of the sales process, so that derivatives transactions become more transparent. A clever piece of bargaining with the director of sales clinched this major initiative. He also began to provide greater support for the bank's heavily marginalized compliance and risk management departments. This initiative Arjun tried to keep 'under the radar' – out of Renton's line of sight – through a complex series of working committees.

Arjun also helped the information technology director to develop more cogent arguments for improving the bank's computer systems – the current ramshackle IT processes were fraught with risk – and stealthily lobbied on his behalf. Arjun argued strongly for this change programme, although it meant a considerable increase in his overall budget. He initiated off-the-record meetings with financial regulators and although they proved to be fruitless in a direct sense – 'we're under-resourced and overwhelmed, as it is,' was their memorable reply – he used them as a springboard for fruitful internal discussions.

As far as his own operational team was concerned, Arjun found it relatively easy to make strides forward, now that he had a clear overall strategy. His recently introduced one-to-one sessions with the team gained a new focus and intensity. He made a determined effort to rein in his 'wild card', Ken, with some tough but empathetic meetings. 'In the end, I told him I was his best hope to achieving the kind of recognition he's looking for,' Arjun said. 'That got him thinking!' Arjun now developed a more sophisticated way of making choices in his own management team, sometimes arguing forcefully, sometimes more subtly and at times employing a democratic approach. 'The key thing for me now, 'he explained, 'is knowing when to let them know where I stand and when it's up to them to take charge.'

In the bank's executive committee, Arjun was now regularly challenging Renton with great subtly and cunning, offering him clever alternative options and, occasionally, the hint of a threat. Arjun's expertise as a communicator, negotiator and master of interpersonal skills shone through in his new relationship with his boss, which was never quite confrontational enough to provide Renton with a clear opportunity to marginalize Arjun. Arjun likened his campaign to a guerrilla war – 'if he ever gets me out in the open, with all his firepower, I'm finished,' he joked. Arjun's subtlety and genuine human care could not fail to impress Renton and in some cases he seemed to shrug his shoulders and accept the wisdom of his strangely changed COO, although someone, somewhere in the bank, probably had to endure an outburst of Renton's anger as a result.

At a personal level, Arjun worked on keeping his self-dialogue positive, building up his assertiveness and focusing on his achievements rather than dwelling on the negatives. This was important because the battle against Renton was not a straightforward progression but a course that was full of frustrating hold-ups and reversals. More confident in his innovativeness, Arjun was also more inclined to point out his new ideas to himself – and to others. His work–life balance also improved. He found that with his new energy he achieved more in the office and so felt less guilty 'leaving early', although he still worked long hours by most standards. This, in turn, meant he arrived home less tired and in a better state of mind than before, so transforming a negative spiral into a positive one.

Conclusion

The result of Arjun's efforts – and his ability to mobilize many other senior executives in the bank – was that when the financial crisis erupted in 2008, Hoskins was far better placed than other banks. It proved to be more resistant to claims of mis-selling, money-laundering and other trading-based scandals than many other UK banks, although it certainly did not escape unscathed. Renton, no doubt sensing the change in climate, moved on, joining a niche investment bank in New York, where according to Arjun, 'he made several multiples of what he'd earned in London'.

As for Arjun, having consolidated his position at Hoskins, 'the unimaginable happened' and he moved into a chief executive role. He was offered the top job at a small but rapidly growing UK bank, known for its reputation for putting its customers first, and he did not hesitate to accept it. It accorded precisely with his values and he saw that it had a strong potential brand advantage at a time when popular trust in banking had hit rock bottom. It seemed that history had vindicated Arjun's belief in honesty and integrity, something I mentioned to him in our final session. He nodded warmly and added:

> I know you are fond of proverbs and I came across an interesting African saying the other day, which runs 'a person is a person because of other people.' I think that probably sums-up what I am about as a leader.

It certainly made me think that Arjun had created a leadership vision which enabled him to connect what mattered to him in his past to what mattered to him in the future. This had helped him to gain a powerful new sense of balance which was why he was now moving forwards as a truly choice-focused leader.

Chapter 7

Coaching the non-delivering leader

'Blocked at every turn': the case of Deborah K.

I'm blocked at every turn. A dream job is turning into a nightmare!

Sadly, non-delivery is the lot of many leaders. They may seem to be up to the job in terms of strategy and resourcing skills but when it comes to putting ideas into practice they grind to a halt. Deborah K. found herself in this situation, after nine months in charge of a nationwide public sector organization. The Agency – I'll just call it that – presided over a disparate portfolio of functions related to legal services and the administration of the courts, which had been put together over many years of wrangling between the Home Office and other ministries. Because of austerity measures in the public sector, the agency was faced with staff cuts of up to 20 per cent, as well as the need to modernize many of its procedures. A series of embarrassing gaffes had led to bad publicity for the Agency and even calls for it to be disbanded altogether.

Up to this point, Deborah had been regarded as a rising star in the civil service, with a brilliant degree from Oxford and a track record of success in a series of smaller public sector roles. The Agency represented a major step up for her in leadership terms and one which she had embraced with enthusiasm. Still in her mid-thirties, she had got 'a dream job', as she announced on social media to her friends. But less than a year later, in spite of her reputation for superb strategizing and elegant resourcing, she was beginning to doubt her ability to achieve anything as a leader.

Slim and chicly dressed, Deborah was dwarfed by her huge, somewhat dilapidated office near Waterloo Bridge, as she told me how the balance between the Agency and herself had fallen so far out of line. She said she had come up against a brick wall in a chaotic, deeply traditional organization, with 'arcane' entrenched routines and a job-for-life culture. 'Frankly, it keeps me awake at night, trying to figure out how it all works,' she confessed wearily. Nor was her immediate boss pleased with her performance. Bernard, an ambitious and irascible senior official in the civil service, had stuck out his neck to appoint Deborah. But now he seemed to think it may have been a mistake.

I felt sympathy for Deborah. Leadership usually boils down to results. To be thwarted at the delivery stage is often the most frustrating form of fractional leadership and one which almost certainly requires some radically revised choice-making if a leader is to avoid total failure.

Deborah's vision

There was nothing intrinsically wrong with Deborah's strategy for the Agency, as far as I could judge. She outlined it in detail during our first session and it seemed a highly intelligent response to a drastic budget reduction. It included restructuring several overlapping departments and streamlining the operations of various call centres dotted around the country. The plan appeared to achieve a delicate balance between voluntary redundancies, transfer opportunities and compulsory lay-offs, which went some way towards cushioning the blow of the dramatic decrease in the workforce. ('Don't blame me, blame the bankers,' Deborah said blandly, when I remarked on the scale of the downsizing.) The plan included comprehensive training and education schemes, new provisions for working parents, a mission statement that was actually memorable and new communication links with other civil service departments. The only fault lines in the strategy which I detected were the inappropriately abstruse language into which Deborah often lapsed – 'policy wonk speak', she would later call it – and her insensitivity to the impact of redundancies on the long-serving staff. Perhaps her management team had experienced something similar when Deborah had first presented the strategy to them. 'I thought I'd sold it to them, she said, 'but in retrospect, I don't think they got it at all.'

And yet at first the action plan seemed to go well enough. The new vision and values and logo were launched with panache and there was a rush to take up the voluntary redundancy places, with their fairly generous compensation terms. Some of the training opportunities were also snapped up, although Deborah was a little disappointed by the general take-up. But when it came to the more substantial restructuring of the departments and the phasing in of the compulsory redundancy programme, the pace of progress slowed down dramatically.

To begin with, Deborah put down the delays in implementing the radical aspects of her plan to the amazingly ramshackle communications systems still in place in the organization. Her management team gave her repeated messages of positive feedback and pledges of support but little action to substantiate them. Soon Deborah found herself caught in a confusing maze of false trails, miscommunication and meetings that never happened, amid an increasingly fervid atmosphere of denial and recrimination. All of this was shrouded in a fog of misinformation as Deborah struggled to find out what was actually going on at the Agency. She spent days poring over inconsistent, badly laid out management information reports, which only increased her feelings of helplessness.

As interactional mapping quickly showed, the biggest obstacle to change on her team was coming from Ray, who was in charge of operations, the largest team in the Agency, and a kind of empire within an empire. He was part of 'the old guard', as Deborah described it, a lifelong civil servant in his fifties, who had spent his entire career building relationships within the Agency and beyond it. Although unsophisticated in his manner, he seemed as happy hobnobbing with government ministers as 'having a drink with the lads' – many drinks, in fact, in Deborah's opinion. Ray was never overtly hostile but surreptitiously resistant to almost every move Deborah made. She could not tell whether his stance was an act of naivety or deliberate obfuscation, and sometimes she was even thrown by his broad Yorkshire accent. Often she came away from their meetings with apparent agreement but with a headache which accurately predicted that these putative gains would soon disappear like water through her fingers.

'Ray-ism', as Deborah called it, pervaded the team. Her only allies in her leadership team seemed to be the head of human resources and the finance director, although they were rather ineffectual executives and generally silent in team meetings. After one particularly dispiriting meeting, with its typical mixture of illusory agreements, confusing recriminations and unreliable information, Deborah had privately confessed her frustration to the HR director and my appearance on the scene had been the result.

The delegator trips up

Deborah was usually a very trusting person. When I asked her to describe her personal qualities 'trustful' is the one of the first words she used. 'I've aways been like that. At home, my parents were very straightforward and open with me. At school, I was always popular. I feel I can spot people who are untrustworthy a mile off and I keep my distance from them.'

This comfort in the space of others – or at least selected others – was the basis of her leadership style. For her, motivation was all about recruitment and delegation, as she explained:

> In my other posts, I set the strategy, made the right hires and let them get on with it. I never had to think too much about it. With hindsight, perhaps I should have, but it all seemed to happen fairly smoothly. I think I'm good at picking the right people for the right roles. Here I've inherited people in key roles – like Ray – and there's nothing I can do about it, at least not in the short term.

In her previous jobs, this resourcing style had consistently delivered positive results, although never in recessionary economic circumstances or with such a large and obdurate organization as the Agency. Deborah was not the first leader to be hired on the basis of leadership skills which are no longer fit for purpose but she seemed unable to see this. Rather than adapting her style to her management team, Deborah rapidly lost trust in them altogether. As they descended into that category of people she normally would prefer to have nothing to do with, she became deeply suspicious of them. She started withdrawing, 'tightening up', she described it. 'When I think of anything in relation to them I feel myself stiffening, as though my skin was shrinking.'

This seemed to affect her choice-making quite strongly. She became more preemptive in her approaches to meetings, planning everything in advance, which clashed with the last-minute style of many of her management team. This increased rigidity actually seemed to be a reaction to the doubts that she constantly had about her strategy. The same can be said of her use of a decision-making style which cognitive psychologist Dan Ariely (2008) refers to as 'keeping doors open', in which a commitment to an excessive number of options distracts us from our real objectives. Deborah began changing tiny details of her plan, constantly fine-tuning her peripheral arguments. To counter this, she put up a wall of resistance against other people's suggestions, an increasingly hollow defensiveness which she tried to present as a strength. So desperate was she to prove that once a decision was made it was never unmade, that she even quoted Margaret Thatcher, telling her team 'U-turn if you want to', which infuriated the Agency's trade union representatives once they got to hear about it.

A gender issue?

When Deborah told me about this incident I asked her if being a female leader presented her with any special problems, especially with some of the more traditional male staff. I had asked her this question several times before but as usual she roundly dismissed this idea:

> That's never been an issue for me. Yes, you have to work harder to get the same recognition as a bloke, but I'm a hard-worker anyway. If anything, it's an advantage being a woman, because it gives you more roles to play.

Deborah's refusal to make any excuses about her leadership on the grounds of her gender was admirable, even though I think she may have underestimated some of the opposition it caused in the Agency. She was clearly right about her range of interpersonal skills. As she reported, she often adopted a bluff, matter of fact, 'macho role', when talking to male members of her staff and a more pliant, people-orientated tone when conversing with women. However, I got the impression that in mixed company she sometimes got the balance wrong, which could have been confusing and even suggest inauthenticity on her part.

At any rate, Deborah's interpersonal skills seemed to do nothing to stop the Agency's monthly performance results from getting worse and worse. Her boss increased the pressure on her. In an acrimonious meeting, Bernard told her that her previous jobs 'meant nothing' and that the current job was all about 'finding out what you do when the going really gets tough'. Now that the challenge was on, and Deborah's poor delivery skills were cruelly exposed, Bernard did not seem to be prepared to give her support or advice, although it occurred to me that this was perhaps what his idea of a leadership test was all about.

Failure as the secret to whole cycle success

When I asked Deborah about her past failures – a piece of oppositional enquiry which contrasted with her usual talk about her past successes – she cited a project early in her career, which had gone disastrously wrong. Some coaches focus exclusively on the strengths of a coachee rather than her weaknesses, but sometimes failure is the secret road to success – and so it turned out here. The failure Deborah described related to her time at the Ministry of Agriculture, when she had been involved in long-winded negotiations over European fishing rights. She had been only a relatively junior member of the negotiating team but had found herself unable to act when called on to take a lead role. 'I just couldn't get my head around it, to be honest. I managed to duck out with sick leave, and friends covered for me, so it didn't go down as a blot of my copy book.'

What was it that was so difficult about this event? I asked her. Her reply was telling.

> It was very confrontational. I find that difficult. I can't think properly in a tight corner. It was also very repetitive, the same discussions over and over again with only minor variations. Of course it's these minor variations, tiny policy nuances, which you have to spot because that's where you get ripped off – or where the breakthrough comes.

The more we discussed the relationship between this project and her current role, the more similarities Deborah began to see, except this time there was nobody to bail her out.

'Getting your hands dirty': key achievement choices

Once she realised that she urgently needed to improve her performance in the delivery phase of the achievement cycle, Deborah was able to look at all aspects of her leadership with a new eye. For example, she recognized that she needed to work on her ability to empathize with others. In spite of her good interpersonal skills and general trustfulness, she found it extremely difficult to put herself in the shoes of people who were not like her. 'I just don't get what goes through the mind of someone like Ray,' she confessed. I asked her to try, just as 'a hypothetical exercise'. 'Pig-headedness' was her first response but after a while she started coming up with phrases like 'loyalty to his staff', 'protecting his reputation', 'fear of change'. Previously, she seemed to have hidden these possible insights from herself as much as from anybody else.

This kind of exercise, so different from her normal policy drafting, caused Deborah to make some modifications to her strategy. She introduced a performance-related payment plan, which represented a striking change in culture for the Agency but one which she believed would have positive results. Initially this was blocked by her finance director but Deborah found a way to persuade him to reallocate some funds set aside for capital expenditure. This enabled her to introduce an incentive plan which seemed to go down well with the staff, especially the most ambitious employees. 'I want to give the best people a reason to stay' was her justification for this measure. After a week of agonising and self-questioning, she even decided to present her strategy to her team as a 'principled U-turn'. Although this perhaps exaggerated the truth, it was a concession she was fully prepared to make, if it helped to get her plans adopted.

Deborah's new, more balanced analysis of her situation also brought home to her just how alone she was in the Agency, in terms of what she-called 'modernizers'. She said she needed 'an enforcer, someone who's on my side for once.' She decided to try and recruit someone to take charge of management information, a role she calculated Bernard would object to least, since he frequently complained about the Agency's lack of reliable data. The real purpose of this new post would be to ensure that Deborah's policies were implemented. She made an impassioned plea to Bernard and won her case, in spite of his concerns about increasing her budget. Within weeks, Edgar, a former colleague, was drafted in from the Department of Work and Pensions. Edgar had none of Deborah's piercing intellect but he had a tough, cheerfully engaging approach and was extremely effective in supporting Deborah to put her plans into action. Deborah also managed to bring in another former colleague she could trust, as a replacement for her personal assistant, who was retiring after forty years at the Agency.

Armed with champions of her own, a revised strategy and a new willingness to empathize, Deborah tried to build bridges with Ray and the rest of her team. During an awayday, she attempted to take Ray into her confidence and a glimmer of understanding seemed to emerge between these very different personalities. However, it was only when Deborah steeled herself to be more assertive, threatening to escalate the issue to Bernard, that Ray started to soften his stance. At the same time, now realising how sensitive the issue of redundancies was, she resolved to negotiate with Bernard for more funds to reduce the impact of the lay offs. Although largely fruitless, this effort went down well with her staff, as did several other measures she introduced, which created the preconditions for real progress. But more was required if Deborah was to actually get across the finishing line.

Actualisation and time

For me, the paramount change which Deborah made was in the time dimension of leadership. The actualizing skills she most lacked were determination and persistence, or to use the earthy, Churchillian motto of marketing supremo, Martin Sorrel, the ability to 'keep buggering on' (Benjamin, 2005). Without this kind of resilience a leader is always likely to be exposed when times get hard. For Deborah, changing her attitude to achievement meant changing her attitude to the temporality of achievement. She realised that success had always come quickly for her. She said, 'I tend to pick up stuff quite quickly and feel most comfortable with people who also get things before anyone else.' Speed of thought and rapid communication can be advantageous but not if a good deal of time is required for the completion of a project. Deborah had to tackle her tendency to get bored or dispirited if progress was not rapid enough and to embrace the experience of repetition which she found so difficult.

So Deborah started repeating herself, so to speak, going back over the same ground, not moving on until the task had been accomplished. In effect, she stopped being so open in the delivery phase, which had led her to constantly modify her position, and became resolutely closed. In this she showed a gritty determination to rebalance herself which, I have to say, surprised me at times. An example of her new attitude to time was her decision to oversee some of the changes which urgently needed to be made in call centre procedure. More than once, she reported feeling disconsolate after spending a long day at call centres in the Midlands or the North of England. In these circumstances, a negative future seemed to envelop her as she envisaged abandoning her visit or, at the very least, losing her composure in a way that she considered was beneath her. But as human beings our resilience is almost always greater than we imagine it to be. So it proved with Deborah, as she endeavoured in coaching and in her daily work to envisage a positive future when the present looked bleak. This increased hardiness enabled her to courageously persist with the measures that she knew would deliver results.

'Hanging in there' became her mantra, especially in her negotiations with Bernard. Wringing new concessions out of her boss became a major theme of her attempt to actualize her vision for the Agency. She frequently expressed her frustration at the task of trying to change the mind of a master negotiator who had a notoriously acerbic turn of phrase. He repeatedly told Deborah that he 'would feel the iron grip of the Treasury around his neck if he missed his efficiency targets by a penny', a negotiating ploy, no doubt, but probably not too far from the truth. Nevertheless, Deborah persisted, combining her charm and intelligence with a new determination that eventually resulted in a series of small but significant concessions, which she was able to present successfully to her management team. Ray in particular could not fail to be impressed by Deborah's doggedness, which in turn influenced the increasingly 'on-message' communiqués, which he and the rest of the managers passed on to their staff.

Another important move in the time dimension of this situation was Deborah's decision to announce that she was committing herself to the Agency for the long term. To begin with, she had tended to see this appointment as a stepping stone to a more glamorous role. Bernard had possibly even sold the job to her on this basis. She certainly seemed to be perceived by her staff as 'a here today, gone tomorrow' type of leader, of which they had had several in recent times. 'I now feel I'm here for the long haul,' she told me, 'for as it long as it takes.' Of course, this genuine change in her attitude to the future manifested itself in a different way of living in the present, which was picked up by those around her in a very positive way.

Conclusion

Fifteen months after our coaching had begun, the Agency seemed like a different place. It had been badly shaken by the departure of many staff and particularly by the compulsory redundancies, although there turned out to be slightly fewer of these than originally envisaged. Deborah had done her utmost to recognize the effect which dismissals had not only on departing employees but on those who remained in post; 'survivor guilt' was a phrase she now used with real feeling. On the positive side, the Agency gave off a quite different atmosphere as you walked through the corridors. The notice boards were packed with initiatives and there was a productive hum about the place that it never had before. The statistics backed this up, with substantially improved performances across the board, as demonstrated by the beautifully laid out management information reports Deborah proudly showed me. The Agency slowly seemed to be gaining a positive reputation within Whitehall, partially as a result of Bernard's growing enthusiasm for the organization. It helped that the public blunders, which the Agency had so often made in the past, had virtually disappeared.

Deborah too had changed. She still had the same enviable facility for talking through her plans but I felt there was now a completely new depth to her as a leader. She had a quiet sense of her own power to do whatever was necessary to implement her goals. This gritty purposefulness might stretch her to the limits but would not cause her to overbalance or behave in ways that she felt were unworthy of her. Increased toughness, combined with greater flexibility and openness, were now enabling her to make effective choices throughout the entire achievement cycle. In my view, she was well on the way to becoming an interactional leader, capable of successfully dealing with whatever challenges the future would hold for her.

Part 3

The multiplicity of leadership roles – and how to coach them

Chapter 8

The global leader, the entrepreneur and the chair of the board

Coaching across the spectrum

The astonishing variety of leadership extends well beyond the three case studies we examined in Part 2, which involved two CEOs and a COO, working in broadly domestic environments. As we will see in Part 3, leadership also encompasses team leaders, potential leaders, thought leaders and leaders of innovation. It is a multidimensional reality which can hang on the leader's ability to develop a group which constructively challenges his decisions, a subject which we explore in Chapter 12 through examples of group coaching.

We begin our exploration of the leadership multirole in this chapter with the global leader, who leads across cultures and continents, the entrepreneur, who starts from a blank sheet, and the chair of the board, aiming to build a productive choice-making environment for his company. As before, the 6D approach will anchor our study. The three phases of the achievement cycle can give clarity to the multiple aspects of leadership, while the dynamics of interactional psychology illustrate once more the importance for leaders to get the balance right between the demands of the self and the claims of others.

1. The global interactional leader

Leading an international company is one of the greatest challenges facing a leader today in our increasingly globalized economy. Multi-national leadership makes demands which are over and above those confronting the head of an organization operating in a single country. The global leader's interactional map is likely to look even more complicated than her domestic counterpart, with additional constituencies in different countries and different rules surrounding corporate legislation, the media, or relationships with shareholders. Creating and maintaining your poise in the face of this vast number of variables, in many sets of interactions, is a test indeed.

The time dimension is also exacting for the international leader. We accept that our subjective experience of time is highly variable; time can 'stand still' or 'fly' depending on the circumstances. But even the relative stability of objective time, the time of the clock, can be shattered by the constant travel across time zones, which many leaders undertake. One finance director who was continually on the move between continents admitted to me that he could not remember the last time he had felt fully healthy and capable of thinking properly. 'You're either on a plane, about to get on one, or recovering from the journey'. In these circumstances, a leader's routine decision-making processes can easily be disrupted. And this is before we even start considering the cultural differences which can fundamentally alter the basic meaning of many of the factors involved in a leadership choice.

Cross cultural leadership and the achievement cycle

Global leadership requires global choices. This means navigating though the maze of habits, expectations and meanings of stakeholders in different national cultures, which usually goes well beyond the cross-cultural dimension of domestic leadership, even in a highly multicultural society like the UK. One of the most influential guides to this cross-cultural labyrinth is Geert Hofstede. His model charts cultural differences along a series of dimensions, which overlap with the 6D leadership model in certain respects (Hofstede et al., 2010). For example, his 'power distance' dimension is closely connected with norms of decision-making in different cultures. According to Hofstede's research, North Americans expect to be involved in key choices much more than Latin Americans, for whom organizational and social hierarchy is more accepted and respected. Hofstede's dimension of individual versus collective values also clearly maps on to the self–others dialectic of the interactional model, which we will explore in relation to team formations in the next chapter.

Time orientation is another Hofstede dimension which parallels the 6D leadership approach in that it makes strong distinctions between the way people are influenced by the future and the past. Some nations, including the UK and the USA, look to the future more than societies which prefer to maintain fidelity to the traditions of the past (e.g. Hong Kong). 'Uncertainty avoidance' is also relevant in the sense that Hofstede suggests that the degree to which we try to avoid uncertainty – by which he means lack of clarity rather than risk – can be culturally determined. This could impact the way different cultures approach the stages of the achievement cycle.

A word of warning is needed at this point, however. Useful as it is, the cross-cultural approach is a key which can lock as many doors as it opens. If it creates strong pre-choices and expectations in advance, it can do more harm than good. Certainly Hofstede's masculine/feminine cultural dimension – although it bears some resemblance to the dominance/supportiveness polarity of the ISO – could easily lead to misunderstandings and an unwanted reinforcement of gender stereotypes. It may be that simply exploring cultural assumptions informally is more beneficial than through the application of a formal questionnaire such as Hofstede's. From the viewpoint of interactional leadership, the further danger is that too much emphasis on cross-cultural differences masks the importance of the achievement cycle. Specifically, it focuses the leader too exclusively on the resourcing stage. After all, a bad strategy is a bad strategy however much cultural sensitivity may be used to communicate it to those who have to implement it.

To underline the point, let me draw on the public domain of leadership and introduce an example of an outstanding contemporary global leader. Carlos Ghosn has succeeded in turning around several multi-national ventures, including ailing Japanese automotive giant Nissan. Ghosn is a Brazilian of Lebanese origin, educated in France, who has had his greatest success in Japan, and so has unusual credentials for assimilating into different cultures and avoiding the pitfalls which might catch others out. Nevertheless, it is his emphasis on all stages of the achievement cycle which seems to dominate his philosophy of leadership. He has said:

> First, you have to give employees the opportunity to create change by discussing and listening at all levels in the company. Then you have to decide and implement. It can be easy to spend too much time listening and planning without effective implementation.
>
> (Magee, 2003: 103)

Ghosn is a whole cycle leader, who pays particular attention to delivery. He claims that the correct focus should be 'ninety five per cent on execution and delivery, five per cent on planning' (Magee, 2003: 103) This seems to tie in with Hofstede's claim that uncertainty avoidance means that members of some national cultures (e.g. USA, UK and Australia) are more comfortable with the strategy phases of the choice cycle, while others prefer the delivery stage. But this does not mean that strategy is not important for Ghosn. In fact, he made a radical commitment to strategy by listening to Nissan employees in Japan, many of whom had never been consulted by their superiors in their entire careers. It is just that culturally, as well as individually, there are variations about how much time leaders prefer to spend on strategy. Indeed, Hofstede and his colleagues offer some evidence that nations which are high in certainty avoidance are more likely to excel at implementation than innovation.

Marlene: 'I'm only creating a strategy for 37 countries!'

The relationship between cross-cultural issues and the achievement cycle was very much to the fore in the case of Marlene, when she became chief executive of a commodities information company. Based in London, it operated throughout Asia, Europe and the USA, and had been suffering from poor results for some time. Her chairman was insistent that much more needed to be done 'at the cultural level'. Marlene accepted this but felt that she wanted to understand the business before committing herself to any course of action. She mischievously described herself as an 'Essex girl' – and it was true that she hailed from that county and had an unpretentious accent and dress style to match. But she also possessed an MBA from a leading French business school, several years experience in the USA and an enviable track record of corporate success. She had little time for 'so-called global leaders whose style doesn't travel'.

The first step for Marlene was to analyse her new firm's strategy. She studied it in depth, trying to keep an open mind and then embarked on a whirlwind tour of the company. She and her management team spent much time in meetings with editors, reporters and sales teams gathering information and encouraging ideas. Marlene wanted this consultation process to bear fruit fairly quickly. She felt she could not keep the company in suspended animation for too long, because, in her experience, extended strategizing was not popular outside the Anglo-American world.

Marlene's conclusion was that the company's existing strategy was a bizarre mix of universal principles and culturally specific exceptions. At first this combination seemed to make sense but she realised that in many cases the relationship between localism and globalism was the wrong way round. For instance, the company's reporting methodology was inconsistent, preventing subscribers from tracking prices from country to country, which led to numerous complaints. On the other hand, the firm's sales teams reported that their activities were rigidly based on Anglo-American assumptions which often were quite out of keeping with the norms of their national cultures. In South-East Asia, for instance, sales people were compelled to take a very direct approach to customers and given little time to build rapport in keeping with local customs. This turned off many customers and even created suspicions that the company's data was biased towards the UK and North America.

For Marlene, resourcing her new strategy largely focused on creating a clear understanding of the changes involved and the standards which needed to be met. She felt that, by and large, the company had the necessary staff, it was just a matter of pointing them in the right direction and providing them with appropriate retraining, where necessary. She used nuanced communication styles when announcing her new vision in different territories. For instance, she employed a more detailed, rule-based approach in Japan, France and Germany than in the USA, Australia and the UK. Here she used a broader brush style, allowing some latitude for interpretation. She felt that in English-speaking countries too many rules stifle initiative. But her down-to-earth philosophy was fairly clear: 'These differences help in getting the message across but in the end everyone has got to follow the same processes to be successful.'

In the final analysis, it was the implementation of the new approach which made the difference. This brought out Marlene's fighting spirit and her patient, steady-eyed toughness in monitoring results. She was adept at spotting problems at an early stage and offering empathetic but essentially practical solutions. If these measures failed, she was prepared to be ruthless, bringing in new managers, for example, or changing remuneration policies, in a way that surprised those diehards in the industry who still harboured suspicions about the abilities of a female leader. With this strong new direction of travel established, this bright, receptive, communicative company soon began to change for the better.

Of course, there are many models of global leadership and the factors involved in working in different industries and countries are likely to become even more complex in the coming years. Multi-cultural coach Philippe Rosinski (2003: 58) rightly emphasizes the need for 'dialectic thinking' in order to turn cultural differences into an opportunity for new forms of integration. This he contrasts with 'binary thinking which assumes one best way' and can create all sorts of cultural impasses. Every successful multinational leader has to come up with her own solutions. But Marlene's emphasis on balancing her whole cycle choices with an awareness of the psychology of cultural difference represents one highly effective example of interactional leadership at a global level.

2. The entrepreneurial leader

What makes an entrepreneur?

Leading a large mature company is one thing, leading a start up is another. Yet every big company was once small, which is why entrepreneurial leaders who get it right are the dynamos of the world economy. Today high-profile, worldwide organizations spring up in a matter of years, rather than decades, especially in the high technology sector, while other successful start ups are swallowed by mature corporate leviathans to provide much needed innovation and growth. In this light, it is perhaps strange that the literature of leadership studies tends to be biased towards large-scale organizational leaders and seems relatively uninterested in enquiring about the special qualities that make for entrepreneurial leadership.

In my experience, entrepreneurs have a particularly strong desire to make their own choices and to build something unique. Being uncomfortable with authority, or at least preferring not to be told what to do by others, may also be a personality trait of the entrepreneur, as well as self-confidence and unpredictability. In terms of the achievement cycle, this could imply that the typical entrepreneur is a possibilizing actualizer, strong on vision and 'getting things done' but poor on resourcing. Some recent research which is specifically focused on the differences between entrepreneurs and large-scale corporate leaders seems to back this up (Bonnstetter, 2013). It suggests that the serial entrepreneur lacks the empathy, planning skills and self-management capability (especially time-management) to be found among successful corporate leaders. Certainly many successful entrepreneurs have a reputation for being hard to work with, which sometimes means that at a certain point it is desirable to replace them, if their companies are to continue to grow.

Another factor often associated with the entrepreneur, which may distinguish her from the typical organizational leader, is an appetite for risk. Almost a century ago, economist Frank Knight (1921) identified three types of risk involved in starting up a business. The first is statistically measurable risk, the second is ambiguity, which is much harder to measure, and the third is 'true uncertainty', impossible to estimate or model statistically. As a former entrepreneur myself, it is this third aspect, the unknown unknowns, which rings most true. Of course, risk is relative and in severely disrupted economic times, when job security is precarious and unemployment is high, it may be that starting your own business represents your best chance of getting a job and holding on to it.

The entrepreneur and the achievement cycle

The importance of the achievement cycle in coaching entrepreneurial leaders cannot be understated. The fact is that the start up operation exposes a leader's choices around strategy, resourcing and delivery like nothing else. These choices come thick and fast, at all levels, from investing in new business cards to changing global strategy, and are not mediated by lengthy chains of command.

Strategy is crucial. The start up is a mission to the future, stripped of the ballast of the past or the reassuring buoyancy of the present. In the often makeshift offices of a typical start up, the company's forward-looking trajectory needs to convey a particularly powerful impression. This is choosing the future in a very pure form. Resourcing a strategy is especially exacting. Financially resourcing a start up is notoriously fickle and hiring the appropriate human resources is an art form itself. When you cannot offer potential employees the job security or reputational advantage of a larger organization, the lure of the future, perhaps in the form of equity in the company, has to be leveraged to the full. The execution stage of a new venture also exerts unique pressures, as there is likely to be limited tolerance for poor results. In fact, all along the high wire of the new business venture there are unexpected hazards. As one successful entrepreneur said to me, 'in big organizations you can get away with some dodgy decisions but when you're starting up, every bad choice could be your last.'

Coaching the entrepreneur

Leadership coaches tend to work with leaders in large organizations more than with entrepreneurs. This is a sad irony in that entrepreneurs are not surrounded by the support systems which most organizational leaders have at their disposal and can often benefit richly from the support and challenge of the coaching process. I suspect one of the main obstacles preventing coaches from engaging with entrepreneurs is a very simple one: payment. Persuading an entrepreneur that she can afford a coach's fees is not easy, particularly given the problems of cash flow in start up operations; but it is not impossible. In my view, the cost of avoiding some of the bad choices which are invariably made at the beginning of a venture can justify the fees involved in coaching many times over. It may even be worthwhile for the entrepreneur to bear some of the cost of coaching herself, which can also help in justifying this expenditure to other participants in the venture.

Other imaginative fees schemes can be devised, such as deferred payments or a percentage payment based on the profitability of the company. There is also the pro-bono option which a coach should always consider in order to enhance and deepen his experience. Of course, these choices represent a risk for the coach – which parallels the risk the entrepreneur is taking – and may not suit everyone. But coaching in the entrepreneurial space can be exciting and illuminating and there are real advantages in being associated with a fast-growing company which succeeds in going against the grain.

Damian: living in a house of glass

Successful entrepreneurs often start early. The founders of high-tech titans, Microsoft, Facebook and Apple, all dropped out of university to start their business careers and some entrepreneurs start even younger, going into business straight from school. Damian had a very different career trajectory but one that is becoming more common these days. He had been the Chief Executive of a successful IT corporation for many years, before retiring in his late forties. He had found retirement boring and decided to fulfil a long-held ambition to create a new software company. He found funding from investors impressed by his plan for a new search engine but six months into the venture he was struggling to transfer his whole cycle leadership skills to an increasingly crisis-ridden start up.

Part of Damian's difficulty was in adapting to his new interactional map. He told me in our first session that in his corporate role he had been supported by a whole communications team. 'It was a bit of a shock to the system', he said, 'to not only prepare my first major pitch entirely on my own, but to have to go out and buy the bloody projector to present it on!' Damian found his relationship to his ten members of staff unsettling and distracting (they all occupied a small office in a rather gloomy building). The software engineers, or 'coders', were young, inexperienced and 'very needy', according to Damian. In the past, he would have received status reports from his managers on software development. Now it seemed he was doing it all himself, 'almost literally hands-on' he said. 'I sometimes feel more like their mum rather than their boss!'

At times, he found the openness of running a start up intimidating. "There's nowhere to hide', he complained. 'You have to get everything right – strategy, hiring, office design – and everyone is waiting for the results. It's like living in a glass house!'

I asked him whether he was having second thoughts about his decision to start a company. He replied that he was fully committed to the venture but it was clear from his tone of voice that he still had some doubts, an impression reinforced by his casual reference to a head hunter who had contacted him about a new corporate role.

Dealing with investors and shareholders

Damian's relationship with his investors was another part of his problem. The relationship with financial shareholders is always a major axis of the leader's interactional map, one which can make or break him. If a major shareholder loses confidence in the person most responsible for his investment, the spiral of mistrust can be unstoppable. In his corporate life, Damian's relationship with shareholders had always been unproblematic, no doubt helped by the fact that he tended to meet his revenue targets with metronomic regularity. On the one occasion when Damian fell short of his quarterly earnings goal, the institutional investors did not protest. At the end of a board meeting to discuss the results, one of them, a famously reserved fund manager, had even placed a reassuring arm around Damian's shoulder.

Things were very different now. There was no distance or restraint. The investors were not managers of others people's money but of their own. Chris, the company's main investor, could be particularly vocal in his criticism of Damian, who replied with scathing comments of his own. 'Chris almost cries when he talks about having to increase his investment,' he said. 'He's a hard-headed businessman but you'd think he was being asked to sacrifice his internal organs!' The other principle investor was a manager of a small fund, which would be in dire straits if Damian's enterprise went down, so the tension at board meetings was great. Yet Damian seemed to treat these meetings with levity, trying to sail through them with off-the-cuff presentations. I got the sense that at heart he felt that the company was immensely lucky to have his services.

Making the right choices

The way forward for Damian only opened up once he fully committed himself to his venture. In a sense, this was all that the coaching series achieved but it was all that it needed to achieve. Damian was a resourceful leader, who could solve most of the problems that arose in a situation, as long as he was not waylaid by counter-choices. Once he made up his mind, the distractions of his new environment faded away and he was able to enjoy the intense, direct, energizing experience it offered. He bought the rights for a new software package to ease his cash flow and invested in his own sales skills to sell more of the company's off-the-shelf products. This new revenue stream, combined with Damian's resolution to put much more effort into preparing for monthly board meetings, began to convince his shareholders that the company was on track. He settled in for the long haul as far as the development of the search engine was concerned, bartering a small share of his equity in order to cover the costs of hiring an experienced software engineer to supervise the coding team.

In short, Damian began to get his basic choices right. By fine-tuning the strategy, improving resourcing and putting a more determined focus on delivery, Damian adapted his achievement cycle skills to the start up. There was no single fork in the road. Sometimes fledgling companies reach an unequivocal tipping point, a major contract, for example, which changes everything. But for Damian there was nothing definitive, just a process of skillfully maintaining his balance in the face of the ups and downs of long-term software development and the monthly sales charts. Over a period of two years, an accumulation of minor victories added up to something bigger and the company began to experience the success which Damian's new sense of commitment deserved.

3. The chair of the board: the non-executive leader

Aside from the chief executive, the most influential role in an organization is often that of the chair of the board. This post is a major driver of a company's decision-making and yet the role itself is quite ambiguous. Is the chair a non-executive, predominately responsible for running the board and in this way facilitating the chief-executive's choices? Or does he have a more direct executive responsibility, even to the point of also performing the chief executive's role? The UK Corporate Governance Code is clear on this point, stipulating that the roles of chief executive and chair of the board should be performed by separate individuals in all publicly listed companies. Several other European countries take a similar line but the USA does not, and even in the UK it is not illegal for a company to have an executive chairman, although it is obliged to justify this deviation from the norm to its shareholders (Padgett, 2012).

Just how important is this separation of roles, known as 'duality', to the quality of corporate choice-making? In certain cases, it would seem clear that the absence of an independent chairman is a disadvantage. Enron's fraudulent accounting, for example, would surely have been more difficult to carry out if, for most of its existence, Ken Lay had not been both the conglomerate's chair and its chief executive. A review of 30 studies of the effects of duality found that 34 per cent suggested better results were achieved by companies with a separation of roles, although the measures of performance are very mixed (Kang and Zardkoohi, 2005). Of course, duality does not necessarily ensure the independence of the board from a dominant CEO, as a powerful chief executive can exert a huge influence over a nominally independent chair. However, from a development point of view, in my experience, duality is probably the best way to ensure that the chief executive has a good platform to improve her choice-making. It frees up the chair to ensure that the board is not so much 'the unworthy appointed by the unwilling for the unnecessary' as the old cliché has it (Garratt, 2010: 47), but a vibrant constructive forum and a distinct leadership asset.

The case of Alexander: the juggler learns new tricks

In practice, every chair of the board has to define his own role, as Alexander discovered, when he took on the role of non-executive chairman for a niche supermarket chain. He had a distinguished background in fund management and a flair for business strategy and was now 'raring to go' in his first role as chair of the board. In his early fifties, he felt he had a good deal to contribute to this company, having always been passionately interested in the retail sector. As we talked through his initial ideas for his new job – and what he wanted to achieve in coaching – it became clear that Alexander's ambitions went well beyond running an efficient board. In fact, his main focus seemed to be on possible acquisitions to move the company up-market. This appeared to go against the strategy of Kevin, the amicable, well-regarded chief executive of the company, who was planning an expansion into local convenience stores. Alexander's attitude to Kevin smacked more of rivalry than collaboration. Certainly the composition of the board and other issues which might aid Kevin's decision-making seemed to play little part in the new chairman's thinking.

The company's first board meetings under Alexander were fairly stormy, with the new chairman seeming to side with whoever seemed most likely to agree with his own views. Kevin seemed irritated by this but tried to shrug it off with good humour, no doubt confident that he was held in high esteem by the board and shareholders. The simmering conflict came to a head, however, when Kevin quite unexpectedly announced advanced plans to take over a down-market supermarket group. Alexander's first thought was to instruct the board to reject this move. But when he lobbied board members unofficially, it became clear this would result in a humiliating defeat for him. So instead he focused on marshalling all the facts against the proposed acquisition. This did little to change anybody's mind and Kevin's proposals were approved, leaving Alexander with nothing more than the consolation that he had at least facilitated a thorough discussion of the issue.

As the acquisition went ahead, Alexander reached a Damascene moment. He realised that it would be extremely difficult to divide and rule the board, as he had hoped, or even to sit on the fence. 'I've either got to back Kevin or sack myself', was his curt but honest analysis of his dilemma. After a coaching session in which we discussed the pros and cons of this choice, Alexander eventually settled for the first option and his mindset changed accordingly.

Having redefined his strategy as chair as one of collaborating with his CEO rather than trying to usurp him, Alexander's excellent probalizing and actualizing skills quickly came into play. He threw himself into promoting positive stories about the company in the media, averting a potential crisis over a suppliers' dispute, and started to excel in the complex business of juggling the interests of different pressure groups in and around the board. A year into the job, I could see that his balancing skills had improved considerably. This did not mean that there were no arguments with Kevin – the border between Alexander's executive and non-executive roles could still be a little fuzzy at times (at least to himself). But broadly speaking, the chair of the company and its executive now worked side-by-side rather than in opposition to each other, a state of affairs which could only benefit the board's commercial decision-making.

What all of these case studies emphasize is that whether chairing the board, running a fragile start up or directing an established multinational organization, every leader has strategic decisions to make and practical actions to implement. Many choices are involved in this balancing act, some are personal, some are collective, but if they have a common link it is surely the leader's relationship with his team, a crucial arena of leadership which it is now time to enter.

Chapter 9

The team leader
Creating the dialectical team

There are no leaders without followers (oppositional logic would not have it any other way). That is why the task of team leadership is so central to the multirole function of leadership. As all the individual leaders we have examined so far have demonstrated, a team potentially represents a more powerful source of ideas and expertise than any single person. The problem is that a team can also have the reverse effect, reducing a group's individual talents to a state of ineffectual confusion. So how do you coach a team leader to get on the right side of this equation and successfully create what I call a dialectical team, able to bring out the best of the resources at its disposal?

In this chapter, I will try to answer this question by exploring how the team leader's art of balance relates to the dual structure of interactional leadership. I want to suggest that the achievement cycle can clarify some of the dimensions of a team and its temporality can offer further insights. I also want to look at the way the self–others dialectic, which is at the core of interactional psychology, can define the individual and collective parameters between which team formations operate. The stories of two coachees, trying to develop very different types of dialectical team, will put this in a practical context.

Defining the team: the role of the achievement cycle

It will come as no surprise to the reader if I say that, from an interactional viewpoint, choice-making is central to the team leader role. This is also the focus of a tradition in organizational psychology, pioneered by Kurt Lewin (Lewin *et al.*, 1939), whose experiments on democratic, autocratic and laissez-faire leadership styles first demonstrated the multiplicity of approaches to team leadership and the difficulty in predicting the effectiveness of any one of them. Meta-choices around style are clearly important for the team leader, as she attempts to resolve the many oppositional forces at play within a group situation, and are also crucial to psychological decision-making. The 6D leadership model can help us to make sense of this intense field of interaction.

To begin with, the achievement cycle offers us a way to categorize the purpose of teams. Some teams have a predominantly possibilizing role, such as strategy groups and think tanks. Other teams are probabalizers, working on planning, resourcing and communicating, for example. Another tranche of teams can be defined as actualizers, functional groups which execute a plan which has been devised by others. Roles within teams can also be analysed in whole-cycle terms. 'Ideas-people', 'planners', 'resourcers', and 'deliverers' all fall into one or another of the three achievement stages. The 'fixer' is often needed at the resourcing stage; while the 'enforcer' makes things happen when it comes to delivery. This kind of categorization can be useful in terms of assessing the strengths and weaknesses of individual team members. Crucially, it can also help to define some of the possible combinations of roles in a team which are likely to bring out its positive potential for change. These dialectical relationships may be oppositional and complementary as well as harmoniously interlocking. For instance, the ideas person and the delivery enforcer may disagree on priorities but their disagreement can produce a constructive energy which powers a team through the whole cycle of achievement.

The counter-voice

In my experience, one of the key roles in creating constructive, oppositional energy in a team is that of the counter-voice. Like the Fool in the medieval court, the counter-voice challenges orthodoxy, says the unsayable, and questions the team leader's strategy. Renowned team expert J. Richard Hackman (2009) called this role that of 'the deviant', rightly arguing that without it a team can become too conformist in its choices. However, there is a vital balance to be struck between this stretching, innovative aspect of the team and the need for the team to be disciplined and uniform in it aims. As is so often the case with real achievement, the secret lies in the interaction between open and closed attitudes. Possibilizing is the time for opening up to every option but hereafter there needs to be a closing movement, as the probalizing stage narrows down choices and the actualizing phase implements them. The team leader usually needs his counter-voices – including his own – to be operating at the possibilizing phase of a project rather then at the operational stage, when dissent can be extremely destructive.

The time of the team

Another factor which can help us to understand the nature of a team is the dimension of time. Consider the differences between the following: a new team, a transitional team, an established team and a one-off team. In fact, all are defined by their temporal parameters. The same can even be said of the increasingly common virtual team, which can be united in time but rarely in space. Team development is also often expressed as a progression through time, as in Tuckman's (1965) well known theory of 'forming', 'norming', 'storming', and 'performing', which highlights the significance of dissent (as well as the mnemonic charm of rhyme). And of course team performance is measured in time, with regular meetings calibrating success or failure, and other time punctuations, such as a sudden crisis or a deadline, bringing out the best or the worst in its members.

Nothing is more fundamental to the meaning of a team than its relationship to the future. Without a forward direction, usually in the form of a clear set of goals and objectives, teams are likely to experience conflict and lowered performance. Groups often break up if their destination is too opaque, perhaps splitting into other formations which have a clearer path ahead of them. However, the past is also important, especially for an established team, as it is the source of its reputation, traditions and myths, which may go back for decades Transitioning from the past to the future is a major developmental role played by experienced team members as they incorporate joiners into the team. This relationship, with all the potential disruption and anxiety it involves, is a significant team interaction. Teams need the infusion of new blood and yet they are often at their most ineffective when they contain inexperienced members. In many organizations, high staff turnover rates dictate constant changes in a team's personnel, which is another balancing act for the team leader to master.

Setting the bar high: the dialectical team

How high should a team leader set the bar in terms of performance? This choice is crucial because in reality, there is frequently a good deal of hype about effective teamwork, as Hackman (2009) frequently pointed out. Often groups are assembled in chaotic or arbitrary ways, without fundamental connections in terms of their work processes, skills or collective purpose. Turning a group like this into a high-performing team may be impossible. Achieving what Katzenbach and Smith (1993) call a 'working group' rather than a true team, may be the best a team leader can realistically expect to achieve.

Nevertheless, if a team leader so chooses and the circumstances are right, teams can achieve greatness. In coaching, the notion of the dialectical team can be helpful to team leaders aiming to build and maintain successful teams. I define the dialectical team as a group able to interact with itself and the outside world in a way that fully exploits the resources of the whole team. It is an integral team, held together by its purpose, competences and execution, and capable of delivering through the whole achievement cycle. At times, the dialectical team can even experience a togetherness, which is not entirely dissimilar to what Sartre (1976) characterized as group 'fusion', a spontaneous commonality which overcomes 'seriality', or individual separateness. A fractional team, by contrast, although it may be successful in some respects, is divided within itself and, as a consequence, is unlikely to experience a real sense of unity.

The choices of the team: the self–others interaction and team formations

In trying to define a team and its prospects, sooner or later we will always return to the meta-choice question: who makes the decisions and how? This is where the psychological interaction of self and others can be helpful conceptually, in that it offers us a spectrum of possible team formations. On one extreme of this range, there is the unilateral or individually-led (IL) group, in which choices are dominated by an individual leader. At the opposite interpersonal pole, there is the multilateral group which is collectively-led (CL), in which choices are mainly made by the group. Often the most effective teams occupy a position on the spectrum between these two poles, varying their style according to circumstances and their stage of development.

The unilateral or individually-led team

In the unilateral or individually-led team, power is invested in a single person to make the right choices around objectives, composition and performance. This kind of team leader may define himself as the embodiment of a formal hierarchy, openly using the authority which is embedded in his line role to distribute rewards and inflict punishment. At best, he sets high standards, leads from the front, and provides clear accountability for performance. Alternatively, the unilateral team leader may lead through charisma or personal influence rather than by using the overt structures of a hierarchy. The team may seem like the embodiment of her personality, as she governs through close personal contacts, only falling back on the real structures that sustain her, when unable to achieve results through her relationships. The unilateral team may evolve because the leader considers herself to be more capable than anyone else in the group – rightly or wrongly, which explains why she assigns secondary roles to the rest of the group.

In any version of the unilateral group, the disadvantages for team members can be a lack of professional and personal development, arising from the limited scope for personal initiative in performing tasks, as well as difficulties in forming relationship within the group that are independent of the leader. Situationally, the IL structure is often most effective in strictly defined circumstances or in emergencies when urgent action is called for or where the possibilities of real team interaction are limited. Psychologically, some team leaders will be comfortable with the high degree of control over others which the unilateral formation often implies. Others will find this stance personally restricting or in conflict with their values and preferred ways of thinking about their relationship to others. Let's examine this individually-orientated style of team leadership in action, before moving on to the multilateral approach.

Case study: Christian: building the IL team

Christian was a newly promoted team leader running a large research team in an insurance company. He needed to make a rapid transition from subject-matter expert to team leader, a common challenge in knowledge-based industries. He was used to going though the achievement cycle as a fairly autonomous agent but his new managerial role called for something quite different.

Christian may have been 'all German precision', as he joked (he originally came from Berlin) but there was nothing amusing about the group he was presiding over. It couldn't really be called a team. Christian directed every research task and presented all the data, overruling anybody who seemed to show any personal initiative. The result was that the team was demoralized and only prepared to work their contracted hours. Christian himself was exhausted and increasingly stressed. He confessed he was sleeping badly and would sometimes spend the night in his office, dozing for a few hours at his desk.

Christian was under pressure from his boss to improve the performance of his team. It soon became apparent that a collectively-led team was not on the cards. Christian's psychological make-up seemed to rule this out, as did his lack of managerial experience. The team itself had been assembled rather randomly, it seemed; some of its members had fairly autonomous, unrelated work processes. At least, it was stable in time, with low turnover, although this probably would not last much longer, given the low morale of the group. The coaching challenge was clear: to help Christian create a team which he would clearly lead but one which enabled its team members to cooperate with each other effectively and develop their skills.

We started by examining the strategy of the group. Christian had many objectives – they were posted all over his office wall in seemingly complex algorithms – but they were all for individual tasks rather than for the team as a whole. The opportunity for cross-fertilizing ideas seemed to be non-existent, so he started to redefine some of the team's tasks to promote group involvement. He also put more effort into getting to know the team. He seemed familiar with their qualifications but when I enquired into their personalities or interests he gave me a blank look. It turned out, that he had once taken them out for dinner but the conversation had been work-orientated, with Christian steering the talk away from leisure interests or family life, preferring to give an impromptu lecture on consumer economics, illustrated by graphs drawn on paper napkins. He now took the team out again and made a genuine attempt to get to know them. He identified one team member as an obvious 'bridger', who was potentially good at liaising with other departments, something Christian admitted he found difficult. He decided that another team member would be good at enforcing a number of data tasks which involved an outsourced company. Having assigned these and other new roles, Christian realised that he had to try to stop micro-managing his team and allow them to develop their skills in their own time.

Team meetings were crucial to this ambition, as these were the only occasions when the entire group came together. Christian focused on making these meetings effective and inclusive experiences, in which team members could report on their work and describe the reactions of their clients. They also evaluated their work regularly, taking plaudits for positive work and trying to learn from their mistakes. Christian sometimes rotated the chair in these meetings and worked hard to bite his lip rather than talk over people. He even tried to cultivate countervoices. One researcher held particularly forthright views and Christian tried to give her a regular opportunity to speak, although he confessed he was once so irritated by her criticisms that it was all he could do to stop himself from storming out of the meeting.

Psychologically, delegation was undoubtedly Christian's biggest challenge, as it meant he had to adopt a new sense of time. To begin with, his impulse was to check on progress with team members almost every day, sometimes more than once. We agreed he needed 'to loosen up' and give people more time but this resolution produced little actual progress. Although he reported it 'felt like weeks' since he had last checked on a team member, it was more likely to be a few days. It became clear that Christian had to turn his strong need for formal control to his advantage. Spontaneity seemed to be out of the question, so he developed delegation routines which had a clear timetable of appointments and deadlines. In this way, he enabled his direct reports to get on with their jobs without too much interference from him. Gradually, his time landscape changed, as he adapted to the weekly intervals that initially 'felt like months' and the monthly intervals that 'felt like years'.

Were there moments of fusion or dialectical productivity? For Christian building the team was undoubtedly a long, uphill struggle. To be fair, the identity of the group and its skill sets, as well as the temperament of its leader, did not lend itself to great spontaneity. But the team's cohesion unquestionably improved, as judged by feedback from Christian's boss and performance evaluations at the end of the year. Christian promoted one of his team members to the role of deputy and two others to managerial roles. As he delegated more of his tasks, his health improved. He even spoke of a number of collective operations which he felt were 'performed to a higher standard than ever before'. Examining these talks retrospectively, he said, 'I often find it hard to distinguish what I contributed from what others put in.' This seemed to me a realistic marker of the progress the team made.

The multilateral or collectively-led team

On the other end of the self–others spectrum is the team which leads itself. The multilateral team may take many shapes, from a conventional team with a flat hierarchy to a fully self-directing, autonomous group. Professional groups, matrix teams and project teams can occupy a position towards the collective end of the team spectrum, as can a self-governing group such as a board of directors.

In the collectively-led group, democratic choice-making is often the predominant way strategy is set. Decisions on resourcing, performance and delivery are also made collectively, within whatever limits the wider organization imposes. Remuneration and other rewards may be based on whole team performance rather than individual results. Dealing with poor performance can be a severe test for the multilateral group. Group processes are likely to be emphasized, with regular group meetings taking place. The extent to which team members can publicly air grievances and challenge each other often determines how effective this kind of group can be.

The advantages of the multilateral team formation for its members can be considerable, as it offers them opportunities to use their initiative and imagination and develop goals and work routines which suit their tasks and skills, rather than follow rules and objectives set from above. This may result in greater job satisfaction and productivity than an individually-led group, although this is by no means guaranteed.

The role of the multilateral team leader can be highly ambiguous. If team leadership is entirely by committee or involves a regular rotation among team members, a single identifiable leader may not exist. But if the group has a nominal leader, who is ultimately responsible for the results of the team, she has a dual role as a member of the team, probably with specialist skills, and as an accountable authority. This requires exceptional psychological flexibility and the ability to learn from the group as well as to lead it. If the multilateral leader can successfully juggle these competing claims, outstanding team performance may follow, as Kirsten's story shows.

Case study: Kirsten: 'redefining the family' or how to run a CL Team

For several years, Kirsten ran a very successful creative team in an advertising agency in which the vast majority of its strategic, resourcing and creative decisions were made by democratic vote. She firmly believed that a team which makes its own decisions is more innovative and productive than a team which is directed by a single leader. Most recruitment decisions were made entirely by an interviewing committee, which didn't necessarily include Kirsten, and remuneration was on a strictly shared team basis.

Kirsten had clear responsibilities to the board of the agency, so there were times when her vote carried more weight in decision-making, especially when important senior management presentations were on the horizon. On rare occasions, she made individual decisions, which she called 'her gentle touches on the tiller'. For the most part, she was simply another member of the team, one who possessed considerable expertise as a graphic designer, but no special rights. This multilateral leadership style provided a clear branding advantage for the agency in a fiercely competitive market place and proved very successful with clients. It also appealed to employees, who liked the prospect of taking on responsibility and developing fast.

However, when Kirsten was persuaded to return to the agency after a two year maternity break, she was alarmed to find that the team had changed radically. Almost all of the old members had left and most of the clients were new to her. This was not entirely unexpected in this high-turnover industry sector but the biggest difference for Kirsten was the way the team worked. Now team members expected to be told what to do. Kirsten's replacement as team leader had been very inexperienced and had adopted a unilateral team leadership style which had not produced the same quality of work as before. The team's aura of freshness and originality had quickly faded, with negative consequences for the overall reputation of the agency.

In our first coaching conversation, Kirsten admitted that, second time around, she found the prospect of leading a team very daunting. Formulating the principles of multilateral team leadership was a major challenge, as much of what she had done before had seemed to flow effortlessly. She said, 'it's like riding a bike, isn't it? It's one thing to do it, quite another to explain *how* you do it.' She realised that she would have to take a more high-profile leadership role to change the structure and culture of the team, a stance that she found difficult to embrace. In the past, she said, 'if I'd told people what to do there'd be some joke about being bossy or even fascist but they'd do it – as long it didn't happen too often.' This humorous banter worked to remind the group of the balance between the nominal leader and the group. Now there was none of this reassuring, good-natured feedback, just silent obedience, a response which initially undermined Kirsten's self-confidence and made her feel 'feeble'. 'I don't want them to act like sheep,' she explained. 'Sheep don't produce great advertising campaigns. But they don't seem to know what to do on their own.'

This was one of Kirsten's many dilemmas, as she struggled to find a new balance in her leadership decision-making. In this respect, team leadership can be compared to a musical producer in a recording studio. He needs a good range of tracks on his mixing desk but the real art lies in finding the right balance between them, fading up the piano to just the right level, for example, or fading down the voice. Tiny changes can make big differences to the final sound. In the past, Kirsten had probably been helped by a seemingly spontaneous complementarity among team members. In this, introverts constructively opposed extraverts, for instance, and there was a spiky but friendly blend between the creatives and the account managers, reinforced by extensive after-work socializing. Creatively, many of the team members had been on a par but in the current group Kirsten quickly recognized that one copywriter, Yannick, was head and shoulders above the rest. His voice often drowned out everyone else in meetings and Kirsten realised she had to tackle him immediately. She spent time with Yannick one-to-one, inspiring him with her plans and making it clear that if he adopted a more generous attitude to his colleagues he would be a beneficiary of the changes Kirsten intended to introduce.

Kirsten now went all-out to explain to everyone how the kind of team she wanted to create would work. There was no point in harking back to the past, she realised. It was all about making a pitch for the future, which she now did with some gusto in a series of daily team meetings. Having unilaterally made some key changes in the ways in which new client development and creative collaboration was structured, she set up collective decision-making votes on campaign selection and even on recruitment (although she retained the final say-so). She was immediately challenged by what she felt was a disastrously wrong collective decision on an important client campaign. 'I agonized over it for ages,' she said. 'If it had been a marginal call I disagreed with I could have gone with it, but this was just plain wrong.' Reluctantly, she overruled the multilateral decision and took the ensuing flak from some team members (a reaction she was not entirely displeased with, incidentally) while trying to clarify the confusion it caused for others.

This setback did not deter Kirsten and she redoubled her efforts, working with the team individually and setting up extensive skills training. She felt that her reputation was on the line far more than it had been during her first stint at the agency and probably more than it would have been if she had decided to lead the team as a unilateral formation. In one coaching session, she confessed to me that she was close to giving up: 'This is not some hippy commune. It's a business, for Christ's sake, and maybe I should just accept that and get on with it.' She was despairing of regaining that gentle touch on tiller that was for her the hallmark of team leadership. She said that she felt she was actually in danger of capsizing her team, with what seemed to her like frequent erratic tacking from one decision-path to another. She also wondered whether she had herself changed, since having her first child. 'The team used to be "the family", she said, 'it's what we called ourselves. Now I know who my real family is and who my employees are. Perhaps there's no going back from that'.

In spite of these doubts, Kirsten persisted with her project. The team recruited two resourceful executives who were fully committed to the philosophy of collective decision-making and they contributed to a brilliant new campaign, which Yannick masterminded. This seemed like a tipping point, as people began to adapt to the principles of multilateral leadership and productively leverage the creative freedom that it gave them. Bit by bit, the number of unilateral decisions which Kirsten made diminished, as did her high-profile role as 'enforcer' of the collective team principle. Her seemingly intuitive sense of when to intervene in a decision and when to stay out of it returned to her, although she never had quite the anonymity within the group she had had in the past. 'It's damn hard work being a leader who is also a non-leader!' she told me in our last session. But Kirsten was amply rewarded for adapting her faith in the collectively-led team to a new reality, as her team began to deliver consistently exceptional results and her advertising company gradually regained its glowing reputation in the industry.

To conclude, Christian and Kirsten developed very different forms of effective team leadership which suited their personalities as well as their situations. In order to do so, they needed to draw on a range of different behavioural styles which crossed the interpersonal spectrum from self to others. The "one-trick pony", who can only lead a team in a single way, will always be perilously vulnerable to changing circumstances. Ideally, this expansion of one's multirole capabilities is something leaders learn early on in their careers; indeed it is a key element in the development of up-and-coming leaders, to which we now turn our attention.

Chapter 10

The potential leader
Coaching the rising star and the gender gap in leadership

The idea that leadership is about choosing the future takes on another meaning, when it comes to developing the next generation of leaders. In this chapter we look at how to coach rising stars in organizations and examine one of the issues most likely to throw off balance many who aspire to the top job: the gender gap in leadership. As we'll see, coaching potential leaders brings out the importance of desire in leadership. Organizational development programmes focus on assessing and developing a candidate's expertise, knowledge, and skills – rightly so because all of these play a significant role in leadership. But positive and negative desires are at the heart of our motivation as human choice-makers, which means that it is crucial to identify what a potential leader really wants to achieve.

Sometimes the desire to lead can emerge suddenly, especially in entrepreneurial companies and in uncertain situations where new leaders may step on to the stage with startling rapidity. Sometimes, the apparently accidental success of the leader is deceptive, as it is really the product of a long-pursued positional strategy aimed at waiting until the route to the top opens up. However, in larger organizations, with the introduction of sophisticated leadership assessment and development programmes, the unexpected becomes a little less likely. The same may also be increasingly true in the political sphere, with the advent of the professional politician, whose every move since school has been designed to promote his political career.

'You must learn to walk firmly on the ground before you start walking a tightrope,' the painter Henri Matisse (1995: 46) once remarked and it is vital to help the potential leader to evaluate her desire to lead because this will determine many of her future choices. Identifying whole-cycle strengths and weaknesses is useful in this respect, as well as being a precious form of development in its own right. Scenarios based on different achievement cycle stages help to illuminate the areas in which the inexperienced leader will excel, as well as the deficiencies which may sabotage her. The 'natural' possibilizer will need to develop her probalizing and actualizing skills, the probabalizer has to work on his possibilizing abilities, and so on. Throughout, the coach will try to balance positive and negative feedback, helping the coachee to master the generics of leadership, while developing her own unique personal style.

The rising star

In any organization, the rising star tends to stand out. The talented, up-and-coming executive may not yet be a driving force in the present but she has the allure of representing the onward direction of a company. 'You're looking at our future', a veteran financial leader once told me, proudly pointing at one of his protégés. Developing rising stars is an imperative for any organization and one which leadership coaching is particularly suited to fulfil. One approach is 'open future' coaching which has relatively few performance goals, as it is aimed at helping the young or inexperienced executive understand more about his values, emotional patterns and his embedded assumptions about life and work. Open future coaching attempts to help the coachee to discover what is familiar about leadership and what is foreign about it. It can also assist him in finding the right balance between being who he is, and who he is not, a useful asset if he is to approach the high wire of leadership with confidence.

Above all, this type of coaching is about helping the up-and-coming leader to see her trajectory to the future, to define what she wants for herself and others. For the coach, it can be rewarding hearing the aspirations of young leaders, their dreams of a future which is very different from the present and their determination to change things for the better. How many of these powerful intentions will become realities is a question which only time can answer.

In large organizations where the competition for top jobs is particularly intense, coaching the rising star often has a more specific agenda. Such organizations put their potential leaders through extensive assessments of their performance – both hypothetical and real – in order to get a clear view of what they need to progress to the top. Specific skills coaching and training may follow on from this. The coach needs to help the coachee to define his leadership aspirations and relate these to the organization's idea of the path to the top. Weighing up the desire to lead against the need to change in ways laid down by others can be a difficult choice, especially if that change appears to go against the grain of one's personality or values. In these circumstances, deciding how much one wants to lead can be a major challenge, as Alberto would find out.

Case study: Alberto: balancing self and others in collaborative leadership

On joining his financial services corporation, Alberto had been identified as a 'natural leader', in that he was a strong, problem-solving strategist and a determined deliverer. For three years, he had been very successful in running a small, highly profitable team which specialized in selling risk-management products. But this success came at a price in relation to Alberto's reputation in the wider company, where he was seen as divisive, hyper-competitive and only loyal to his own team. In his boss's words, Alberto was 'trampling on far too many important egos' to be considered promotion material and his star was definitely on the wane.

In whole-cycle terms, Alberto's problem seemed to be his resourcing skills, which may have been adequate for his role as a team leader but was not considered up to scratch for him to progress to the next stage in the steep hierarchy of his current employers. To do this, he urgently needed to develop his capacity for collaborative leadership.

In our first session, Alberto spent a good deal of time telling me about his leadership skills. He listed his impressive achievements and quoted testimonials from satisfied clients, as though I was interviewing him for a job. He went on to explain what his team did in selling interest rate derivatives. 'It's all about pricing risk,' he said. 'Essentially it's an insurance policy, so you never get surprised by the future.' Alberto was young enough to have spent most of his present career in the period following the financial crash in 2008. He told me, 'anybody before the credit crunch who'd said interest rates would be at virtually zero for years would have been put in a strait jacket because there was absolutely no historical precedent for what's happening now'.

Alberto also said something which struck a common chord with me: 'This business is all about the future – you try to anticipate what you can never totally predict.' Alberto's world of financial risk management was wholly directed at – you could almost say obsessed by – making choices around the future. I brought this up a little later, as we discussed Alberto's leadership plans and his reluctance to embrace the collaborative leadership style his bosses and talent management team wanted from him. Why, I wondered, was he so keen on selling the future to others but thought of his own future as a mere continuation of the past? This kind of conversation – it was no more than that – enabled Alberto to develop a more open mind to expanding his repertoire of leadership behaviours.

The real psychological challenge for Alberto was to move along the self–others spectrum. He seemed to view his team as a kind extension of himself. He declared that 'I am the team, they are me,' and he used the terms 'the team' and 'I' interchangeably. Now he had to learn to build relationships outside this enclosed space with those he regarded as potential competitors for business, promotion and even remuneration (all his team's bonuses came from one divisional pool). Suggesting that he transfer some of his sales strategies and techniques to his peers and internal customers helped. This use of the sales model of interactional skills, which I have discussed in more detail elsewhere (Harvey, 2012), enabled him to adapt to decision-makers within in his own company the probalizing skills he normally only used on customers. Once he had perfected the script for these targeted roles he seemed able to play them to perfection, even though he confessed that staying in character when adopting a more cooperative and empathetic attitude was initially 'exquisite torture'.

Alberto's run at collaborate leadership paid off. He progressed far enough to assure his organization that he could make the behavioural changes necessary for promotion. As to whether he would ever make it to a top corporate leadership position, I rated the chances at about 50/50. He was now capable of incorporating a collaborative dimension into his everyday activities, without, I suspected, entirely believing in it. Perhaps this would come with time or perhaps he would start his own company and put all his possessive and competitive zeal into that, without having to think too much about 'others' in a wider sense. Whatever the future held in store for him, now at least Alberto had the priceless asset of knowing much more about what his leadership choices would involve.

Case study: Jay: 'talking the talk' versus 'the religion of doing it'

If Alberto's dilemma was around resourcing, Jay's was about delivering results – with a peculiar twist. He was a young manager in a large public relations and lobbying company, who had been picked out for great things. But his leadership ascent had now stalled, as his boss began to undercover a disturbing lack of consistency between the brief that clients gave Jay and the results he delivered. Jay seemed to be 'in denial' about his failure to meet his goals, trying to conceal this discrepancy by retrospectively changing the brief. This 'reverse engineering', as his boss called it, was putting Jay's future in doubt. 'He can charm the birds from the trees, alright,' she said, 'but if he can't walk the walk, he won't go any higher here or in any top-tier agency'.

Jay had chosen to be a leader, there seemed to be little doubt about that. From the outset of the coaching, he was clear about his determination to get to the top. This fierce ambitiousness was combined with self-deprecating humour and a surprising openness which made for a strong leadership presence. His conversation was studded with memorable phrases and pithy quotes from everyone from Nietzsche to Homer Simpson.

But when we discussed the inconsistency between his strategy and his results, Jay's ability for self-evasion and denial became apparent. He did not agree with his boss's diagnosis of his leadership failings. He claimed that he had all he needed to become 'a signature leader' and we ended the first session on something of a stalemate. A fortnight later, he launched into another defensive monologue at the start of the session but after a while it became clear that Jay was ready to address his faults. Deep down, the criticism of his professionalism had hurt him and he could no longer protect himself from the accusation that he was deceiving clients. It took more time before he could bring himself to be completely honest, but when he did so it brought a refreshing 'unburdening of the soul', to use his phrase. It meant his development as a choice-focused leader could begin in earnest.

First, Jay had to reinterpret his tendency to deviate from his original brief. This he initially saw as creative improvisation, 'an impromptu variation on a theme', which added 'spice to the whole process'. The realisation that this bending of the rules brought out the risk-seeker in him gave him 'a perverse pleasure'. So weighing up these previously unacknowledged aspects of his personality against the new goal of whole-cycle performance was by no means a straightforward choice. Jay hankered after the 'old Jay', 'the reckless improviser' and 'verbal magus.' 'Sticking to targets will be a hard slog,' he complained, 'since all the interesting decisions have already been made.' At the same time, he was ready to accept his challenge: 'It's the religion of doing it,' he said, 'and I have to become a devoted acolyte.'

In the end, Jay found it easier than he suspected to develop a tougher approach to pushing through his brief. His relationship skills already existed in abundance and he found that he could be resolutely consistent with his team if necessary. At times, adopting a closed attitude rather than an open one seemed 'too much like hard work' to Jay but when he successfully used it on an important assignment he became convinced of its effectiveness. After that it became much easier for him to deliver the results he had promised. 'Walking the walk' became a habit for him, however precarious the path ahead. It enabled him to channel his creative skills in ways that complemented the achievement cycle rather than subverting it – and this meant that his positive leadership prospects in his company were soon revived.

The gender issue in leadership: who's really choosing?

So far we've looked at potential leaders who are male but it is common to find as many women on organizational leadership development programmes as men. And yet if we look at the top management layers of these organizations disproportionally fewer women are to be seen. Although women make up almost half of the UK workforce – and dominate in certain professions, as well as in current UK university undergraduate attendance – the percentage of women in senior corporate leadership positions is still depressingly low. For example, only 4 per cent of FTSE 100 chief executives are female (as of January, 2014). The statistics in the US are almost as dismal: only 21 of Fortune 500 companies have female CEOs and just 15 per cent of the executive officers of these companies are women. In the political sphere, there are a few well known women leaders, such as Angela Merkel of Germany, but only 20 out of 193 UN-recognized countries have female leaders (Williams and Dempsey, 2013).

What happens? Why do so many potential female leaders fail to become actual leaders, especially in large organizations? It is not as though women leaders make a lesser contribution to their organization than men. One longitudinal study in the USA found that, in terms of financial profitability, Fortune 500 companies with the best record of promoting female executives outperformed their median competitors (Adler, 2001). This appalling waste of human resources could get worse, if Leimon *et al.*, (2011) are right and demographic changes in Western Europe mean that we are heading for a 'leadership cliff' by 2030, caused by a significant gap between leadership-age population supply and demand. So why do big organizations continually fail to choose women as leaders? Is it the system that decides, or women themselves who make the choice?

There are of course many possible explanations for one of the greatest of all imbalances in the contemporary world of leadership, although here there is only space to scratch the surface of this subject. One view is that female executives do not push hard enough. Facebook CEO Sheryl Sandberg (2013) argues that women are held back by a lack of ambition – 'an ambition gap' – which causes them to 'lean back' rather than 'lean in'. Without becoming over-aggressive, she believes that women need to be more forceful in asserting their authority as executives. Others take a less individual-centred position, arguing that the whole work system is skewed against potential women leaders, especially if they are parents. Political scientist Anne-Marie Slaughter (2012) argues that women are more family-orientated than men but that the whole structure of work reflects an opposite bias. For example, if someone leaves a high-profile role job 'to spend more time with the family', for a man this is a likely to be a euphemism for being sacked, whereas for women it is often the real reason they are leaving (2012: 4). When it comes to a choice between the job and the children, Slaughter asserts that men find it easier to choose the former. She quotes US Senator Jeanne Shaheen, who says in this situation, 'There really is no choice'; for a woman, the 'maternal imperative' wins every time (2012: 9).

It is certainly true that the very dimension of time at work seems to militate against women. Anthropologist Edward T. Hall (1986) makes a distinction between monochronic time (which is sequential) and polychronic time (in which events run in parallel) and suggests that women are often more comfortable in polychronic time. Certainly many organizations run on what has been called 'macho time', consisting of long hours, client entertainment evenings and extensive travel, all of which come at the expense of time spent at home. When we talk about the art of balancing choices, the family tends to represents a special challenge to the female leader. Indeed, in coaching, female executives with children often define their roles predominantly as 'juggling between work and family', with the school run imprinted on their consciousness in a way that is probably not true for most men. Women have different choices around parenthood and work. I've never heard a man saying that he decided not to become a parent because he felt it would interfere with his leadership ambitions. I know several women who have not only talked about this choice but have made it, with the result that their careers in the higher echelons of organizations have come at a considerable personal cost.

In spite of the difficulties, it is not impossible for women to reach the top. Psychologists Alice Eagly and Linda Carli (2007) argue persuasively that the glass ceiling metaphor for the limits of female leadership is misleading and a more appropriate trope is the labyrinth. There are many challenges which women have to navigate to succeed as leaders, beyond overt discrimination and sexual harassment. Women can be at a disadvantage in building social capital in organizations where the social bonding that influences promotion happens during male-oriented activities such as fishing or hunting. Eagly and Carli also pinpoint the double bind which women can experience as far as communication and leadership style are concerned. For example, women are expected to be supportive and communal in their approach – although they are not necessarily credited for this – but blamed if they are not dominant enough.

In this context, it is worth remembering how one of the twentieth century's outstanding female political leaders, Margaret Thatcher, was criticized early in her career for sounding too 'shrill' and aggressive and so lowered the pitch of her voice to sound more reassuring (Moore, 2013). (When was a male political leader criticized for being shrill?) Yet Thatcher also demonstrated some of the potential advantages of the female leader. She could act like a stereotypical man in terms of decisive action – and she was certainly no feminist friend to women. But she skilfully used a range of traditional female roles, such as mother, teacher, housewife, and even flirt, to gain the support of her allies and fatally disarm her opponents (Campbell, 2012).

To some extent, we come back to the cardinal question, 'what do you want? The question 'can women lead' is totally redundant (if it was ever otherwise) and needs to be replaced by the question 'why do some women not want to lead?' Specifically, we should address this question to large organizations, corporate, public sector and governmental, where the most influential choices are likely to be made, as there is evidence of growing female leadership in smaller organizations (American Express OPEN, 2013). It is one of the biggest questions for the whole future of leadership. At the same time, we should not lose sight of the fact that every potential leader, whether male or female, always has to make his or her own choices, in a particular situation, at a particular moment in time.

Case study: Lauren: do you really want to be a leader?

Many of these issues of gender and leadership come together in the case of Lauren. She was a rising young executive in a large credit card company, whose fast-tracked career seemed to be threatened by a bout of headstrong, undisciplined behaviour. Unlike our previous potential leaders, Lauren was not lacking in any aspect of her leadership competence. Although only just 30, she was an accomplished whole-cycle leader, with strong possibilizing and probalizing skills and a record of achieving exceptional results. But she now seemed to being 'having difficulty with some of her peers', according to her manager, who also felt she was no longer 'pushing herself beyond her comfort zone'.

Lauren initially described an incident in which she had lost her temper with a male colleague as 'a storm in a teacup' but later admitted that it had been provoked by what could be considered sexual harassment. 'It's just that kind of "dumb blonde" remark which is basically good humoured banter,' she explained. 'You've got to take it but it can still catch you off guard sometimes.' She said it was one of a number of things which had made her question for the first time whether she was ready for a promotion to a senior role, which later that year was a distinct possibility. She denied that she was considering leaving the company but she clearly was having fundamental doubts about her future.

She faced a series of dilemmas. She was increasingly bored by the kind of 'alpha male' behaviour of her peers, which, if anything, seemed more problematic at the next level up in the organization. She said she found it increasingly hard to be enthusiastic about some of the client entertainment events, in which predominantly male clients were invited to football matches or lap dancing bars. She also questioned whether promotion was a real option. She had better qualifications than her colleagues and better results but she had recently lost out on promotion to a 'relatively lacklustre' male colleague and was beginning to wonder if the organizational cards were stacked against her.

Increasingly to the forefront of Lauren's mind, were her concerns about the 'crazy' work–life balance which seemed to be the norm for the company's exclusively male senior management. Now in a committed long-term relationship, Lauren was seriously thinking about having children for the first time but she was trying to figure how she could plan this in a way that made her leadership ambitions possible. Should she wait for a few years or have children now and hope to come back into the market in her late thirties? We discussed these considerations over several sessions and eventually Lauren came to a decision, adopting a positional strategy. Her choice was to do everything she could to secure promotion, as apart from anything else, she felt that she should set an example to the women executives in her team. If she got a senior job, she would try to negotiate its terms to make it as compatible with her values and family ambitions as possible. Only then would she really be in a position to make a definitive choice.

For the best part of a year, Lauren gave it everything she had. She showed tremendous energy and resourcefulness in developing a new balance of strategies and behaviours which would enable her to weave through the labyrinth of promotion. She worked on her communication skills, trying to blend assertiveness with supportiveness. She varied her position on the self-others spectrum in a way that accorded with her understanding of how women are expected to behave: generously and caringly but not weakly. She also targeted the senior leaders, who were the arbiters of promotion, and ensured that they knew who she was and the results her team was producing. In the past, she would have hung back from this approach, regarding it as 'toadying', but she was no longer prepared to leave the field open to her male colleagues.

Lauren also made an effort to be 'one of the lads' in client entertainment events (although she decided that the idea of supporting a football team was 'a bridge too far'). At the same time, she cultivated female clients and subtly tried to change the entertainment events schedule by advancing cost-cutting arguments to her finance director ('lap dancing bars aren't cheap, you know', she said). She worked hard to improve her presentation skills to ensure that on the occasions when a larger audience saw her, she stood out from her colleagues. Above all, she made sure that her team was in the top ten percentile in terms of all-round performance.

I have to report that Lauren did not break through the glass ceiling in her organization. In the end, she lost out on promotion, narrowly, it was said, in a way that put her in a strong position for the following year. But it was not to be. She became pregnant quite soon after, whether by coincidence or not I couldn't say. She did not return to the credit card company after the birth of her daughter, preferring to join a smaller, family-friendly outfit, which allowed her to combine work and childcare in a satisfying way. Whether at some stage in the future, she may decide to return to the corporate fold and compete for a top leadership job is hard to say. No doubt it will depend on how much she wants it. One thing is clear: it is not only individual women who have to make hard choices about becoming leaders; society also needs to ensure that these choices take place in a free, open and balanced environment. Hopefully, requiring a woman to want to lead more than a man in order to make it to the top will become a thing of the past.

The next in line: succession leadership

Finally, I briefly want look at another way in which organizations choose the future, which involves a very different matrix of choices for the potential leader. Succession planning is an increasingly important part of organizational life, designed to provide a smooth, efficient leadership pipeline. It is required by many corporate governance codes, which recommend that key positions have an internally appointed successor, who can take over in the case of the unexpected departure or temporary unavailability of the post-holder. Leadership succession involves adopting a long-term time horizon, planning for the future and trying to minimize disruptions, and as such it is a sensible course of action.

What is not always appreciated, however, is just how ambiguous the successor role can be. In fact, it is a challenging balancing act in its own right. If the successor is too distant from his leader, his suitability to succeed him may be questioned but being too close to him can also cause problems, especially if the leader is unpopular. Many politicians have had to walk this particular tightrope, with mixed results. For example, in the 2000 US presidential campaign, Al Gore chose to distance himself from his former boss, Bill Clinton, in order to avoid being tainted by the Monica Lewinsky scandal. But this tactic may have lost Gore enough votes among core Democrat supporters to tip the election result against him (Pomper, 2001). It underlines the difficulties of reacting to a situation which in reality gives the would-be successor no rights to, or guarantee of, a job.

Case study: Sean: embracing ambiguity

Unlike the example quoted above, Sean's role in a large retail company had few implications for world history but, as the officially designated successor to the head of a division, it was complicated enough. He was eager to take over from his boss, Eloise, when the occasion arose, but careful not to put pressure on her, as the two were very close personally and professionally. Indeed, most people in the division saw Sean and Eloise as being more or less engaged in a joint leadership operation. This might have been fine for Sean, were it not for the fact that the business was going through a downturn. As his boss's performance was put in question, so was Sean's. Suddenly the next-in-line role began to look like a poisoned chalice. He realised that he had been acting on the assumption that the organization had worked out everything for him but he now realised that it was up to him to develop his own response to his increasingly precarious situation.

In coaching, Sean began to develop what he had lacked before, a strategy for succession. He decided to subtly distance himself from Eloise, without offending her. He would offer her support in management meetings but also be prepared to challenge her. He also worked a lot harder to impress his senior managers with his view of what needed to be done, balancing respect for his boss with an enthusiastic account of the changes it was in his power to instigate as a team manager. In time, he came to regard his position as one of 'as if'. He explained: 'I have to act like the job is mine but there are absolutely no guarantees. I've got an edge in the race but the rest is up to me.' This interpretation seemed to give Sean the new balance of choices necessary to take him to a successful conclusion to his role as successor. Indeed, it is not a bad summary of the situation faced by the potential leader in general.

Chapter 11

The thought leader
Coaching creative and intellectual leadership

In our age of knowledge, nothing is more important to social and economic progress than thought leadership. In this chapter I want to focus on four aspects of this wide-ranging subject, starting with thought leadership as a component of general leadership and then moving on to the role of the leader who is directly responsible for promoting innovation. The role of the leader in the thought industry itself is also illustrated, through the case study of a leading academic, before we examine the role of the internal consultant or subject-matter expert, an area which underscores the value of communication in leadership.

One way of interpreting thought leadership is in relation to the writers, philosophers, scientists, artists and political thinkers, who create revolutionary new ideas that lead a generation forward. James MacGregor Burns (1978) sees the intellectuals of the eighteenth century Enlightenment in these terms and if we turn to the twentieth century, three thought leaders who stand out for me are: Albert Einstein, Jean-Paul Sartre and Bob Dylan. These very different individuals had one thing clearly in common, namely achievement cycle skills beyond the dream of ordinary mortals. They all possessed possibilizing visions which challenged the status quo, the resourcefulness which comes from copious individual talent and the ability to enlist others to a cause. They were also astonishingly productive when it came to delivering results. Einstein published over 300 scientific articles, Sartre wrote 50 books consisting of some 15,000 pages (Cohen-Solal, 1987) – that is almost a page a day for 50 years! – and to date Dylan has released more than 40 albums. But taking this analysis further is no easy matter. Intellectual and artistic genius seems to elude precise definition, in part because great thinkers alter the way we experience the world, setting new parameters which normalize radical change.

In the management field, intellectual leadership is unlikely to produce the exhilarating shock of innovation, which major artists or scientists provoke. Nevertheless, thought leaders in this arena still have an important role to play in promoting the best practices of actual leaders and in influencing real leadership. Who comes first? Is it a Peter Drucker or a Tom Peters, or the innovative organizational leaders who inspire them? And to what degree does leadership theory influence leaders, as it makes its way from the lecture hall into leadership development workshops and, indeed, the coaching room?

The ideas dimension of leadership: every leader should be a thought leader

Whatever the source of bold, new organizational ideas, one thing is incontestable: when it comes to the practical domain of leadership, thoughts can be like lightning bolts. The idea travels faster than any corporate restructure or recruitment drive. The chief executive who ignores the ideas dimension of leadership is missing a prime opportunity to break out of the physical confines of her daily routines and communicate her goals, values and advice to large audiences, inside and outside her organization. Speeches, newsletters, emails, videos and texts can all be means to get the message across. Allan Leighton (2010), for example, talks of sending regular emails to inspire and surprise his staff or simply to remind them of agreed objectives. In his autobiography, former BBC director general, Greg Dyke, recounts how he assiduously used emails, internal broadcasts, video and the BBC's in-house magazine, 'with the aim of creating a one-to-one relationship with nearly thirty thousand people' at the broadcasting organization (Dyke, 2005: 202).

Coaching the intellectual dimension of leadership may focus on helping a leader to develop her thoughts about anything from her ethical responsibilities to the trends in her market sector. Brain-storming is likely to be a part of this process with the coach acting as both a source of stimulation and as a sounding board. Often the coach will encourage a leader to seek out concrete opportunities for thought leadership, such as strategic reviews, internal forums and innovation campaigns. Volunteering for industry conferences can also be a wonderful way for a CEO to concentrate his mind on what he really stands for.

The leader's use of ideas is not without its dangers, however. It is easy to lose one's balance and veer in the direction of messages that are too prescriptive, formulaic and clichéd in their content. Employees and other stakeholders are rapidly turned off by anything that seems phony or intended to manipulate them. Organizational bosses can also be at a disadvantage compared to other thought leaders, in that they may be loath to take risks with their ideas or create any inconsistency with previous messages. That is why authenticity is so important for the thought leader. It is often better for the coach to help the leader develop her ability to speak from the heart rather than try to compete with silver-tongued opinion formers.

Telling stories is at the core of authentic leadership communication. Stories move the leader away from the language of the boardroom, which is often abstract, analytical, jargon-filled, to engaging, concrete narratives about real people in real situations. Leaders sometimes seem to forget that they have access to a much wider range of places and people within an organization, as well as beyond it, than most employees or stakeholders. Telling stories is also an effective way for a leader to influence organizational culture. Narratives of success, expected and unexpected, and stories about the right kind of failure, will gain attention, be remembered, and at their best, be repeated, producing a viral effect which ripples through an organization.

Leading innovation and creativity

Directly overseeing creativity and innovation is another vital aspect of thought leadership. Without new products and services and refinements of old products, most companies have limited prospects for survival. In order to avoid the extinction event which could be just around the corner, the leader of innovation needs to instil a sense of urgency without creating so much anxiety that he overwhelms creativity. Perhaps 'worry but don't worry' is a mantra that captures this paradoxical set of balances for the creative leader.

A major role of the CEO in creative industries is to create a culture where innovation can flourish throughout the achievement cycle. Leaders of innovation rarely innovate themselves. Steve Jobs was an exception in this respect, in that he not only developed a powerful culture of innovation at Apple, but had his name on many of its patents (Isaacson, 2011). Greg Dyke in his period leading the BBC offers an example of a more hands-off approach to creating an innovative culture. Dyke started by offering a daring creative vision to a huge organization, which had become mired in bureaucracy, and backed this up by providing the new financial resources, which were necessary for innovation in programming and digital development. He also restructured the organization to facilitate creative production and launched 'Making it happen', a comprehensive programme of training and cultural change (Dyke, 2005).

So what is the secret to leading a culture of innovation? In my view, understanding the nature of innovation has to be the starting point. Oppositional logic is central to this analysis: creative breakthroughs are often achieved by doing the very opposite of what you think you are supposed to do. Fortunately this topsy-turvy, jump-cut way of thinking is entirely compatible with the more down-to-earth logic of the achievement cycle. In fact, it is only by understanding the striking differences between the three achievement phases of innovation that we can reconcile the seemingly contradictory aspects of the process. Mix one phase with another at the wrong time and the volatile compound of creativity can blow up in your face. Probably no other field of leadership demands such a delicate yet determined touch.

Possibilizing: lighting the spark

Possibilizing really comes into its own with innovation. This stage is about creating an environment in which the rules of probability do not apply and where anything goes. Possibilizing is the quantum mechanics phase, when the seemingly senseless makes sense and the logic of illogic rules. But that does not mean the bar should be set too high. Going for total novelty or blockbuster innovation, perhaps in direct imitation of a competitor or a previous success, can inhibit creativity. Sometimes small ideas can lead to big achievements. Innovation is not all about visionary power; it also involves seeing the new possibilities inherent in what already exists.

In Blake S.'s story, in Chapter 4, we glimpsed some of the tactics a creative leader can take to encourage the generation of new ideas, such as cross-team development which gets employees talking to each other, and creative forums, which bring in outside influences. A key factor here was banishing the blame culture, so that people could possibilize without fear of the consequences of getting it wrong (the 'don't worry' phase of our mantra). If employees fear that their creative suggestions will be ridiculed or that they will be reprimanded if a new idea fails, they will often refrain from volunteering suggestions.

Embracing oppositional logic is also important for a creative leader because this is dominant in the possibilizing stage of innovation. We see this in the role of accidental discoveries, where one successful product emerges out of the failure of another. The law of unintended consequences is particularly prevalent in the pharmaceutical industry, as we noted earlier through the example of Viagra. Other serendipitous drug discoveries include the first major antidepressant, Iproniazid, which was originally intended as a treatment for tuberculosis, Warfarin, a leading anticoagulant which was developed as a pesticide against rodents; and, perhaps strangest of all, Mustine, an anti-cancer drug, which first came into existence as the chemical warfare agent, known as mustard gas (Roberts, 1989).

The role of happenstance in innovation turns upside down our normal definition of failure. Indeed the ability to learn from failure is a major asset in innovation, as creativity can all too quickly be dissipated by anxiety or shame. Encouraging what Tom Peters (1987) calls 'fast failure' is one way leaders can help to redefine the meaning of success. This can be done by promoting projects which go through the achievement cycle quickly and cheaply but realistically enough to determine that they are not marketable. If you have enough of these 'good' failures, you can start playing the numbers game of innovation to your advantage. As Soichiro Honda, founder of legendary innovators Honda Motor, said:

> To me success can only be achieved through repeated failure and introspection. In fact, success represents the 1 per cent of your work which results from the 99 per cent that is called failure.
>
> (quoted in Peters 1987: 259)

Another surprise is that creativity is not all about inspirational eureka moments: it can be achieved by using a methodical, unflappable approach. Sometimes innovation is about wearing down the truth, trapping it by eliminating improbabilities. This involves steady, patient work, for example, by trying to find what went wrong with an invention and experimenting with new solutions. It is an approach which psychologist Michael Kirton (1989) praises in 'adaptors', such as Howard Carter, the discoverer of the fabulous tomb of the Egyptian Pharaoh, Tutankhamun. Carter simply divided the Valley of the Kings into sections and kept digging year after year until he discovered what many more flamboyant archeologists had missed.

Possibilizing is the key to fostering the creative spirit. Nothing douses creativity like prematurely introducing practicalities into the creative process, such as financial resources, the similarity of a fledgling idea to an already existing entity or the statistically low chances of actually producing a viable new product. The very notion of probability can be an impediment to creative thinking. And yet, when the time is right, moving into the probalizing stage of the achievement cycle is vital for successful innovation.

Probabilizing: resourcing creativity

Probabilizing is about resourcing innovation, making the choices that give it the best possible chance of succeeding. The statistics around successful innovation may be discouraging but there is still a good deal a leader can do to improve his company's probability factor. Choosing which ideas to develop is central to this, a crucial forking of the road, which consigns many possibilities to oblivion. The trick at this stage is retaining the excitement of the possible while realistically identifying the resources that exist for actualizing it. As Rosabeth Moss Kanter (2006) suggests, having a pyramid of development projects, separating the major from the minor, can provide guidelines for making intelligent decisions about what ideas to develop. Setting timelines for development projects and clarifying expectations may also be useful.

Selecting the development team is another significant set of choices. The wrong skills can throttle a good idea at birth. Often technical skills need to be balanced with team-working skills. The most effective leader of an innovation process may not be a technical expert but someone with outstanding people skills. If the team is resourceful enough and able to bring out all its potential – in other words, if it is a dialectical team – it will be able to solve problems which would defeat a weaker group.

The physical environment is another resource which can play a role in supporting and stimulating the development team. The research lab that has the right equipment, the offices that allow for dreaming space, the sponsored canteen that brings together people unexpectedly and in relaxed circumstances – all these factors can make a difference. Does the office look as though it fosters creativity and unusual conversations, like Google's 'nooks'? Are the meeting rooms blandly corporate or do they provide creative focus and connection with the user, like UKTV's gadget-filled, clubby conference room, which reflects the male-orientated spirit of the Dave TV channel (Kingdon, 2012).

Inevitably, financial resourcing is also a vital component in innovation and often the decisive factor in successful development. An innovation leader's fate frequently depends on her ability to provide the appropriate budget for a development project. Sometimes this can be furnished by clever deals, imaginative accounting or by recognizing unexpected sources of funding. For instance, a surprisingly large number of profitable innovations in the high tech sector were only possible because of huge investments by the US government in scientific research, which led to the creation of the Internet and other crucial pieces of technological infrastructure, as Mariana Mazzucato (2013) has shown. Yet it is also true that the very absence of financial resources can sometimes produce the best in human ingenuity. Inspirational leadership and teamwork can often enable people working on shoestring budgets to make major creative breakthroughs.

Actualizing: delivering the end product

In the end, driving ideas through to completion is the real test of innovation. As a head of innovation once opined to me, 'doing the fluffy stuff is fine to create a feel-good factor but it's turning out monetisable end products which takes the real creativity!' Or as management guru Peter Drucker (2002) said, 'Innovation is work rather than genius.'

The nitty gritty labour of the actualizing phase of innovation can look very different to some people's notion about creativity. It is a skill set that calls for persistence, perseverance and even, in Sir James Dyson's words, a 'sheer bloody minded refusal to give up'. As we will see in Chapter 13, Dyson's innovations have been made in the face of numerous setbacks. He openly celebrates 'stubbornness' and rejoices in 'the virtues of a mule' (1997: 40). He is also a great believer in improvement by increments rather than breakthroughs, which means fully inuring yourself to the regular disappointments that come with trial and error.

Deciding whether to persevere with an innovation or abandon it is a key choice at the actualization phase. If you contemplate terminating your project too early, the hard, detailed, repetitive labour involved in any successful innovation may suddenly seem pointless. On the other hand, many innovations are never going to make it to the finishing line – or only at a cost which is ruinous. In this respect, as in so many others, innovation is all about timing, knowing when to open up your thinking to new possibilities, and when to keep it resolutely closed.

Clearing the way for creativity

Leading innovation usually means creating an environment in which others can flourish. Some leaders find this multirole shift difficult. It may require a leader to break with a paradigm which has been formed by previous innovations, moving away from the past, with all its apparent certainties, to the blank canvas of the future. It may seem to the leader that she is deskilling herself whereas in fact she is acquiring a different set of skills as a facilitator of innovation, which may prove to be even more valuable.

Clearing the way for creativity is often about removing the red tape that ties up new developments in knots. Especially in large organizations, the real enemy of innovation is not out in the world; it is within, where bureaucracy and old ways of working form a potent inner resistance movement. The larger the organization, the greater is its potential to delay, deflect and destroy new ideas. The choice-focused leader of innovation needs to deal with this resistance head-on if she is to create a successful culture of creativity.

This is what Rosalyn discovered. She was the chief executive of a publishing company, which she eventually realised had become 'incredibly effective at sabotaging its own best ideas'. In coaching, she resolved to put all her energy into changing the process by which new publishing proposals were actioned. Turning her back on her own much-vaunted expertise, she decided to leave new book ideas to others, acknowledging that 'there are no end of writers in the world and commissioning editors to read their proposals'. Instead, she focused entirely on the 'less travelled road' of working with her board, finance department and production teams to create a smoother journey from the book proposal to the printed (and digital) page. For Rosalyn, this meant 'cutting out the intellectual vanity and putting on some strong gloves to clear away the brambles'. The result was that in due course she cleared a path for a whole series of innovative publishing successes.

The intellectual leader and 'the thought industry'

Thought leadership is not only about facilitating other people's ideas, of course, it is also about producing your own. This is particularly true once we step outside the corporate arena into the world of 'pure thought' inhabited by organizations devoted to the development and dissemination of knowledge. Universities, think tanks, research laboratories, institutes and consultancies all play a phenomenally important role in our knowledge-based societies. Although traditionally coaching has not been common in this world, the principles of interactional leadership apply to it as well as to anywhere else.

In fact, coaching may be particularly needed in intellectual organizations, as the story of Hugh below shows. Although these workplaces may differ in all sorts of regards, one thing many of them have in common is a focus on individual work. According to Goffee and Jones (1998), thought organizations are often characterized by a 'fragmented' organizational culture, the motto of which is 'all together alone'. This culture is built around individual thinkers and researchers who, typically, are self-critical and critical of others. Academics are employed to teach and even manage others but for many of them it is their research which really motivates them and this does not necessarily involve teamwork or close collaboration. So what happens if your productivity starts to fail? In a fragmented culture who can you turn to?

Case study: Hugh: 'whatever happened to possibility?'

Hugh was a historian at a well-known university, who was a renowned authority on the Tudor period. Early in his career, he had enjoyed great success. But he had not written an original work for a decade and now was desperate to start a new book. By an unusual route, through a mutual acquaintance, he came into coaching, which gave him the opportunity to describe the problems he was facing. It also enabled him to fully explore for the first time the intimate processes of writing and the hurdles it involved.

Contrary to what his readers and students might have thought, in the past Hugh had experienced difficulties at every stage of the achievement cycle. For example, at the probabilizing stage, he had sometimes found it a challenge to convert a good idea into a workable chapter structure. He had once had a 'very strong idea' for a book on Henry VII but had ended up 'writing endlessly' searching for the precise subject. 'I got there finally', he said, 'but the writing took me down a lot of dead ends.'

Hugh had also experienced problems at the actualizing stage of writing. Like many writers, he experienced various kinds of difficulty getting down to writing. Sometimes, he was blocked by the contrast between the possibilities of the book and its actuality. He poetically called this clash, 'the riches of the imagination versus the poverty of the page'. 'You've just got to accept that you can only do your best but it often takes time to come to terms with that.' Time also seemed to play a part in reminding him of the huge amount of work involved in writing a book, which could take him up to five years. 'The thought of all those years of manual labour hangs over you!' Our coaching dialogue took place during the summer of the London Olympics and Hugh compared this choice to that of an Olympic athlete, who has just won a gold medal and is asked if he would be competing in the next Games: 'He probably has a vision of another four years of unremitting work, renouncing so much pleasure, and he thinks: 'Do I really want to do that all over again?''

Yet for Hugh, time could also deliver the solution. 'You just run up to the point where the deadline becomes serious and that seems to change the whole paradigm'. The 'metaphysics go out the window', he said, implying that the possibilizing and probabilizing phases are suddenly superseded by the sharp urgency of 'getting something done'. Once this happened, he suggested, the positive role of indecision in creative choice-making was revealed. 'You realise then that you had spare time, time for all that to-ing and fro-ing, which was fruitful in its way. But now your time is up and you start writing.'

These fascinating insights brought Hugh back to the real difficulty he was facing in writing his next book, which was a basic possibilizing problem: what exactly was he going to write about? He revealed that he felt trapped by his reputation as a Tudor historian and felt that he had now exhausted that territory. He realised that he had become too reliant on his reputation which had been sealed by the time he was in his early thirties, a quarter of a century before. He had become too safe in writing a string of books, which never strayed beyond his specialist historical period. In his twenties, he had boldly, even selfishly, set out on his course, but now he seemed to have moved to the other pole of the self–others spectrum. It was other people's opinion of him which appeared to dominate his thoughts and his publishing strategy. He was, I ventured to suggest, 'a prisoner of yes', who had become frightened of saying 'no'. This was particularly true in relation to Hugh's publisher, who was keen to keep the historian supplying the profitable Tudor market.

Something had now been released in Hugh by talking through his experiences. Over the next few sessions, he began to focus on a range of totally new possibilities for his next work. I could see his creativity returning in the sheer quantity and originality of the titles he began to consider. It was an intense, fervid, creative process, criss-crossing between what was desirable and what was doable. In the final analysis, it was Hugh's ability to connect with his most profound personal values which was decisive. His concern with the problems of contemporary political democracy and particularly what he saw as the erosion of civil liberties was a recurrent theme. In the past, he felt he had been self-evasive, 'fudging choices', by discussing some of these issues in relation to 'the Elizabethan police state' but not relating them to the current European context. This is what he finally chose to do, setting out a plan for an ambitious work which promised to root itself in contemporary history but provide illuminating links to the past. Once he had persuaded his initially reluctant publisher to back this new departure, Hugh settled down to writing his book without hesitation.

Communicative leadership: the subject matter expert

Our final form of thought leadership concerns senior executives in organizations who have no managerial responsibility but whose job it is to inspire, stimulate, and inform others. These subject matter experts and internal consultants have an increasingly significant role to play in today's knowledge-rich organizations. Although they may have no line authority, their knowledge and analytical expertise can significantly influence the choices which people make in their organizations.

As with intellectuals like Hugh, the subject matter expert's thought leadership is based on the quality of her ideas and the depth of her knowledge. But it also depends to a great extent on her ability to communicate her ideas to her colleagues, most of whom, almost by definition, are less expert than she is. Acquiring knowledge and transferring it to others are very different skills. Communicating a message to an audience has its own achievement cycle, which involves the passage of an idea through expression to comprehension. Ineffective expression can leave an audience confused and allow for different – even opposite – interpretations than those the communicator intended. In other words, making your ideas understood is often as important as the ideas themselves, as Theodora was to find out.

Case study: Theodora: 'why don't they get it?'

Theodora was a brilliant economic analyst working for an international charity. She had no formal line authority but she exercised significant influence in providing accurate and insightful information about the political, social, and economic conditions in different operating countries. This analysis enabled managers in the field and at home to make the logistical and timing decisions around aid provision on which many lives could depend. Unfortunately, Theodora's intellectual gifts were far superior to her ability to communicate her expertise to others. Her colleagues complained they simply did not understand much of her advice. Like many quick thinkers, Theodora had little time or aptitude for anything that lies between the possibilizing and actualizing phases of the achievement cycle.

She had started her career working for a high-powered team of international economists but had taken a significant drop in salary joining her non-profit organization. She said she was happier working in an environment which was not dominated by 'cut throat competition'. She seemed to think, however, that this would allow her to escape from the communication problems she had experienced in the past. If anything, these shortcomings were more acute in her current role because she was not working with economists, who at least understood her terminology. Her internal clients now were charity workers, often having to make incredibly difficult choices in the field. Poor lines of communication, including unreliable mobile phone signals, made clearly expressed content all the more vital.

'Why don't they get it?' she complained to me, demonstrating just how prescient her economic forecasts were. But when we started examining her ideas, not through the articles she proudly gave me, but actual recordings of conference calls and email communiqués, her problems in communication became evident. She didn't engage in dialogue but offered a monologue: she didn't wait for questions but provided her own, which she then answered through circumlocutions. After analysing these recordings, Theodora confessed that even she did not always understand what she was saying.

So she started putting much more effort into framing her communiqués, using probability ratings, rather than complex hypothetical scenarios. She began using metaphors instead of reams of statistics to make her point, and tried to explain her argument as though she was talking to a friend. She stopped acting as though she was in an academic tutorial and focused on presenting information, which provided a platform for urgent decision-making. In the end, it was Theodora who 'got' it. She diverted her energy from content to communication, training her formidable intellectual talents on her real job, which was to help her colleagues to help others. In doing so, she made the move from isolated individuality to a group-orientation, which is a significant milestone in many people's progression towards interactional leadership.

Chapter 12

The influence of the group in leadership

Coaching the board

The leader cannot do it all on her own. The primary issue facing her can often be put very simply: how willing and able is she to surround herself with a team that optimizes her choice-making? In Chapter 9, we looked at some of the ways in which specialist team leaders can create productive interactions between themselves and their teams. Now let's return to the chief executive and the influence of two crucial constituencies on her interactional map, her management team and the main board. These leadership groups can be her greatest assets or her greatest liabilities.

'Be careful what you wish for' is the caveat for the leader whose ideal team is one that uncritically supports him. Throughout history, surrounding oneself with 'yes people' has led to calamitous choices. For instance, what historian Ian Kershaw (2007: 290) calls 'one of the most extraordinary miscalculations of all time,' Joseph Stalin's failure to anticipate the disastrous German invasion of the Soviet Union in 1941, was largely due to the Soviet leader's absolute intolerance of counter-voices. It was this which lay behind Stalin's decision to purge the Red Army of its best, most independent-minded generals a few years earlier. But if total group unanimity can warp decision-making, excessive conflict and dissent can have the same effect. So how does the interactional leader get the balance right?

In this chapter, I attempt to answer this question by outlining the process of group coaching and showing it in action with the main board of a failing engineering company and a hospital management team in crisis. We also look at the phenomenon of leading upwards, before moving beyond corporate leadership to explore political decision-making in the immensely consequential context of international foreign policy. The connection between the CEO of a humble engineering company and the world-historical choices made by George W. Bush or Barack Obama is closer than you might think.

Group coaching: basic processes

Throughout this book, I've concentrated on coaching as a one-to-one form of development and there is no reason why this format cannot be used to help a leader develop a constructively challenging leadership team. Individual coaching has certain limitations, however, in that the coach's knowledge of the team is entirely filtered through the coachee. Although this drawback can be ameliorated by the coach's observation of the leader's team at work or by interviewing individual team members, it is sometimes better to turn to another form of coaching intervention. Group coaching is a powerful medium for developing coherent, confident teams. It can work as a stand-alone method, forming the coach's only contact with the group, or in a hybrid form, in which group work is combined with one-to-one coaching with the leader and/or members of her team.

Whatever the format, the initial procedures of interactional group coaching are similar to those of one-to-one coaching, starting with the cardinal questions. 'What do you want as a group?' begins to identify the group's vision and perhaps some of its divisions and shortcomings, as far as the future is concerned. 'What resources do you have to achieve this vision (both individually and as group)' takes us further into the group's skills and self-image. 'Who do you need to interact with to achieve this?' encourages interactional mapping, which identifies the state of relationships within the group and beyond it. These lines of inquiry are often enough to establish the interactional frame, the oppositions and dilemmas which define the group's choices, and this, in turn, is likely to set the direction for the coaching. It is also important for the coach to get a sense of who makes the choices in the group – and how, something that often merges spontaneously from group interactions.

For the group coach, it is the whole team in front of her which provides her main source of information. It may be easier for her if the group is inclined towards a collectively-led structure, as its established leadership mechanisms are likely to ensure that the whole group is included in discussions. If the group seems to be much more individually-led, the coach needs to work harder to bring out the collective dimension, and to enable group members who do not normally speak out to express their views.

Some of the factors which determine whether the group can improve the quality of the leader's decision-making are similar to those conditioning its ability to go through the achievement cycle. The composition of the group needs to include the right range of expertise, knowledge and voice and counter-voice. It needs to be structured in a way that allows members to be informed about up-and-coming decisions and play a significant part in deliberating on them. Discussion points are often most effective if researched in advance to ensure that all the appropriate options are included. This is an important aspect of the possibilizing stage, which influences everything else. Ideally, communication in the group grants everyone a platform to speak and prevents individuals from monopolizing discussions. And of course, the relationship between the leader and the group in terms of who actually makes final decisions will be critical. These issues apply to all groups, from management teams in tiny start up companies to the boards of giant multinationals and the gatherings in the citadels of governmental power, in which policy choices are made that affect us all.

The choice-focused board

As we saw in Chapter 8, the main board is a specialized group, consisting of executives and non-executives, which generally functions as the organization's formal decision-making forum. Corporate governance codes provide guidelines for the composition of the board and the role of the chair. But it is up to each and every board to create an environment which enables its chief executive to make the best possible choices. If the chairman is too weak or the CEO too strong, the risk is that the board becomes not a vibrant decision-making forum but a rubber stamp for whatever the CEO wants. Gender diversity can help in this respect. For example, according to a Leeds University Business School study, simply having one woman director on its board reduces a company's risk of going bankrupt by 20 per cent (Wilson, 2009). Yet too often organizational boards deprive themselves of a balanced roster of directors.

As a result, rigorous group procedures such as properly analysing alternatives or conducting penetrating information searches often fall by the wayside. Erratic decision-making can become the norm, as revealed by the Groupthink tradition of analysing group choices initiated by Irving Janis (1972). This shows that the sense of security offered by a group can actually lead to much worse decisions than an individual alone might make. We have already touched on one corporate example of this in RBS's disastrous takeover of debt-ridden Dutch bank ABN Amro, which happened with the full backing of a compliant board, yet seemingly without proper due diligence or risk management assessments (Martin, 2013). Sadly, it is far from being an isolated case.

Case study: boredom in the boardroom – learning how to disagree

In the boardroom things are not always what they seem. On paper, the board of the engineering company which Colin ran was united behind its chief executive but in fact it was churning with disagreement and discontent. Adrian was the chairman of the board and in the past he had been very supportive of Colin's decisions. The two were old friends and related by marriage but this cosy relationship hit the rocks when the company's tender for a lucrative tunnelling contract in the Benelux region had abruptly ended in failure. According to insiders, the company had been in pole position to win the contract, which would have elevated this medium-sized company to an entirely new level. But the proposal which Colin had pushed through the board without serious discussion had been badly drafted and mispriced and was rejected at an early stage. This shock had finally caused Adrian to wake up and address the issue of his CEO's competence to run the company.

Before declaring his hand publicly, Adrian asked me to have a session with the board, which I subsequently worked with entirely on a group basis. My first impression was that the main mood of the group was boredom. I've often found that this is a misleading phenomenon and, sure enough, when the team members began to voice their opinions, it became clear that beneath the soporific atmosphere of the boardroom, there was seething frustration with Colin and his chairman. Part of the problem was the level of detail which Colin brought to discussing every point. This not only required a high degree of concentration but excessively thorough preparation. Colin would not accept comments from anyone who was not, in his words, 'on the top of the brief', i.e. totally familiar with the formidably long documents he had issued. Some board members complained that the agenda which Colin circulated always contained more points than could be discussed and that the minutes he compiled provided one-sided accounts of meetings.

Psychologically, there seemed to be a deep-rooted dislike of confrontation among the directors. Initially, at least, they were reluctant to say very much, especially the non-executive directors, who often glanced towards Colin apprehensively, if they were at all critical of him. Colin had been heavily involved in the recruitment of the non-executives, seemingly selecting only those he thought would be loyal to him, even though one of the primary roles of a non-executive director is to question the CEO's decision-making. There also seemed to be a widespread assumption among the whole group that effective teamwork is about harmony not disharmony. Colin actively promoted the view that team members who disagree with each other were failing in their responsibilities. He could also be quite intimidating to anyone who questioned his position, publicly reminding them of past mistakes or, behind the scenes, issuing veiled threats to their favourite projects. All of these factors had contributed to the creation of a board which was deeply uncreative, swamped in detail, and so committed to unanimity at any cost that it virtually enabled Colin to make whatever decisions he wanted.

For the coaching, a starting point was to challenge the assumption that good teams never disagree. After some discussion, in which several examples of 'the right kind of disagreement' were offered by the group, 'learning how to be confrontational in a productive way' was adopted as a key coaching objective. After two sessions, the company's director of operations began to assert himself for the first time and other board remembers became more comfortable in offering dissenting views. It seemed the Benelux fiasco had finally dispelled their fear of Colin's mild-mannered bullying. They asked Colin to explain himself less long-windedly and requested that Adrian shield board members from Colin's public criticism of them. The chairman began to shoulder his responsibility for providing a realistic agenda and ensuring that the minutes were accurate. The board also passed a resolution never to approve a major commercial decision without 'a cost-benefit debate', even if this meant appointing someone to play the role of devil's advocate. There was also an improvement in the succinctness of the briefing documents, which encouraged the non-executives, in particular, to read and discuss them.

The result was an engaged, informed and empowered board in which boredom was a thing of the past. Colin initially had been very defensive about his leadership style but he soon realised that the stakes were high as far as his own job was concerned. To begin with, he complied with the emerging spirit of the board reluctantly, sometimes displaying moody fits of anger which he barely controlled. But in time Colin began to see the benefits of the constructive opposition which the board were now offering him. He revealed two beliefs which he realised had held back his leadership. The first was a need to justify every decision in immense detail, and the second was that leaders have to have all the answers, otherwise they will be judged to be weak.

The new, constructively challenging board helped Colin to ditch these assumptions and become a more effective leader, which encouraged Adrian to keep him in the job, at least for the time being. Inevitably not every outcome of the board's new decision-making process was successful. But the debating process became much more robust and psychologically balanced than before and, so it seemed to me, far more likely to produce beneficial business results in the long run.

Case study: conflict in the management team: negative opposition

The right kind of oppositional logic in a group brings out its positive dialectics. But there is also the wrong kind of opposition, based on negativity, prejudice and conflicting goals, and this can result in constant frustration for all concerned. The leader does not need uncritical yea-sayers – although sometimes he might secretly hanker after them – but nor does he need automatic nay-sayers; they can be just as debilitating. Too much opposition of an inflexible, biased kind can impair the group's choice-making intelligence as effectively as enforced unanimity.

This was Nelson's problem as CEO of a National Health Service (NHS) healthcare trust overseeing several hospitals. His management team was polarized by the intractable opposition between himself and his medical director, Pavel. In recent times, there have been several well-publicized scandals in Britain involving failures by NHS healthcare trusts to properly care for their patients, in some cases resulting in needless deaths. Fortunately, Nelson's organization did not yet fall into this category but the inability of its executive team to implement urgently-needed new reforms for monitoring patient care meant that it was flirting with disaster. After all, if the top team cannot even agree on basic strategies what might be the consequences lower down the chain of medical care?

There was no doubting the gravity of the problem, as I interviewed Nelson and his team on a one-to-one basis before our first group session (in what turned out to be a hybrid group coaching format). On paper, the executive team was well constituted in terms of expertise and responsibilities, and its meetings appeared to have accurate, properly advertised agendas, but the reality was that the group was in crisis. Decision-making was dominated by the fiery opposition between Nelson and Pavel, which influenced every strategic and operational discussion. This had the effect of polarizing the group. Some executives adopted factional positions which resulted in bitter, marathon arguments, while others withdrew from participation, confused or angered by the binary choices, with which they were presented. Every issue was immediately reduced to the simple calculus of how it would play with Nelson or Pavel rather than any consideration of its intrinsic merits. 'It's hell in those meetings, frankly' was one team member's weary summary of the situation.

Nelson's frustration with Pavel was apparent in our first one-to-one meeting. He desperately wanted to sack his medical director but recognized that this was impossible. Pavel had a brilliant reputation as both a medical practitioner and researcher. He also spoke up fearlessly for the medical staff, who strongly supported him in most of his actions. It did not help that Pavel's heroic vision of the medical profession seemed to ignite a slight sense of inferiority in Nelson as 'a mere technocratic manager'. He confessed that 'the whole aura of the doctor sometimes makes me feel like a bean counter.' Perhaps for this reason, alternative courses of action in solving the dispute with Pavel didn't seem to have occurred to Nelson. If he could not beat his medical director at his own zero sum game, he was out of options.

From the interactional viewpoint, conflict is a fundamental type of interaction which can never be entirely absent from human relationships. Sartre (1992) suggests that one way to resolve conflict is through the concept of 'the appeal', a process of finding commonality among people who are at odds with each other. After a lengthy discussion of this and related issues in coaching, Nelson decided to meet Pavel informally and they agreed at least on one thing: the impasse could not continue. For the first time, Nelson seemed to treat the deadlock as a pragmatic negotiation rather than a battle of egos, and although no specific concessions were made, the hazy outlines of a possible agreement appeared. For his part, Pavel seemed relieved to perceive some give and take in his chief executive's position.

The conflict with Pavel also blinded Nelson to the fact that it made the rest of the group redundant. Highly experienced professionals were reduced to sullen silence or to playing the role of a screeching chorus for one faction of the other. Once Nelson fully faced up to this, he resolved to try to interview each of the team individually to hear what they really thought. As it turned out, he did not need to. Most of the team saw the group coaching as a final opportunity to break out the frustrating stranglehold of the group and in the next group session they began to assert themselves vigorously.

Several of the female members of the team were particularly vocal. They felt that they had been sidelined by what one of them called 'a typically male locking of horns'. They had reacted to this in different ways. For instance, Kelly, the finance director, had become so frustrated that she had started supporting Nelson even when she knew he was wrong, which made her feel guilty. Chona, the head of data operations, who was of South-East Asian origin, admitted that she found male conflict 'quite normal' and realised that she had been falling back on a traditional female role of passive subordination. This she now shed and began actively trying to help the group find a solution to the problem of the new reforms.

Sorting out the many complex details of the new patient care agreement took time but it was achieved because of a new spirit of open communication in the group. Much of this was aimed at providing alternatives to the winner-takes-all communication style into which Nelson and Pavel had forced the group. For example, when Nelson lapsed into his usual confrontational manner, giving Pavel an 'all or nothing' set of targets for patient care surveillance, Kelly suggested, 'Why not give him the choice and see what he comes back with?' Nelson looked doubtful but it produced a slightly different response in Pavel, who realised that the responsibility now lay with him. He proposed a level of surveillance which was lower than Nelson had demanded but much higher than he had been prepared to accept before. In this way, common ground was glimpsed. The final agreement was hammered out by the group after several further meetings. It was not completely satisfactory to everyone but what compromise ever is? The main thing was that it freed the hospital trust from the log jam that had held it back. Nelson and his team were now able to move forward on other reforms which were vital to the care of their patients.

Leading upwards: individual support for the leader

In the final analysis, groups consist of individuals, who can play many different roles in relation to the leader, both inside and outside the group. For the leader there is much to be gained by exploiting another aspect of oppositional logic, which says that individuals who complement you, in terms of skills and personality, can be more valuable to you than those who share the same characteristics. This is part of the phenomenon known as leading upwards and it can make a big difference to life on the leadership high wire.

Many senior managers may exert upwards leadership. The chair of the board holds the most defined role in this respect – although in her case perhaps we should refer to it as leading sideways. And we have seen how important it can be for her to compliment and constructively oppose a CEO rather than operate unreflectively on the same wavelength as him. Other heads of function within an organization can play a similarly productive role, especially senior managers in the talent management and learning and development teams.

Perhaps the best known role of this kind is the deputy or 'trusted lieutenant'. As second in command, he can provide powerful support to a leader, especially if he possesses skills and resources which the leader lacks. In the corporate world, Michael Eisner's twenty year leadership of media giant Disney provides a good example of this type of relationship. Steve Jobs had an inside view of it and his assessment was typically trenchant: 'For his first ten years as CEO, Eisner did a really good job. For the last ten years he did a really bad job. And the change came when Frank Wells died.' As President of Disney, Frank Wells provided the managerial and operational skills that enabled Eisner's special creative skills to flourish. Once he was deprived of these resources, Eisner's 'dark side' emerged, in Jobs' view, and he became 'a terrible manager' (Isaacson, 2011: 437).

In the political sphere, a notable example of the trusted lieutenant was Willie Whitelaw. who was deputy prime minister to Margaret Thatcher from 1979 to 1986. Whitelaw is widely credited with smoothing over conflicts and creating a platform which enabled his prime minister to implement many of her policies, as Thatcher herself recognized in her bon mot, 'every prime minister should have a Willie' (Campbell, 2012: 121). For many political commentators, it was in part Thatcher's failure to find an effective replacement for Whitelaw, which led to the deterioration of her relationship with her ministers, culminating in her being ousted by her own cabinet.

However, the phenomenon of leading upwards is not always positive. It can have a darker face, if it is covert, when it may more properly be described as 'leading from behind'. There is a fine line between open support for a struggling leader and surrogate leadership. When responsibility surreptitiously shifts away from the nominal leader to someone who is not formally acknowledged, the consequences can be negative. The classic 'power behind the throne' may resort to all sorts of psychological subterfuges and Machiavellian ruses to maintain his influence. This highly untransparent situation can create a crisis of accountability, which is as unproductive in its consequences as a leadership vacuum. For some political commentators, the relationship from 1997 to 2007 between Tony Blair, as Prime Minister, and Gordon Brown, as Chancellor of the Exchequer, falls into this category of negative upwards leadership (Richards, 2010). Although the two men were complementary in some ways, their tortured and tortuous competition for power dominated many aspects of governmental policy, marginalizing other cabinet members, and, it could be said, preventing both of them from fulfilling their political ambitions.

Choices that have changed the world: lessons from foreign policy decision-making

Corporate decisions, then, are not the only type of choices which can be strongly influenced by the dynamics between the leader and the group. Let's continue the theme of political decision-making and concentrate on some major foreign policy decisions of modern times. When it comes to choices which really do change the world, we can again see the advantages for the leader who chooses to form a leadership group around him which challenges and complements him rather than reinforces his prejudices.

The influence of the leadership group on foreign policy decisions

The basic idea behind Janis's (1972) original concept of Groupthink was that groups can create a mindset which negatively influences their decision-making. As an example of this phenomenon, Janis studied the attempt by the United States to bring about regime change in Cuba in 1962, following Fidel Castro's revolution. President John F. Kennedy's leadership group contained a host of secretaries of state, military and intelligence advisors and some of the brightest minds in the country. And yet it sanctioned a mission of myopic foolishness, which ended in the military fiasco of the Bay of Pigs invasion.

The plan was not completely unopposed. Arthur Schlesinger wrote Kennedy several memos warning him that the invasion would risk all the good will the administration had achieved. But, crucially, Schlesinger and other counter voices were silent in meetings, in deference to the President's apparent desire for a unanimous decision. This strong impulse, combined with poor information search, the stereotyping and underestimation of the enemy and the influence of 'mind guards', caused the group to approve a duplicitous and extraordinarily inept military plan (Janis, 1972). In effect, the collective intelligence of this brilliant group was severely impaired, leading to a humiliating defeat for the USA and a massive propaganda victory for Castro. As Che Guevara wrote in a note to Kennedy, 'Before the invasion, the revolution was weak. Now it is stronger than ever' (Anderson, 1997: 509).

The remarkable ability of a group to undermine the choice-making of governmental leaders has been studied extensively by political scientists Mark Schafer and Scott Crichlow (2010). They have updated and amplified Janis's methodology to include not only decision-making factors but psychological, structural and situational factors. This approach resembles 6D leadership theory in so far as it places the psychology of self and group interaction within a framework of situational decision-making, although with a total of 37 factors it is a much more complex model.

One choice Shafer and Critchlow study in depth is President George W. Bush's fateful decision to invade Iraq in 2003. According to a panel of foreign policy experts consulted by the authors, this was a poor decision, in both process and outcome. It initiated a war that cost hundreds of thousands of lives (not to mention some three trillion dollars) and had the effect of stimulating, rather than deterring, anti-Western terrorism. So what went wrong? According to Schafer and Critchlow, the flaws in the decision-making of the leadership group were manifold, including biased information processing, lack of surveying of objectives or alternatives, stereotyping of the out-group and overconfidence on the part of the president, who was biased towards the invasion from the start.

What is surprising is the extent to which counter-voices were deliberately excluded from the leadership group, even if they had expertise and up-to-date knowledge of areas which might have been thought indispensable for sound decision-making. Amazingly, key meetings were held without officials from the Department of Defence, the Department of State and even the CIA, all of whom were in a position to provide the best possible intelligence of the situation in Iraq and the state of US military preparedness. The role of vice-president Dick Cheney in the group was also unusual, according to Schafer and Critchlow. Although nominally second-in-command to Bush, he seems to have acted in an extremely dominant way. Rather than complementing the president, he was often a driving force behind his decision-making. The result, according to one political analyst, was a leadership group dominated by 'an inexperienced and rigidly self-assured President who managed to fashion, with the help of a powerful vice president, a strikingly disfigured process of governing' (Danner, 2006).

Where the group helps the political leader

By contrast, let's consider the group process which led to a US foreign policy choice which many hailed as a triumph, president Barack Obama's decision to send an assault force to Pakistan to kill Osama Bin Laden in 2011.This decision, like many recent American foreign policy choices, was not without its controversial elements, not least because it involved a violation of Pakistan's sovereign territory, but in its own terms it was highly successful, both in process and outcome. According to Mark Bowden's (2012) excellent account, Obama's tendency to carefully deliberate on decisions, in this case over many months, was a strong factor in this crucial choice. In this, incidentally, he contrasted strongly with the choice-making style of George W Bush, who after a debate, 'unhesitatingly, often on the spot, made a decision' (Bowden, 2012: 159).

In early 2011, ten years after the attack on the World Trade Centre, al-Qaeda leader Osama Bin Laden appeared to have been finally tracked down by US intelligence to a secretive compound in Abbotbad in Pakistan. At this point, Barrack Obama seems to have had three main options: a drone strike on Abbotbad, a Special Forces raid, or 'wait and do nothing'. The arguments for the drone strike were strong, such as no risk to US personnel, but the chances of killing Bin Laden were fairly low and the task of proving this to the world even lower. The 'do nothing' option was also attractive, especially as there was no guarantee that Bin Laden was actually in Abbotbad (Obama never rated this as more than a 50/50 probability). But in the leadership group's final meeting, the majority of the politicians and military and intelligence chiefs present argued for the Special Forces option (Bowden, 2012).

There was no enforced unanimity in this group. Secretary of Defence, Robert Gates, dissented from the majority and argued for the drone strike. He was a veteran defence expert, who had been in the White House in 1980 when the decision had been taken to free the US hostages in Iran, a choice which had contributed heavily to Jimmy Carter's election defeat later that year. On the other hand, Vice President Joe Biden argued vigorously for the 'wait and do nothing' option. According to Bowden (2012: 201), Biden 'never hesitated to disagree at meetings like this, something that the president encouraged him to do'. In fact, Obama has always been explicit about Biden's constructively challenging role, stating that:

> The best thing about Joe is that when he gets everybody together, he really forces people to think and defend their positions, to look at things from every angle. And that is very valuable for me.
> (Cummings, 2009)

Biden's vigorous role as 'the skunk at the family picnic', as one aide described it, (Cummings, 2009), is very different from that of some other vice presidents. For example, Ronald Reagan's second in command, George H.W. Bush, appears to have played a low-key role, exerting negligible influence on the President's decision-making (Schafer and Critchlow, 2010: 20).

On April 28th 2011, after his family had gone to bed, Obama spent three hours pacing up and down in the White House, before announcing next morning: 'it's a go. We're going to do the raid.' (Bowden, 2012: 208). He said that 'he had all but made up his mind' when he left the meeting. This was not a multilateral group. It simply provided its leader with the best possible support and challenge for a decision, which in the end would always be his and his alone.

The raid, of course, was successful, although far from incident-free. Obama watched it live (captured in a famous photograph), in what he called 'the longest minutes of his life' (Bowden, 2012: 227), an interesting addition to the lexicon of the time dimension of leadership. After the event, he was realistic about the choice-making process: 'this is one of those times where you make a decision, you're not sure that it's going to work out and, in retrospect, you can say that it did work out'. (Bowden, 2012: 257).

Coaching for politicians?

In the light of all this, is there a case for saying that political leadership groups should have some of form of choice-focused coaching? One-to-one coaching for politicians may already be on the rise. In May 2013, according to *El Pais*, a prominent regional politician in Spain, Alberto Fabra, president of Valencia, declared that he was working with a 'personal coach' who was an expert in leadership and claimed that other politicians were doing the same. Perhaps predictably, this caused some controversy, with his political opponents asking, if Senor Fabra could not lead already why had he been elected in the first place? (Ferrandis, 2013).

Whether group coaching for political leaders would be subject to the same kind of objection is hard to tell. Politicians are surrounded by highly paid advisors and consultants but the suggestion that their leadership skills need improvement may be too much for some voters to swallow. Yet high political office is a job for which there is no real training. 'You learn as you go', Tony Blair admitted (2011: 643). This learning has to be done very fast, under immense pressure, and this can only increase the chances of error. If choice-focused development can help politicians make better decisions on the part of the electorate, it is surely worth serious consideration. At any rate, it is one direction that leadership coaching may take in the future, a subject which we will return to in Part 5 of this book.

Part 4

Interactional leadership in the public domain

Chapter 13

From Steve Jobs to Hamlet
The art of the choice-focused leader in business, politics and literature

Part 4 is a little different from the rest of the book. In it, I take a break from discussing coaching examples of choice-focused leadership and move into the public domain. I want to give the reader a sense of how the interactional approach might apply to some well known corporate chief executives, politicians and even some fictional protagonists. In other words, what does an interactional leader whom you've heard of look like? In trying to answer this, I'll prioritize the achievement cycle, as without the coach's inside knowledge, it is less easy to be precise about a public leader's interactional psychology. What follows, then, are more like 3D portraits of leaders than full 6D analyses, although where appropriate I'll offer psychological commentary, as well as ethical observations.

Some of these portraits focus on fractional leaders who initially lack one or other of the three main achievement cycle skills but overcome this deficiency to achieve interactional status. In other cases, these fractional deficits, or other imbalances which develop in the course of a career, limit a leader's achievements and even bring about his downfall. As well as examining choice-focused corporate leaders, I'll try to identify what the careers of some recent British prime ministers can teach us about the balancing art of leadership, before turning to one of the greatest of all writers on leadership, William Shakespeare.

The non-resourcing leader

As many of our case studies have suggested, however impressive a leader's strategy may be, she is unlikely to achieve much unless she has the appropriate resources. Failing to convert a vision into an action plan, mobilizing the necessary human resources, concluding watertight deals with suppliers, or making licensing agreements: these and other resourcing snags can trip up the most forward-looking leader. Action focus and a burning desire to get from A to B are not enough if a leader is let down by her ability to create an environment for turning ideas into successful products or services. Sometimes an organization can compensate for the non-resourcing leader's shortcomings, although the strain on the organization may be heavy. Rash, headstrong decision-making can lead to mistakes and wide-spread disaffection among the key players in a company. It is a fractional pattern that is repeated in the careers of many talented leaders, including that of one of the most legendary of visionary actualizers, Steve Jobs.

Steve Jobs: the making of a choice-focused leader

As a corporate leader Steve Jobs is probably unrivalled in contemporary history. He was a business hero who in 1976 co-founded Apple with a few thousand dollars, a company which by the time of his death in 2011 had become the biggest corporation in the world. He was also a hero to those indifferent, or even opposed, to all that goes with building a multinational corporation. For them he was, and still is, a design genius who changed peoples' lives with his beautiful, intuitive, revolutionary technology.

As an interactional leader, Jobs's credentials were impressive. We can see his choice consciousness in his statement on the importance of renunciation in decision-making I quoted in Chapter 1. This is not to say that he was orthodox in his choice-making. He often obstinately maintained a contrary opinion and only changed his mind if others argued against him persuasively enough. Jobs could even be surprisingly indecisive at times, according to Walter Isaacson's (2012: 315) compendious, authorized biography. It was in choosing the future that his choice-making reached the level of genius. His novel and timely vision of a consumer-orientated, highly aesthetic technology, 'at the intersection of liberal arts and technology', as he described it (p. 494)[1], distinguished him from an industry obsessed with engineering rather than art.

This ability to see the future before it had happened was central to his distinctive talent: 'Our task is to read things that are not yet on the page,' he said (p. 567). But this visionary perspective was combined with an exceptional concentration on getting right every detail of the finished product. He was a superb deliverer, with a determination to see his ideas implemented which tested his co-workers to the limit. His refusal to accept his engineers' thirty-eight reasons why his vision for the iMac could not be produced was one example of this exceptional focus on execution. Another was his insistence that the circuit boards of Apple PCs should look perfect, even though they were housed in sealed cases.

It was as a resourcer that Jobs was most susceptible, especially in the early days at Apple. At the age of twenty-one, he made an inspired resourcing choice in joining forces with the computer genius of Steve Wozniak. But Jobs was not easy to work with. He was often adversarial in his relationships with others, causing major splits and resentments in his teams and a permanent headache for senior management. He could fly into furious tempers and regularly burst into tears at important meetings. At this early stage of his career, his behaviour was problematic enough to be cited by Jay Conger (1990) – perhaps only slightly unfairly –as an example of 'the dark side of leadership'.

The end result of this failure to develop the interpersonal and self-management skills commensurate with the success of Apple was that in 1985 Steve Jobs fell victim to leadership hubris, as he was effectively forced out of the company he had co-founded. This is perhaps the ultimate fate of a non-resourcing leader, who lacks the probabilizing skills to create an appropriate environment for his ideas.

By the time Jobs returned to Apple in 1997, things were very different. 'I've got thousands of key decisions to make' (p. 315) he told his expectant board. But he had learned from his roles as chairman and CEO of NeXT and Pixar to make choices in a different way. His multirole experiences had taught him a good deal about the art of leadership, including developing people and being both directional and opportunistic in his strategy. At Pixar, in particular, where film animation was far from being his original strategic priority, 'he learned to let other people flourish and take the lead' (p. 426). Becoming a father had also changed him. He said of this experience, "it's like a switch gets flipped inside you and you can feel a whole new range of feelings' (Blumenthal, 2012: 157).

Jobs's first actions at Apple demonstrated this new emphasis on resourcing. For example, he introduced a remuneration plan to properly incentivize the staff, stating that 'people are the key' (p. 318). He also formed a clever pact with Microsoft, ending years of intense competition. Strategy of course was still to the fore, as he quickly narrowed down Apple's plethora of products to just four product development areas, recognizing the need to renounce possibilities in order to create the probability of success.

Job's new resourcing skills were also obvious in 2002 through his creation of a market for Apple in the music industry, which was soon to account for more than half of its revenues. Many people had had the idea for a digital music service before Apple but no one could bring together the notoriously uncooperative heads of the main music companies until Jobs did so with a mixture of charm, vision and pressure. iTunes was not so much a triumph of 'where' but a victory of 'how'. Technologically, as a resourcer, Jobs was always quick to spot opportunities created by government financing. The ground-breaking iPhone was heavily reliant on technical innovations which had been forged in military and scientific establishments and other publically funded bodies (Mazzucato, 2013). On the human resourcing front, Jobs's ability to encourage talented designers like Jonny Ives was also a key to the success of Apple after 1997.

This is not to say that probabilizing was ever Jobs's greatest strength. He was never exactly known for his smooth diplomacy and at times he seemed to ignore the rules of ordinary social intercourse (p. 262). His board at Apple after 1997 was made up of admirers who did not, on the whole, challenge him constructively, but his day-to-day interactions with his staff were robustly two-way. As his successor as CEO, Tim Cooks, said of him, 'if you don't feel comfortable disagreeing, then you'll never survive' (p. 460).

Ethically, Jobs often worked on the borderline. His so-called 'reality distortion field' (p. 117) led people to think they could achieve the impossible, often correctly as it turned out, although in other circumstances this trait might have taken Jobs across the ethical divide. His vision of Apple as a self-sufficient world was certainly at odds with the open-source Internet idealism that Steve Wozniak represented. Who knows where this vision – and 'the holy war on Google' which he promised (Bradshaw, 2014) – may have led Jobs? But his death at the age of 56, at the very peak of his fame, robbed the world of the answer to this question and deprived us of the innovations he might have brought to the market. It also probably consolidated his reputation forever, and today he stands as a corporate leader who is revered by the establishment and the anti-establishment alike, a rare feat in a century whose faith in leadership has been so badly shaken.

James Dyson

If Steve Jobs was a great instance of an American interactional leader, Sir James Dyson represents an exceptional British example. There is less information available about Dyson, in part because his company is privately owned, but his vivid autobiography gives us enough material to form a picture of a man of extraordinary choice-focus and determination to succeed. He may not operate in as glamorous an industry sector as Jobs but he too has an extraordinary ability to work against the odds to change consumers' lives. His vision in understanding the potential for Dual Cyclone technology was outstanding, as was his resolution to follow through on his innovation. The 5,127 prototypes he developed for his invention are ample proof of his philosophy of 'progress through iteration' (Dyson, 1997: 168). This exceptional ability to operate in a world that has not yet happened is made possible by his resilient attitude to delivery. He has written that 'As an inventor... You are never happy. There's always another insuperable problem to overcome' (Uhlig, 2010: 146). This stubborn combination of 'stamina and conviction', (Dyson, 1997: 207) is the lesser known side of many successful visionaries.

Yet, like Jobs, resourcing was Dyson's problem area, at least in the formative stages of his professional life. As he recounts in his autobiography, he made some serious resourcing mistakes in his early career, especially in the treacherous world of licensing agreements where the wrong contract can mean signing away the profits from – and even rights to – your innovation (Dyson, 1997). In the end, he chose to build a company around himself, rather than rely on others, and appears to have mastered the arts of resourcing, by developing a harmonious, design-led culture, which can deliver outstanding financial results.

Psychologically, Dyson is hard to fathom, as he keeps a low public profile. He says that in the past people have considered him 'arrogant, rude, stubborn and solipsistic,' but that, in hindsight, these were the qualities necessary for to achieve a vision. He adds, 'when all has come right, the kind of man who persisted despite constant ridicule from the controlling forces will be said to have possessed vision.' (Dyson, 1997: 40) He appears to be extraordinarily comfortable working in the future and yet his autobiography also reveals a deep contentedness about being in the present. His account of his years leading up to the success of his first vacuum cleaner, as he worked in his workshop, often alone, conveys a sense of the master craftsman and passionate scientist patiently searching for practical solutions to complex problems. From this, he has gone on to master multirole leadership, as designer, chairman, chief executive, marketing frontman and champion of innovation and science (Uhlig, 2010).

For some, Dyson's ethical reputation was tarnished by his decision in 2002 to move much of his UK workforce to Malaysia, a strategy that he claimed was necessary for his firm's survival. Whether this decision was an ethical one is debatable. It almost certainly was not a choice that was made easily. His company has grown considerably since the move and in 2014 he announced his intention to recruit 3000 new engineers for his UK operation (Dyson, 2014). This would seem to justify Dyson's overall strategy and provide further evidence of his ability to make the tough decisions involved in choosing the future.

The non-strategizing leader

The leader who lacks the strategic skills to create a forward path for her organization is always likely to struggle. If she is fortunate enough to have inherited an effective vision, it may be enough for her to simply resource and deliver it. But in this case, it might be said, we are really talking about a superior manager rather than a leader. The leader's ability to work in the future is what marks her out from the crowd. At the same time, a vision can emerge in many ways, as we've seen, especially if you have the outstanding resourcing and delivery skills to force it into revealing itself.

Richard Branson

For me, Sir Richard Branson is an unusual, entrepreneurial example of non-strategizing leadership. Whereas James Dyson works in one industry, Branson is the very incarnation of multiplicity and has worked in dozens of different sectors. He has developed many successful businesses, although there have been a good few failures along the way (e.g. Virgin Cola). In one sense, his choice focus is exceptional. He has the juggling ability to keep many corporate balls in the air, as he focuses on a huge variety of projects, in which he variously plays the role of executive, shareholder, publicist or project development champion. As a resourcer, he appears to be capable of effective if unorthodox financing, inspired recruitment and successful delegation. He has a genius for self-publicity, which earns countless millions of pounds of free advertising for his ventures, an almost unique resource which is one of the few constant features of the Virgin brand.

In delivery terms, Branson's approach is highly energetic, pragmatic, and action-focused. He is a classic actualizer, as befits a businessman whose motto is 'Screw it, let's do it' (Branson, 2006). He has said, 'we often do things and then work out afterwards what the strategy was' (Bower, 2008: 197). This back-to-front approach to the achievement cycle may have some advantages, especially if you are prepared to cut your losses if a business does not thrive, as Branson is certainly prepared to do. But if you start with a situation and then try to create a strategy for it, it is hard to develop a coherent long-term vision.

Indeed, as far as the achievement cycle is concerned, Branson's weak spot is strategy. In spite of his achievements, especially in traditional industries such as aviation and railways, Virgin has no compelling long-term or overarching vision. Branson has often hived off one company (Virgin Music) to pay for another (Virgin Atlantic). In the 1980s, he said, 'I had a vision of Virgin as the largest entertainment group in the world outside the United States' (quoted in Bower, 2008: 73), but this ambition of rivaling Rupert Murdoch's empire has come to very little. He has not shown Murdoch's ability to work in the long term, taking major risks with new ventures such as satellite television. (Nor, it has to be said in Branson's defence, has he been associated with the dubious ethical behaviour of a Murdoch outlet such as *The News of the World*). Branson is more pragmatic, short-term focused and this has led to a lack of coherence and perhaps missed opportunities, especially in the media. He appears to be a master juggler, a supreme entrepreneurial self-starter, but not a visionary leader.

The non-actualizing leader

Effective leadership action can be blocked by many things: flaws in strategy, planning or resources, the inability to adjust to unexpected events, psychological rigidity, a lack of action focus or a culture of low performance standards. In the end, it all comes down to a damaging lack of adequation between the strategy and resources being used and the actual situation on the ground. Expressed in these terms, it may seem that the non-delivering leader will rapidly be found out. In reality, this type of leader is often a master of disguise, able to conceal his lack of results through many means, including the dark arts of creative accountancy. In recent times, nobody illustrates this type of fractional leader better than Jeffrey Skilling of Enron.

Jeffrey Skilling

Although he only officially held the title of chief executive of Enron for a short time, Jeffrey Skilling was probably the most influential leader of the multinational gas and trading conglomerate, which by the time of its bankruptcy in 2001 had grown to be the fifth largest company in the USA. Skilling is currently serving 14 years of a 24 year prison sentence for conspiracy, false statement to auditors, securities fraud and other offences. And yet, we have to remind ourselves, during the 1990s he was hailed by investors, analysts and politicians as a business genius, a visionary leader who could do no wrong, in the same way as Steve Jobs is today. But whereas Jobs was obsessed with the execution phase of the achievement cycle (for him, as for Dyson and Branson, strategy without implementation was meaningless), Skilling seemed to have been remarkably indifferent to delivery. At times, he appeared to be almost contemptuous of real results, as long as they could be presented positively to Wall Street. This deficiency put him out of touch with reality and directly contributed to one of the most devastating corporate failures of this century, depriving 20,000 Enron employees of their jobs and many of their life savings.

In terms of choice-making, strategy was almost everything for Skilling. He was so comfortable operating in the future, especially with forward accounting practices, that the present could seem almost irrelevant to him. He is a rare example of a leader who not only uses the future but abuses it. As one of his former colleagues said, 'Enron borrowed from the future until there was nothing left to borrow' (McLean and Elkind, 2004: 158). Skilling's strategy seemed to be dominated by a single constituency on his interactional map: equity analysts. As long as he could convince the capital markets of the progress of Enron and maintain the upward rise of its share price, the conglomerate's bewilderingly complex accounting practices and investments could pass muster. If the share price went down, the house of cards would tumble. For Skilling, this meant that everything had to be sacrificed to keep the quarterly earnings targets on track, even if this meant distorting what was actually happening on the ground.

Skilling was weak at resourcing. As authoritative Enron chroniclers Bethany McLean and Peter Elkind suggest (2004: 28, 55) 'his management skills were appalling' and his philosophy of management summed up by his belief that 'all that matters is money... you buy loyalty with money'. He built his teams around intelligent, like-minded people, paid them well, and did not expect them to challenge him. In terms of execution, he was even more fallible. He was 'a designer of ditches not a digger of ditches' (p. 28)[2], a brilliant innovator who saw no great need to follow through on his ideas, as long as he could convince outsiders that others were doing this for him. He seemed to have a disdain for the nuts and bolts of building a business, expressing the surprising view that long-term planning was irrelevant to building a multinational corporation. He also seemed to lack personal resilience. When things got hard, especially when he was finally promoted to chief executive, he struggled. 'Jeff doesn't do hard,' was the crushing verdict of a fellow Enron executive (p. 339).

As a consequence, strategy was increasingly severed from delivery. For instance, Enron Broadband, which was touted by Skilling as the future of the company, and at its peak was valued in the accounts at $36 billion, in reality was never much more than a failing start up. This preference for strategy above delivery did not inevitably cause the extraordinary collapse of Enron. We also have to take into account Skilling's dubious personal morality. In this he was not alone, of course. For example, his chairman, Ken Lay ran a handpicked board which, according to one of its directors, operated 'more like a family gathering than a board meeting' (p. 96). Lay was willing to exempt the company's chief financial officer, Andy Fastow, from corporate governance regulations around conflicts of interest, which enabled Fastow to amass a fortune by trading with his own company – at rates of return of up to 17,000% (p. 206). Skilling might have stopped short of malpractice but his dissociation from reality meant that this was highly improbable. The biggest bankruptcy in US history, before Lehman Brothers, was the outcome.

Not all non-actualizers fall as hard as Jeff Skilling, They are often more mundane, lost in muddling incompetence or stuck in frustrating impasses, like the many leaders on which John Kotter's (1996) influential studies are based, which claim that most leadership change programmes end in failure. But the inability to funnel down into the resourcing and executional levels to see the possible implications of a strategy is always a liability, especially in that most consequential arena of leadership choices, the merger or acquisition. For example, take the merger between AOL and Time-Warner in 2001, the biggest in media history. It was intended to transport both companies into a new commercial era but within less than a year, it had lost them up to $200 billion in shareholder value and the union was soon unwound. The outsized egos of the two companies' chief executives was one factor in this catastrophic alliance but their inability to drill down and understand the profound incompatibility of the two companies – in addition to the divisive structure of Time-Warner itself – was probably the major cause of the disaster (Munk, 2004).

The political high wire: four prime ministers

Political leaders are also subject to the achievement cycle, although evaluating them is always likely to be a controversial topic. One of the few contemporary leaders to rise above narrow partisan prejudice is Nelson Mandela, who has already been referred to in this book as a man who provides a compelling example of interactional leadership. As the poet Seamus Heaney (2001) wrote, 'the name Mandela...is the equivalent of a gold reserve, a guarantee that the currency of good speech can be backed up by heroic action'. Mandela was undoubtedly an interactional leader with extraordinary vision and resourcefulness, who executed the most improbable balancing act in first bringing down an oppressive Apartheid regime and then dedicating his presidential career to reconciliation. The fact that most of his political career was conducted in prison makes his story even more exceptional.

What can we can learn about the art of choice from political leaders working in more conventional circumstances? We've already referred to several American presidents, so let's now look at the lessons about interactional leadership offered by some recent British prime ministers. I want first to focus on Margaret Thatcher and Tony Blair, who (along with Clement Atlee) came top of a survey of over 100 UK-based academics, who were asked to rank the achievements of all postwar British prime ministers (Theakston and Gill, 2011). Thatcher and Blair both had strong, radical visions of change, the resourcing ability to persuade others and the determination to transform their policies into social and economic realities. They each won three consecutive general elections, and yet both were finally pushed off the tightrope of power, not by the electorate, but by some of their own closest colleagues.

Thatcher and Blair: the hubris of vision

Margaret Thatcher's strengths were her vision of a market-oriented British economy and her extraordinarily determined, can-do ability to deliver her policies. As a resourcer, in the early years of her premiership, she exhibited a much underrated ability to mix boldness with caution and maintain a subtle balance between the supporters of neoliberalism and the traditional, 'wet' elements in her party. Buoyed up by the unexpected popularity of her conduct in the Falklands War (without which she may not have been re-elected in 1983), she led a strong, effective cabinet, which implemented many of her most cherished policies.

Yet her resourcing skills would be her downfall. She was ultimately an ineffective team leader, because, as her biographer John Campbell (2012: 410) observes, 'she did not trust her colleagues...and could not tolerate rivals'. Willie Whitelaw, as we noted earlier, had a crucial role as deputy prime minister in reconciling the voices and counter-voices in the cabinet but after he resigned in 1986, Thatcher relied increasingly on her own vision for policy guidance at the expense of her colleagues' opinions. First, she insisted in implementing the deeply unpopular poll tax, which alienated many of her own party. Then she showed an increasingly erratic and autocratic attitude to the issue of the single European currency, which eventually caused even her most loyal minister, Geoffrey Howe, to turn against her. The end result was that she was ousted not by the electorate but by her own parliamentary colleagues, another example of the hubris which may await the visionary leader who ignores the needs of her leadership group.

Tony Blair was also undone by a foreign policy, and a cabinet he ultimately failed to unite. Blair's clear strategy of modernizing his party, his outstanding communication skills and his initial ability to balance a cabinet, which was torn between left and right factions, enabled him to introduce many of the reforms he aimed at as prime minister, although he regretted not being more radical in relation to public services (Seldon, 2005). The timing of Blair's resignation even enabled him to evade some of the blame for the 2008 credit crunch, although he later admitted 'We didn't spot it' (Blair, 2011: 667). But it was Blair's foreign policy, and his failure to master the multirole challenge of combining very different realms of leadership, which brought down this exceptionally able politician.

Emboldened by foreign policy success in Kosovo and Northern Ireland, Blair's decision to back the US invasion of Iraq in 2003 without a full and open discussion with his own cabinet – or indeed parliament – was a fateful choice. He still insists that this was the right decision but he is acutely aware of its implications and has sympathy for those who fell in the war, commenting that 'They have died and I, as decision-maker in the circumstances that led to their death, will live.' (Blair 2011: 272). This compassion was not enough to prevent the intense personal unpopularity which the Iraq war brought him and the Gordon Brown faction in the cabinet finally forced Blair to resign as prime minster in 2007.

Blair's political touch and intuitive sense of balance, initially so precise, deserted him over his Iraq war choices. Some lines in his autobiography referring to his last months in office perhaps indicate why:

> I had started by buying the notion... that being in touch with opinion was the definition of good leadership. I was ending by counting such a notion of little value and defining leadership not as knowing what people wanted, and trying to satisfy them, but knowing what I thought was in their best interests and trying to do it.
>
> (Blair, 2011: 600)

As a description of a highly talented, interactional leader moving out of touch with reality this is hard to surpass.

The fate of the successor: Major and Brown

The least successful of recent prime ministers, according to Theakston and Gill's (2011) survey, were John Major and Gordon Brown. They are examples of leaders of considerable talent who ended up as non-actualizers, incapable of delivering positive results. Both illustrate the often difficult fate of the successor. In Chapter 10, we discussed the ambiguities of the leader who is next in line but the challenges can be even greater for a leader when power is finally achieved. John Major, who succeeded Margret Thatcher as prime minster in 1990, after a stellar ministerial career, was never able to create a distinctive public image for himself. He failed to restore the balance between the factions in his cabinet over Europe, which Thatcher's departure had exacerbated, and his party was increasingly dogged by a reputation for 'sleaze' and corruption. Major had a relatively clear, free-market, pro-European vision but this was poorly communicated and his premiership was generally seen as weak and ineffectual, with few domestic achievements. His one memorable reform, the privatization of the railways, is still viewed today by some as a costly disaster.

When Gordon Brown finally became prime minister in 2007, after a relentless ten-year campaign which had sapped a good deal of energy from Blair's premiership, he seemed to find himself surprisingly bereft of strategic ideas with which to distinguish himself from his predecessor. Brown entered 'a policy vacuum', quite distinct from his complex, often audacious strategizing as Chancellor of the Exchequer. His negative evaluation of Blair was not replaced by a positive vision of his own. His erratic choice-making around calling a general election in 2007, which might have enabled him to make his mark, was a fatal blow. First he seemed to indicate that the election was on and then he changed his mind, leaving his party confused and his reputation in disarray. One sympathetic biographer argues that this indecisiveness, 'in the full media glare', more or less 'destroyed Brown's premiership' (Richards, 2010: 285), barely months after it had begun.

Only Brown's response to the 2008 financial crash enabled him to find something like a vision, even though politically it could be seen as the polar opposite to his strategy as Chancellor of encouraging the growth of the financial sector in order to provide increased tax revenues for alleviating poverty. Like John Major, who came up trumps when faced with what looked like certain defeat in the 1992 election, Brown found a brief clarity of purpose, when events were forced on him, which eluded him at other times. His defeat at the 2010 general election, which was not helped by his ineffective attempts to improve his communication style ('Emotional Intelligence, zero.' was his predecessor's harsh comment (Blair, 2011: 616)), only served to emphasize that a leader needs good resourcing skills, if real results are to be attained in politics – or anywhere else.

Choice-focused leadership in Shakespeare

Finally, in this wide panorama of leadership examples, I want to turn away from factual reality to the world of literature. As a former student and teacher of English Literature, I've long revered William Shakespeare as the greatest of all writers – and an outstanding thought leader. More recently, I've also come to appreciate him as a great writer on leadership, if a highly ambiguous one. His plays portray historical and semi-historical figures in a way that compels an audience to experience the emotional reality of leadership as well as its substantive issues. In coaching, referring to Shakespearean characters and other fictional examples can illuminate new parallels and pathways for the coachee. Nor is it a surprise to find that several modern leadership theorists have been inspired by the Bard's work (e.g. Whitney and Packer, 2000).

I would argue that Shakespeare's concept of leadership, although largely developed through negative portrayals, closely parallels certain aspects of interactional leadership. Shakespeare's tragedies, in particular, have an intense focus on choice-making, as the dramatist is drawn again and again to the delicate balance of forces which can overthrow an emperor like Julius Caesar or the psychological factors which can topple a great military leader like Mark Anthony. Shakespeare never portrayed a fully interactional hero. Perhaps Henry V comes closest, a medieval warrior-king who is both of his time (and thus often shockingly cruel) and strikingly modern. His authenticity in listening to his men before the Battle of Agincourt provides the inspiration for his powerfully motivating, visionary 'band of brothers' speech. However, it is through his great tragic heroes that Shakespeare shows most vividly the connection between choice-making styles and the fate of a leader. Through these negative imprints, shadows of what have been, the great dramatist sketches the balancing art of choice, enabling his audience to imagine for themselves what a good leader would look like.

Othello: the fallible resourcer

In Shakespeare's tragedy, Othello, the hero is depicted as a brilliant military strategist and a proven man of action who is destroyed by his resourcing choices. Not that replacing Iago, his former lieutenant, with the suave aristocrat Michael Cassio is a bad move in itself. It may even be an astute recruitment decision, suggesting that Othello is thinking carefully about his new political role as governor of Venice and recognizing the difference between this and his previous life as a military commander.

Othello's problem and 'tragic flaw' is that he fails to realise the impact this tough decision may have on his erstwhile deputy. The noted nineteenth-century poet and critic, Samuel Coleridge, famously accused Iago of 'motiveless malignity' but no one who has been passed over for a promotion would be quite so quick to make this judgment. In a sense, of course, Othello would have agreed with Coleridge, because he fails to perceive the interpersonal implications of his dismissal of Iago, which, whether right or not, requires a disciplined, self-renunciatory personal response on Othello's part. In continuing to trust a man whose career he has ruined, Othello engages in a negative parallel choice, trying to have his cake and eat it. King Lear does the same, in renouncing his formal power yet attempting to retain his real authority – an act of a bad faith, incidentally, which many a family firm has had to deal with on the supposed retirement of its founder.

However, it is not only a poor recruitment choice that undoes Othello. Like many a leader before and since him, he is let down by a lack of emotional self-management. Of course, Othello is up against a man of diabolical brilliance in reading and manipulating other people's emotions. Indeed, Iago's political skills suggest that he might have become a far better diplomat than his replacement. But Othello's lack of self-knowledge also shows in his relationship with his newly married wife, Desdemona. He does not seem to know her as a person or know how to get to know her. In the end, Iago's cunningly phrased accusations of marital infidelity carry more weight than Desdemona's fervent denials. The tragic conclusion of this imbalance is that Othello ends up killing a woman whom he genuinely loves and who genuinely loves him. The distorting pressure of leadership could not be more clearly articulated.

Macbeth: delivery without vision

Shakespeare's Macbeth offers the chilling spectacle of the pure actualizer, the ruthless executor of a strategy he does not really believe in. Macbeth is a leader driven by ambition rather than vision. In fact, his vision has to be literally displayed in front of his eyes – by the three witches and a phantasmagoric parade of future Scottish kings – and reinforced by his wife's raw ambition before he can make his monumental choice to assassinate his own king. This is not a vision which emerges from his own deep values and emotional self; it is more like an opportunistic spur to action.

The fact that Macbeth's violent and individualist strategy for usurping his king contains no ethical legitimacy – or at least none that Macbeth can truly commit himself to in a collectivist society, eats away at him psychologically. But this does not stop him from embarking on a campaign of ever greater ruthlessness and cruelty to protect his new power base. Lady Macbeth is haunted by the real moral meaning of her murderous action, as her husband enters an ethical void.

Macbeth becomes a leader as much at war with himself as with his society, embodying a pure will to action. He is defeated only when the very landscape in front of him seems to alter its shape – as it may seem to do for leaders during moments of great change – and Birnam wood appears to move to Dunsinane. By then, life has long ceased to have meaning for him: 'it is a tale/Told by an idiot, full of sound and fury/Signifying nothing' (Shakespeare, 1997: V.5. 26–28). I wonder if other, more contemporary, leaders have experienced the same emptiness when faced with the prospect of total failure. In any case, Macbeth offers a chilling example of the barbaric chain of actions that can occur when a leader's strategy has been reduced to nothing more than self-perpetuation and all his other responsibilities have been thrown to the wind.

Hamlet: to lead or not to lead?

If Othello lacks resourcing skills and Macbeth an authentic vision, Hamlet seems to have all the achievement cycle skills – and none. He has the potential to be an interactional leader but does not actualize anything. He provides Shakespeare's most celebrated and complex examination of the vagaries of choice and non-choice and the multiplicity of leadership roles. Like Macbeth, Hamlet is presented with a vision, the ghost of his murdered father, but he cannot fully embrace this vision or turn it into a consistent set of intentions. Part of the problem may be the personality of Hamlet's father, who is lauded as a great leader but who seems to have spent most of his time in overseas wars. He was charismatic but possibly a neglectful husband and father, in contrast to his murderous brother, Claudius, the polished diplomat, who at least clearly loves Hamlet's mother, Gertrude.

Hamlet's choices come and go. Sometimes they appear to him in sharp detail, at other times blurred to the point of invisibility. He can make blindly impulsive choices (stabbing Polonius) but when confronted with a reactive choice (Rosencrantz and Guildenstern's assassination attempt), Hamlet's responses are razor-sharp. As a resourcer, Hamlet has wonderfully versatile interpersonal skills and winning charm, if he cares to use them. His behaviour at court, an intellectually dazzling and disarming mix of mystery, madness and menace, buys him some time but he squanders this. Ultimately, Hamlet 'forgets'. In this most incisive portrayal of choice evasion, the prince seems to drift off into a world where the sword of Damocles of choice disappears, until the brutal facts of the court cause him to regain his memory (too late, for Claudius has now made his choice).

Put like this, we can see Hamlet as a portrait of the ultimate non-actualizing leader – a kind of 'how not to do it' text on effective leadership, which is largely how leadership theorist John Whitney (2000) interprets the play. But are we asking the right questions of Hamlet's mission? Instead of wondering, 'Why does he not do what he sets out to do?' perhaps we ought to ask, 'Why should we expect him to be able to cope with his situation?' After all, he is a young man with no experience of leadership. Thirty is Hamlet's conventionally accepted age but he may be considerably younger. His apprenticeship in leadership seems sketchy, with his university in Wittenberg providing a largely academic education. Compare this with the historical Henry V, who had an apprenticeship in real kingship at only twenty years of age.

In other words, Hamlet may be best interpreted as a potential leader. In this light, he does what many a talented but inexperienced leader does, when pitched into a situation which is way beyond his experience. Let's face it, being thrown in at the deep end doesn't get much more demanding than having as your first task the assassination of the king, who just happens to be your uncle and the man your mother loves! Some of the ways Hamlet copes with this unlooked-for role are brilliant. What a paradigm of probabilizing intelligence is the play-within-a-play which he stages to gauge Claudius' reaction. As a device to find evidence that turns the possible into the probable it is a stroke of genius. But Hamlet flounders, zigzagging between options, and in the end follows events rather than leading them, a fault of many fledgling leaders.

I would argue, however, that Hamlet finds his real leadership role in yet another guise, that of thought leader. Nowhere is the lonely responsibility of leadership so incisively articulated as in his words. He is the poet of uncertainty, a brilliant, inspirational analyst of the difficulties of making high-risk choices and putting them into action. Hamlet is the master of paradox, exhibiting a nihilistic art of balance, enabling him to live on his wits, until defeated by the brutal realpoltik of his uncle's accomplished, if deeply unethical leadership. Given time, Hamlet might have learned to integrate his thought leadership with his other talents. Allies would have helped: why did he not confide in the loyal Horatio, for example? Or perhaps he might have found a mentor, one more appreciative of the ambiguities of power than the simple-minded Polonius. One thing is certain, this mixed-up, would-be interactional leader, created some four centuries ago, can still provide a treasure trove of lessons for today's leaders.

Notes

1 All page references in the section on Steve Jobs refer to Isaacson, 2011, unless otherwise indicated.
2 All page references in the section on Jeffrey Skilling refer to McLean and Elkind, 2004, unless otherwise indicated.

Part 5

Choosing the future

Leaders and coaches

Chapter 14

Engaging with choice
Ethical issues for leaders and leadership coaching

Leaders and leadership coaches face some extraordinarily tough choices in the coming years and in the final part of the book it is time turn the spotlight on them. Before fully opening the lens to view the challenges of choosing the future in Chapter 16, we return to the ethical dimension of leadership, in this chapter and the next. Ethics is concerned with choices about right and wrong and, in this sense, is an extension of the balancing art which leaders practice every day. But in the future a new focus on this arena of choice-making seems to be urgently needed, if the scale of ethically problematic organizational behaviour which has emerged since the Great Recession is anything to go by.

The banks and other financial institutions have led the way with unethical and illegal activities around rate fixing, money laundering, illegal trading and mis-selling of insurance products, to say nothing of fraudulent funds and Ponzi schemes. Phone-hacking and other illegal accessing of private data by media corporates and governments have also been headline news. Generous compensations schemes for dismissed executives have been criticized for 'rewarding failure', while 'gagging orders' prevent others from speaking the truth about wrong-doing. Corporates have been accused of tax evasion, facilitated by accountants and lawyers. Nor have public sector organizations escaped opprobrium, with politicians falsifying their expenses, the police involved in bribery and other scandals and the NHS covering-up medical incompetence and wasting billions of pounds on failed information technology. And all this is without even considering the ethical status of entire industry sectors, such as tobacco or the arms trade.

Whether this spate of revelations suggests a real increase in organizational wrong-doing or simply a new intolerance of practices which have existed for some time is a moot point. After all, an economic boom has a way of raising the threshold of moral acceptability. What is undeniable is that the ethical dimension of leadership is now in the foreground as never before and is likely to stay there in the future. Leaders urgently need to engage with this new reality – and leadership coaching has to provide an intellectually consistent basis for doing so.

In this chapter, we try to beat a path through the moral entanglements facing the coach and the leader, sketching some principles of an interactional approach to ethics and contrasting this with an undialectical, universalizing morality which attempts to eliminate, rather than embrace, contradiction. I'll also try to define what the concept of challenge really means in leadership coaching and give some coaching examples of the ethical dimension implicit in the interactional leadership model.

Four principles of interactional ethics

This is not the place to develop a full-blown account of an interactional ethics, even if I were capable of providing it, but I feel it is worth outlining four broad principles which may help to guide the choice-focused leader and the interactional coach.

1. Ethics is about engaging with choice

The first of these interactional principles states that the quality of our engagement with choices is perhaps the only guarantee of ethical behaviour which we have. This engagement requires an intense openness to, and involvement with, our experience as it presents itself, which Heidegger (1962) sees as the heart of authenticity. We search for an anchor – loyalty to a family, a nation, a universal formula or even to oneself (after all, amorality is kind of morality), but this search for a 'pure knowledge' is self-contradictory. There is only what Sartre calls 'the point of engaged knowledge.' (1958: 308). In the end, the search for perfect outcomes is equally futile, the process is all that we can guarantee. This at least can help us to avoid giving in to others heedlessly or surrendering to our own unreflective impulses. It can also prevent us from ignoring that a choice exists (the phrase 'I had no option but to...' usually needs to be treated with great suspicion).

2. Ethical choices involve a situational interaction of self and others

To engage with a choice is to engage with a potential opposition between the interests of the self and the interests of others. Resolving this is no easy matter. A decision that appears to be 'selfish' may be the right option, when it creates real possibilities for others. Equally, apparently selfless choices, made in the name of others, can turn out to be deceptive or unsustainable. Only the context can reveal the truth and that context is the lived human experience where real choices are made. This means that the culture and customs of an individual, her beliefs and values, her psychological differences and her socio-historical period are all components of a situational totality which influences her sense of what is right and wrong.

Ethical choices are particular as well as general; they take place not in principle but in a unique concrete situation. This is not to embrace an all-out moral relativism but to suggest that the search for universal moral principles which hold true for all situations, such as Kant's (1999) categorical imperative, is misleading. Universals can divert us from the real contradictory context in which choices take place, easing the decisions of armchair generals and back room statisticians, but distorting or concealing many of the elements which make for real moral engagement.

Real choices are also saturated in time, both subjective and objective. This doesn't mean we are locked into the present perspective, on the contrary we know how valuable the future is in decision-making but we cannot make choices in the future. Nor can we decide in the past, using the hindsight which is much loved by rationalistic students of decision-making, although of course we can perhaps learn something from these past choices. The present, as it is lived, is all we have.

3. The ethics of freedom

If there is a lodestar for an interactional ethics, it is the existentialist notion of freedom, which Simone de Beauvoir puts like this: 'the precept will be to treat the other... as a freedom so that his end may be freedom' (1948: 42) Nelson Mandela, (1994: 751) summed up this principle eloquently when he wrote 'I am not truly free if I am taking away someone else's freedom.' Oppressive, manipulative behaviour treats the other not as a freedom but as a thing. It aims to deprive people of the right to make free choices and substitute these for the choices of the oppressor. This not a universal formula: it does not give infallible instructions for moral action but it can provide a basic compass to guide oneself by. It can even help us understand that sometimes we must close down choices in the short term to open them up in the future. As de Beauvoir (1948) says, to expect a child to behave like an adult is to deprive her of her real freedom, which can only come with maturity.

4. The ambiguity of choice

Our final principle concerns ambiguity, which conventional morality sees as a problem but which, from an interactional perspective, can form part of the solution. Ambiguity is not vague or unclear thinking – this is no use to anyone – but a recognition that the boundaries of choice are rarely fixed. Moral dilemmas often take us into a world which seems closer to the apparently contradictory complexity of modern quantum mechanics than to the comparative simplicity of Newtonian physics. Accepting, rather than rejecting, the daunting, elusive and multi-faceted nature of ethical choice can be a source of moral strength, if it directs us to the concrete interactions which are always present in real human choices. It was probably for this reason that Hegel (1931) argued that social institutions are indispensable to ethical thinking, as they invariably promote or hinder moral action, and rejected the view that sees ethics as a purely individual matter. Abstract thinking takes us away from authentic moral struggle, whereas the perception of ambiguity can be a sign that we are engaging with the oppositions which structure real choice-making. If an ethical choice seems too good to be true, it probably is.

Undialectical ethics – the price of rejecting ambiguity

These principles of interactional ethics might seem rather tentative compared to the reassuringly forthright and even commanding language which is often used in talking about ethics. This is the language of ethical codes, moral guidelines and clear imperatives. Of course this language has its place. In the case of the coach, such codes highlight the coach's contractual and legal obligations and promote an awareness of ethical issues. But at a deeper level, I would argue, there is a danger that the discourse of codes oversimplifies real choice-making. It can even promote complacency and unquestioning obedience, which prevent a real engagement with ethical choices, in coaching and in leadership.

Let me try to illustrate this contentious point by examining three pieces of advice which coaches Peter Welman and Tatiana Bachkirova (2010: 154) advance in their attempt to argue – mistakenly, I feel – that power is not inherently present in the coaching relationship. These well-meaning precepts have recurred in moral philosophy through the ages and, if interpreted flexibly may be useful. But, if read too literally, in a binary, either-or fashion, I believe they can be misleading. At worst, they are symptomatic of what I call undialectical ethics, an attitude which traps us in the certainty snare, blinding us to the inherently ambiguous nature of the world and the choices we make in it. The three precepts in question are as follows:

1. *Know thyself.* This is a proposition which I certainly endorse in principle. However, the human self is a complex, changing phenomenon which is as much about 'unknowing' as knowing, as Ernesto Spinelli (1997) has shown. It is worth reminding ourselves of Sartre's (1958) paradoxical contention that as human beings we are who we are not. He means we differ from ourselves, in time, in that our past is different from our future, or in company, as we behave differently in one social context to another. Self-knowledge is about recognizing this inconsistency and acknowledging our failings as well as our strengths, so as to be able to focus on when we can be effective and when not.

    Self knowledge is positive if it promotes this genuine, light-and-shade understanding of our own experience and cultivates a constant readiness to go deeper in reflecting on the assumptions which underlie our behaviour. Self-knowledge is more negative if it is based on the idea that self-reflection leads to ever greater consistency, implying a self who can say 'I am who I am'. This can lead to over-confidence in our ethical choices, putting us dangerously out of touch with reality, because the unambiguous self is a myth.

2. *Do no harm.* This phrase might seem self-evident. It is hard to imagine an ethical position which would advocate doing harm to others but the problem is in defining what 'harm' means. In medical ethics, this may be relatively straightforward but elsewhere one person's idea of harm may be another person's notion of creativity, as in Joseph Schumpeter's (1994: 83) influential belief that 'creative destruction is the essential fact about capitalism'. Short-term 'harm' can be the necessary prelude to personal well-being. This is enshrined in the idea of being 'cruel to be kind' or its therapeutic equivalent, the elegantly dialectical notion of 'tough love'. And what about coaching itself? The coaching conversation often produces emotional responses in the coachee, such as anxiety, anger and confusion, which could be considered harmful – and that we would probably try to avoid in normal social intercourse – but which may be essential for positive change.

    The fragility of this precept was revealed in an organizational context, when high-tech giant Google's well-known corporate value, 'Don't be evil' (which featured in its 2004 flotation prospectus), was criticized by a British parliamentary committee in 2013. Accused of unethical tax avoidance – Google paid just £6 million in corporation tax on UK revenues of £2.5 billion in 2011 – chairman Eric Schmidt replied that 'we fully comply with the law' (Arthur, 2013). This may be true but for many it was a disturbingly overliteral interpretation of 'not being evil'. After all, there is no legislation that stipulates that you should help a friend in need or donate to charity. For that matter, none of the seven deadly sins is actually prosecutable in a court of law. To march under this kind of moral banner can induce a self-righteousness which prevents employees from asking honest questions about what is really harmful and what is not. For the coach likewise, this precept can mask the fact that harm needs to be defined contextually. 'Define what you mean by harm situationally and try to avoid inflicting it' might be a more accurate, if less snappy, guideline for the coach to follow.

3. *Do nothing to anyone that you would not wish done to you.* This so-called Golden Rule can be very useful if interpreted as a reference to the importance of reciprocity in human behaviour and the virtues of empathizing with others. Taken more rigidly, however, it closely resembles Kant's categorical imperative (1998) which argues that we should treat a moral action as though it were a universal law. This is an application of the law of non-contradiction, which, as I suggested in Chapter 3, is essentially fallible. I readily concede that it is better to be morally consistent if possible, but real choices do not always allow for this.

    Consider the example of a parent who smokes cigarettes but urges his children not to. Ideally, you might say, he should give up smoking but if he can't (or chooses not to), should he then be morally consistent and encourage his children to smoke? In this case, his plea to 'do as I say not as I do', might actually be his most moral course of action, even though it involves him in contradiction. In leadership situations, too, sometimes the lesser evil is the only realistic choice about right and wrong which is available. Overall, guidelines have their place but we must guard against those that offer mere moral comfort food rather than real ethical sustenance.

The ethics of the coach

So what guidelines can realistically support a coach's ethical practice? In an interesting essay on ethical coaching, Ho Law (2010) lists the many codes coaching organizations have produced in an attempt to address this question. These codes rightly warn against such actions as giving too much business advice, unduly prolonging coaching, taking advantage of the coachee financially or sexually, creating psychological dependence, and so on. Other ethical borderline issues may involve the coach performing the managerial duties which the sponsor of the coaching should be carrying out, coaching the boss's direct reports or accepting assignments with conflicting goals.

Ethical codes are an important part of the coach's ethical approach but following these guidelines should never be a matter of mindless obedience. It is always a question of trying to achieve a working balance between the best and worst that can be achieved in a situation, which is partially dependent on the judgements you have made in accepting the assignment in the first place. Appreciating the ambiguity of ethics can help. For example, the coach may risk the overdependence of a coachee, if he feels the consequences of terminating the coaching will be that the coachee relapses into his former behaviour. Likewise, coaching a leader's direct reports may be problematic but possibly the right thing to do, if this is the only form of intervention on offer. As is so often in the precarious world of ethical choice, the correct answer is: it depends.

Law (2010) also discusses organizational corruption in relation to Enron and poses some intriguing questions about the officials, to whom a coach in this kind of situation might have reported suspected wrong-doing. For me, this evocation of a concrete ethical dilemma raises many considerations, not least, whether a whistle-blowing coach would have suffered the same vilification which was directed against equity analysts who downgraded Enron (McLean and Elkind, 2004). Unfortunately, Law does not attempt to answer his own questions but shifts from a real moral quandary to an account of how to create an ethical culture in an organization through educational workshops and the like. Admirable as this commitment is, this shift in grammatical mood from 'is' to 'ought' is sometimes a sign of an undialectical approach to ethics. Creating an ethical organizational culture, which avoids messy compromises and agonizing choices, would be ideal, but we do not live in an ideal world and probably never will.

The 'challenge' in coaching

Another response to the problem of coaching in an executive world where ethical wrong-doing is a distinct possibility is proposed by John Blakey and Ian Day

(2009) in their provocatively titled book, 'Where were the coaches when the banks went down?' Implicitly, they suggest that coaches may have contributed to the 2008 financial crash by being too fixed on the coachee's agenda. This may be a veiled reference to positive psychology's tendency to focus one-sidedly on the coachee's strengths at the expense of her weaknesses. As I have suggested elsewhere (Harvey, 2012), any approach to coaching, which is either too positive or too negative, can miss the important meanings which emerge from the constant interaction between these two dimensions of existence.

Blakey and Day's solution is to move away from the coachee's agenda and insist on forthright feedback, accountability, a systems perspective and a deliberately 'challenging' approach. Up to a point I agree with their project but if we abandon the coachee's experience of the world, whose agenda do we replace it with? If it is the coach's, we decisively shift the balance of power away from the coachee. If the organization's agenda predominates, we risk losing the uniqueness of the coaching dialogue, which in part lies in its difference to the organizational conversations the coachee is having every day. This shift is doubly problematic in the case of leadership coaching, because it is the leader who often sets the agenda for the entire organization. In either case, we are in danger of losing the spontaneous, unstructured and relational elements of coaching and turning it into yet another form of training.

From the interactional perspective, the real challenge for the coach should emerge from engaging with the coachee's choices. Trying to understand the dialectics of the coachee's world, without prejudgments, and helping her to transform these into a positive outcome: this is the essential challenge of coaching. The more the coach preloads his conversation with assumptions and requirements, the less he is able to identify what is really going on in a situation, let alone bring to light the coachee's underlying moral dilemmas. Setting up as an ethical, or deliberately challenging, coach is acceptable if this is transparently signalled and agreed in advance. But as a general proposition, it represents the start of a slippery slope for coaching, which could wither its experiential and relational core and reduce its capacity for promoting real change.

The ethics of the leader: authenticity

So much for the coach, what about the leader? To what extent does the interactional leadership model encourage her to engage in authentic, ethical leadership? Because choice is at the heart of the interactional approach rather than added to it as a kind of bolted-on extra, the ethical dimension tends to emerge more or less of its own volition. As we've seen, this sometimes leads to spectacular turnarounds in coaching; at other times, the changes in a leader's choice-making can be much more modest. The aim is always to encourage leaders 'to work the dialectic', to find the best possible balance between the interactions at work in their situation. It is not to prescribe or promote a particular line of action.

In fact, a more ethical approach to leadership can emerge from the interactional model in a number of ways. To begin with, the achievement cycle can help to focus the leader on the ways in which the dialectic of strategy and resources influences delivery. This can at least identify some unethical routes to actualization such as falsifying results or manipulating targets. It may even show up forms of resourcing which are exploitative, in that they fail to respect the freedom of others.

The ethical status of a leader's vision and values is more complex. Imagine an aspiring leader, who is prepared to do anything that it takes to realize his goal of setting new boundaries and overturning the existing state of things. Superficially, this description might apply equally to a heroic leader or a villain, to a Nelson Mandela or a Kenneth Lay of Enron. It is not easy to judge where a leader's determination to break the rules will take him or whether his determination to succeed at all costs will prove to be the seeds of his own undoing. No model of leadership can pronounce sentence on this in advance but at least the interactional model can raise these questions from the start.

The way a leader engages with his choices throughout the achievement cycle can provide a clue to his moral style. Let's try to imagine the sequence of choices which results in serious wrongdoing. If the leader starts with a vision that is clearly illegal, we are talking about a fraudster or a gangster, but in most cases of corporate wrongdoing I think it more likely that the leader begins with a legitimate set of objectives. The starting point for his slide into illegality may be a negligible choice, a small deception, perhaps, or a relatively innocuous infringement of the rules. When he gets away with this, he is encouraged to make another small decision of the same kind. Perhaps, without deep reflection, as though habit has now set in, the leader makes another choice which takes him past the point of no return. It is now easier to continue than turn back and the result is a headlong rush towards wrongdoing. We have to ask: if the leader had been truly committed to the interactional goal of engaging with his choices – which might have led him to surround himself with a constructively oppositional team – would he have been able to embark on this destructive trail of incremental decisions in the first place?

In many ways, this is a question of personal integrity. As leadership expert Jon Howell (2013) points out, this is the one leadership quality which the charismatic, visionary, innovative, and communicative Ken Lay lacked (and which Nelson Mandela had in abundance). Integrity under conditions of uncertainty is a fundamental characteristic of the authenticity of the interactional leader, as I suggested in Chapter 2. Authenticity is a commitment to experience, to openness in viewing possibilities, and to taking responsibiliy for the choices which you have made. Such a commitment leads to real self-knowledge which recognizes the many-sided complexity of the self. It can also manifest itself in a compelling presence and a tendency to make a deep impression on others. Being honest about the real dilemmas and difficulties of leadership can also intensify this sense of a leader who can trust and be trusted.

Respecting the freedom of other people's choices, our third interactional principle, represents another aspect of authenticity. The leader who engages in systematic deception violates this principle by closing down other people's choices. Once an organization ceases to be a relatively open network of interactions and becomes a fortress of lies, it prevents almost everyone involved in it from seeing the truth. People cannot make informed choices about this organization because the information provided is carefully arranged so as to present a very different reality from the actual one. Transparency is replaced by deliberate opaqueness. It is commonplace to say that the cover-up is sometimes more serious than the crime but it is often true. Systematic deception warps ethical sensibility and spreads like a contagion well beyond the original offence, twisting every factor in a choice into a kind of parody of good decision-making. In these circumstances, the leader can start living a lie – and impose that lie on everyone around him. Keeping the notion of the freedom of others as an end may help to prevent this turn of events or enable the leader to find the strength to escape from it, if it does occur.

Another interactional principle, respect for ambiguity, can help the leader to understanding that contradictions can never be entirely eliminated from a situation. Her goal can only be to turn them into the most positive form which is available. If her choices seem as subtly complex as the line of the horizon in a heat haze, it may well be that she is getting them right, although of course it is also true that sometimes the correct choices seem to select themselves.

To return to the case of Enron, could a respect for ambiguity have made a difference to the many people who were taken in by the company? Part of the problem in assessing Enron is that some of what it did was genuinely innovative. Just a year before the company filed for the biggest bankruptcy in US history, management guru Gary Hamel (2000: 212) praised the company's 'genius of innovation'. He said that, '...Enron institutionalizes a capacity for perpetual innovation. No wonder *Fortune* magazine named Enron America's most innovative company for five years running.' For sure, it was not easy to detect the boundary between the real innovation which Enron created in a deregulated gas market and the rankly illegal accountancy which it practised for many years. Nor did interpretations of Enron take place in a timeless, placeless zone but in a real historical situation, which just happened to be the frenzied dot-com boom that led to the stock market crash of 2001, when Internet companies which were little more than business plans could be valued in billions of dollars. Yet it is still worth suggesting that an appreciation of the ambiguous nature of innovation – and the fact that certain rules need to be broken and others respected – might have helped some of the accountants, analysts, management consultants, lawyers (and possibly even coaches) involved with Enron to get on the right side of that ambiguity.

The language of authenticity

To conclude these remarks on ethical leadership, I want to look at the way the language of leaders can reflect their authenticity and their engagement with choice. The language of deliberate deception can easily become institutionalized, masking the real choices which lie beneath it. Think of the of the Watergate scandal which ended in President Richard Nixon's impeachment, famous for the phrase 'plausible denial', i.e. 'a lie you think you can get away with' (Janis and Mann, 1977). The language of redundancy often contains a similar tendency to euphemism, perhaps because it is one of the most difficult and ethically challenging acts a leader has to undertake. Here is just a small sample of the amazing array of metaphors for corporate downsizing uncovered by management academics Dunford and Palmer (1996: 102):

> Slimming down, paring to the bone, getting rid of the bulge, preventive medicine, belt tightening, biting the bullet, tossing managers overboard, purging, scything, pruning, shedding, getting rid of dead wood, leakage.

I once worked with a CEO who, although using nothing like such a florid vocabulary, was particularly attached to the phrase 'letting go', as he embarked on a major series of redundancies. For him 'letting go' had implications of releasing employees from an onerous obligation, as if he were freeing captive birds, even though the chances of these workers getting alternative work were slim. As we delved deeper, it became clear that his use of language obscured an unease on his part, which was creating a kind of recklessness. He may even have been dismissing more people than was necessary. His rigid use of a euphemism was an indication that he was not fully focused on accepting responsibility for his choices. Once he did, he was able to deal with the downsizing process in a way that was more beneficial to himself, his remaining colleagues and possibly even his departing workers.

Sometimes a phrase is enough. A financial leader I coached talked repeatedly about 'giving something back', referring to his occasional charity work. Finally, I couldn't help asking him, 'What exactly do you have feel you have taken?' After an initial rebuff, this led him to reveal his disquietude about his level of earnings, following a bitter row with his teenage son, whose criticism of his pay in relation to that of the average worker at the company had deeply disturbed him. Or take the marketing director from the North of England with a love of sporting imagery, a rich source of metaphors in business. This coachee used football metaphors to talk about a rival company, claiming that you had to 'catch them offside at every opportunity' and put in 'some hard tackling behind the back of the referee'. It was only when we started exploring the actual state of this business relationship that it became apparent that the two companies were not bitter rivals at all. In fact, they more closely resembled partners in an undeclared industry duopoly, which was on the verge of engaging in unfair competitive practices.

In the end, of course, ethics has it limits. Morality and the law need to work hand-in-hand. We cannot expect the law to do the job of the ethical consciousness but the law can provide regulations to guide the morality of leaders. If some politicians have their way, this will entail increasing legislation around transparency and governance and the introduction of legal sanctions around the reckless behaviour of leaders. Hopefully, this will accomplish the tricky task of strengthening the rules which promote ethical behaviour, without weakening the ability of leaders to break the rules which need to be broken if genuine innovation is to occur.

Chapter 15

Coaching difficult leaders
The paradox of leadership coaching

In this chapter, I want to continue with the theme of the potential damage caused by leaders who overstep the mark of ethical behaviour. The fact is that since Jay Conger's path-breaking article on 'the dark side of leadership' (1990), we have added a desperately long list of 'difficult' leaders to the infamous roll call he outlined, years before the Enron crisis, the 2008 financial crash and the revelations of malpractice since then. If in the future, coaching is to have a positive impact on choice-making at the top, it is plain that it cannot ignore these difficult leaders but needs to find a way to work with them.

This brings us back to what I call the paradox of leadership coaching, a problem which I raised in the case of Blake S. in Chapter 4, which states that those who need coaching the most, often want it the least. If we return to that bold question about 'where were the coaches when the banks went down' (Blakey and Day, 2009), I suspect part of the answer is very simple: they were somewhere else. My guess is that nobody was coaching most of leaders who were responsible for the credit crunch or who were engaged in other forms of wrongdoing. Coaching is probably the last thing that these leaders would have wanted. And who had the organizational authority to persuade them to change their minds?

The difficult leader is often beholden to few. He may have succeeded in shifting the balance of power between self and others to the extent that the entire organization has become a kind of unilateral team, completely under his sway. In theory, a chairman outranks the chief executive; in practice he may be powerless. In the case of Dick Fuld of Lehman Brothers, he was for 14 years one and the same person. The human resources director is the obvious person to sponsor a CEO's coaching but does she have real status in the organization? Is she even on the top management team? And in an organization dominated by the all-controlling leader, the option of reporting wrongdoing to any internal authority may be virtually impossible.

The reluctance of some leaders to engage in coaching is not confined to bosses in the financial sector (if my hunch above is indeed correct). According to Tappin and Cave (2008), only 40 per cent of FTSE 100 chief executives receive coaching, which means that the majority do not. I would not want to suggest for a moment that every uncoached leader is overbearing or bullying but it is important to consider the practical and ethical problems of coaching those who are. One conventional approach involves a kind of triage, which distinguishes the 'coachable' from the 'uncoachable' (Bluckert, 2006). This may be prudent and yet if we accept that some leaders are beyond the pale, we run the risk of only preaching to the converted, which simply reinforces the paradox of leadership coaching. So, in this chapter, I want to consider how to mitigate the risks of working with difficult leaders and examine a coaching case of what I call 'the Soprano syndrome', before returning to the question of what organizations can do to engage those leaders who seem to need coaching but emphatically do not want it.

Requirements for coaching difficult leaders

One qualification for the coach who engages with challenging leaders is exceptional openness. Peter Burditt, a financial coach who claims to work with 'difficult people who eat other coaches for breakfast', gives a nice example of this. After ten minutes of his first session with a particularly domineering chief executive of an asset management company, Burditt said to him:

> I don't think I can work with you. I feel physically sick...I am feeling intimidated, bullied, interrogated. If you do this to your people, no wonder you have the highest turnover in your company.
>
> (Hall, 2013: 20)

The upshot of this declaration was that Burditt was hired and a five-year coaching relationship ensued.

Openness worked in this case, and there is no doubt that a leadership coach working with difficult coachees needs to be prepared to walk away from a relationship, if he decides that there is no possibility of honest interaction. The danger, however, is that by peremptorily terminating the assignment the coach and the coachee lose out on the transformational, relational qualities of coaching which only emerge over time. Coaching is often a long-term process, where change may happen not in minutes or even months but over a much longer period, through the fits and starts and other curious rhythms of change, by which a coachee alters his patterns of choice-making.

A second asset for the coach working with difficult leaders is strong psychological foundations. Having trained as a psychotherapist and occasionally worked with clients with extreme diagnoses, such as schizophrenia and long-term depression, I have found this experience can sometimes come in useful when coaching particularly challenging executives. Experience here is probably more important than any particular psychotherapeutic model but, given the wide range of psychological coaching models on offer, it is worth speculating here on which approaches may be most appropriate for coaching of this kind.

One of the most prominent and insightful of leadership coaches is Manfred Kets de Vries, a psychoanalyst, who has been coaching, and writing about, challenging bosses for many years. His approach is partially illustrated by the title of one of his books, *Leaders, Fools and Imposters* (2003). Indeed, at times, he seems to see the desire for leadership as a problem in itself, as a kind of ego deformation. This clearly arms him against some of the disappointments and seductions of leadership coaching, as does his model of therapy in general. Classical psychoanalysis offers a cautious, even pessimistic approach to changing human behaviour, often summed up in Freud's well known therapeutic goal of transforming 'hysterical misery into common unhappiness' (Freud and Breuer, 1955: 393).

Perhaps this sceptical bias provides the analytical coach with a better set of equipment for working on the dark side of leadership than person-centred therapy, with its commitment to treating its clients with 'unconditional positive regard', in Carl Roger's (1961) famous phrase. But is psychoanalysis committing the same, if opposite, one-sidedness? From an existential viewpoint, the philosophical limitations of the psychoanalytical approach have been exposed by Sartre (1958) and many others (e.g. Spinelli, 1994). They accuse it of relying on prejudgments about the formation of personality in very early childhood and a concept of an unconsciousness which is shut off from self-reflection by the client but mysteriously accessible to the analyst. For me, the analytical model reduces the importance of human choice and shifts the balance of power in the coaching relationship too much towards the analyst.

More orthodox scientific methods can offer alternative ways to add authority to the challenging coaching relationship. For instance, measuring a leader's performance through 360-degree surveys or other forms of multi-rater assessment introduces a valuable collective element into the coaching dialogue. In the coming years, neuroscience may add another dimension to the process, with brain scans adding a wealth of information about a leader's emotional patterns and ways of choosing. Real-time scanning may even be an option, with the coach able to see a coachee's amgydala light up as he gets angry or his frontal cortex come into play as he tries to plan for the future. Assessments of this kind should not encourage the coach to see herself as no more than an expert technician, administering results. All evidence, however 'hard', is always a matter of interpretation. But accurate data can add another string to the bow of an experienced coach and help her to sympathetically challenge a coachee's entrenched view of the world. Of course, the reader may object, what will make the difficult leader submit to a 360-degree survey, let alone a PET scan? That task may be beyond the coach's remit, although her persuasiveness can make a difference. Ultimately, it is an area, for which the organization – mainly through the chair, the board and the talent management department – needs to take increased responsibility, a subject we will return to in a moment.

'The Soprano syndrome'

One of the most important requirements in working with the dark side of leadership is to be fully cognisant of the risks involved. As in coaching, so in making choices about a coaching assignment, a worst case scenario can be useful. The least desirable outcome of working with a difficult leader is not, as might appear at first sight, that the coaching series ends prematurely. It is actually something more subtle and potentially more threatening, which, deliberately shockingly, I call the 'Soprano syndrome', after a reference made by Melvin, the coaching client whose story is recounted below. Throughout the acclaimed TV drama, *The Sopranos*, which charts the career of mafia boss, Tony Soprano, the protagonist – very unusually – is engaged in therapy. In working with this client, his psychiatrist, Jennifer Melfi, is confronted by an acute dilemma. Tony clearly needs psychological help – among other things, he suffers from debilitating panic attacks – but is Melfi herself part of the solution or part of the problem? Do the occasional insights which Tony receives into his own feelings and the effect he has on others change him for the better or simply make him able to operate more sustainably in his pitch black ethical world? In short, does therapy make Tony a better person or simply a better gangster?

An equally important issue is whether Dr Melfi herself is corrupted or, at least, severely compromised, by her long-term professional involvement with a criminal leader operating in a sociopathic world. She is a psychiatrist, working within a medical model of therapy, but this does not prevent her relationship with Tony from becoming very personal at times. She spurns his attempts at sexual seduction and heroically resists the temptation to enlist Tony's special brand of rough justice when she is raped by an assailant. But Melfi's clinical supervisor, once he discovers Soprano's identity, becomes increasingly insistent that the therapist should terminate the therapy for her own good.

Mercifully for the leadership coach, these issues are never likely to present themselves in such an extreme form but the Soprano allusion is a useful reminder of some of the queries which need to be made repeatedly when working on a long-term basis with a difficult leader. Is the effect of coaching to make a leader more secure in his role without fundamentally changing his ways? Is the coachee's progress as unambiguously positive as it may seem? Does the coach become blind-sided by the apparent success of the coaching or by more deliberate attempts to compromise his integrity by a powerful coachee? We might add another Dantean circle to this spiral of dilemmas by asking, whether even compromised coaching is sometimes better for the difficult leader, not to mention his long-suffering subordinates, than no coaching at all? I don't pretend that Melvin's case study answers all of these questions but at least it may allow them to assume a more concrete shape.

Case study: Melvin and 'the Soprano syndrome'

Melvin was a devious, scheming leader heading up the tax division of a large accountancy firm, who had a reputation for intimidating his staff and for extreme competiveness. His 'hair dryer' rants were notorious and there were several cases in which he had driven employees out of the organization in bitterly acrimonious and litigious circumstances. He had been regarded as 'untouchable' by his board because the revenues of his division were so high and because they feared he would defect to a competitor if reprimanded. But eventually Melvin's violent outburst of anger in a meeting, as he attempted to justify less than stellar results, proved the final straw for his board. The chairman had instructed the HR director to construct a remedial programme for Melvin, the centrepiece of which was leadership coaching.

In our first meeting, Melvin made a joke about 'feeling like Tony Soprano'. My attempt to establish some common ground around our mutual admiration for the crime drama came to little, with Melvin only muttering grumpily that 'therapy almost got Tony killed by his own crew'. But the reference certainly started me thinking more intensely than usual about some of the issues involved in this type of assignment. It would be wrong to say that Melvin explicitly tried to compromise me in our first session, although he clearly floated the possibility of more work for me if the assignment 'turned out to our mutual satisfaction". He also pointedly mentioned his authority to appoint a coach for his direct reports, many of whom, he joked, were 'pretty screwed up'.

To begin with, Melvin's attitude was more intimidatory than seductive. He was constantly rescheduling sessions, cancelling them at the last minute or trying to take telephone calls during a session. Then in our third session, he tried to renegotiate my fee – downwards. He said he wanted to make it depend on performance like his own remuneration. It is hard to tell how serious he was (much later he referred to it as 'a wind up'). He knew that my fees had been set by the HR department and would be paid by them but it was, at the very least, a deliberate attempt to unsettle me and to remind me of his power.

Melvin's tactics were useful because they gave me first-hand experience of some of the methods he had been using in his leadership role. When I raised this issue with him, he seemed amused but I wanted to draw out some of the implications of his choices, especially when it came to respecting the freedom of others. The conversation continued like this:

Michael: My point is that your attitude tries to close down my choices. We enter into an agreement on a date and then you change it repeatedly. You cut short a session because of a telephone call and so on. All the choices are on your side.

Melvin: That's business, mate. It always takes priority.

Michael: It's how you do business – that's what we're here to talk about. Is it right to disrespect others' choices?

Melvin: If they get something out of it, yes. People don't know what their best interests are. People call me a bully but I take on people and push them harder than they've ever been pushed. I work them in the galleys – like I was worked as a junior – and in the end they find something they've never had, as well as starting to earn big money. That's the game.

Michael: And the casualties along the way? You mentioned careers being cut short by stress.
Melvin: I always make sure everyone knows where the exit to the building is. They can walk through it at any time.
Michael: But did they join this organization and go through their training on the basis that they'll come to this take it or leave it choice?
Melvin (shrugging his shoulders): Ask them. My choice is to give my job everything I've got. I don't take prisoners – or carry passengers.
Michael: That's why were here, isn't it?
Melvin: So you keeping saying, mate.

To what extent this kind of discussion modified Melvin's view on other people's freedom of choice is hard to say. Business-focused considerations were probably more important to him. For example, when we examined his leadership style from the viewpoint of the achievement cycle, we found that although he was a clever strategist, he often failed to get his proposals accepted by his peers. He was a terribly poor resourcer, and this was becoming critical as fewer and fewer people in his organization wanted to work for him. Although a renowned deliverer of results, the cost of his methods was becoming too high in an organization which was looking to improve its ability to attract talent. Initially, Melvin justified his leadership skills vigorously, reciting detailed results from previous years' profit and loss accounts, but there was something strangely empty about his arguments. Sure enough, in our next session, he conceded some points about his leadership style. I was beginning to learn that Melvin often made up his mind by ferociously defending a position until he arrived at the opposite conclusion. He was his own devil's advocate.

So when Melvin began praising the coaching process, several months into the series, using certain phrases enthusiastically, like 'pull' rather than 'push' advice, my first thought was that he was trying on the language for size, so to speak. He said his staff seemed to be reacting favourably to some of the changes he was making. Of course, my overall reaction to this was positive and yet there was something unconvincing about some of Melvin's remarks, especially as they were followed by a strong hint that I should relay these changes to the chairman (I was contracted to report to the board halfway through the assignment). It was at this point that the example of Tony Soprano reared its head again. I wondered if Melvin was changing his bullying ways or simply becoming a little more cunning and resourceful in his intimidation, a better bully in fact.

The answer was not clear cut. Melvin seemed to be pursuing a kind of parallel strategy – changing in some respects, staying the same in others. It was a puzzling mix and it must have been confusing for his staff, doubtless something that Melvin could use to his advantage, although I suspect that he was sometimes confused by it himself. The process of change was ambiguous for Melvin, perhaps like all real change, but even ambiguity was a breakthrough for someone who had always seen the world in strictly binary terms: good or bad, win or lose.

Another thing struck me in our final session, when Melvin, 'apropos of bugger all', to use one of his favourite phrases, mentioned that he had decided to ditch a new tax avoidance scheme which he had boasted about to me earlier in the coaching. At the time I had questioned him on this product, less out of ethical zeal, than out of curiosity in relation to a high-profile entertainer, who had publicly admitted to using a similar tax avoidance device. Melvin had been brusque to the point of rudeness when I pressed the matter, so this final turn of events – and Melvin's decision to bring up the issue unsolicited – was perhaps an indication of a wider change in his thinking. Or of nothing of the sort. This ambiguous parting shot was at least in keeping with the theme of *The Sopranos*, the final episode of which leaves it to the viewer to decide what the mobster's fate will actually be.

If Melvin's coaching was a contest – and unquestionably he always saw it as one – I think it is fair to say that it concluded in an honourable draw. Towards the end, I definitely felt that we were working together, rather than on opposing sides, more often than at the start. In short, I felt that there were enough positive changes in Melvin's choice-making for the chairman of the board, and others charged with the responsibility for upwards leadership, to create an environment in which these changes could become permanent.

The role of the organization

Melvin's case highlights the importance of psychological experience when coaching difficult leaders and the usefulness of an approach which links business and leadership theory, from which ethical questioning can flow organically. But for me it also clearly illustrates the need for decisive organizational involvement in this type of development. Coaches need help. Underpinning this intervention was a strong triadic relationship between coach, coachee and the sponsor, which here included both the chairman and the head of human resources. This meant that the embedded choices before, during and after the coaching were very different from what they were in the Blake S. case. There it was the coach who persuaded the leader to engage in coaching in what was initially a completely dyadic configuration. Choices about leadership need to come from a wider community, not simply from those at the very top.

A role for corporate governance?

To press home this point, let me reintroduce the subject of corporate governance. This branch of economics and finance theory is specifically aimed at formulating regulations and mechanisms which help organizations, and especially their chief executives, to make the best possible decisions (Padgett, 2012). As we have seen, seemingly dry issues such as the composition of the board, the division between non-executive and executive chairpersons and the role of the remuneration committee are all linked to a single purpose. In other words, like interactional leadership coaching, corporate governance is a fundamentally choice-focused discipline.

Is there a case, then, for making some form of choice-focused development mandatory for CEOs and other key decision-makers? This may be in the form of recommendations, or even legally-binding provisions, aimed at encouraging boards and executive committees to evaluate all the resources available for improving their choice-making. It might include a collective obligation to consider the option of coaching for a chief executive, making it much harder for difficult leaders to decline this type of intervention. In short, measures like this could go a long way to addressing the paradox of leadership coaching.

For some, the disadvantage of this suggestion is that it could put undue pressure on coaches, exposing them to the influence of the board or shareholders or employees and potentially making them scapegoats for poor choices. Against this, I would stress that the coach would have a free choice whether to engage in this type of coaching and that, in any case, the choice-focused approach insists that the coach can only facilitate choices by offering supportive expertise; he cannot direct them. Nor does this only involve one particular type of coaching, as arguably all leadership coaches work with choice-making in practice, although this is not necessarily accurately identified by their theoretical models. Group coaching for the board would be an alternative to one-to-one coaching or perhaps an addition to it, as in the hybrid coaching format used with the hospital leadership team described in Chapter 12. Either way, I suggest this kind of extension of corporate governance could be an important consideration for the environment of leadership in the coming years, especially as leaders face the hugely consequential choices for human society, which we explore in the next chapter.

The importance of supervision in balancing the coach's choices

Finally, we should not end this chapter without emphasising the importance of supervision for the ethics of coaching, especially in the case of difficult leaders. The coach's own interactional map needs to contain a powerful support and challenge system to help him maintain his own sense of balance. This system is not likely to be an extended network, because confidentiality is an issue here, but will normally focus on the coach's relationship with his supervisor or a small supervising group. This is the coach's version of the leadership group, providing clarity, a counter voice, alternative options, support and constructive criticism. In short, supervision supplies the coach with upwards leadership. It offers a powerful forum for identifying and reflecting on a coach's choices in an assignment and can help him see what he may be missing. If I can make a final reference to *The Sopranos*, it is worth pointing out the crucial role Jennifer Melfi's supervisor plays in keeping a constant monitor on Melfi's emotions, dilemmas and doubts, finally enabling her to realise she has done all she can for Tony. This second pair of eyes and ears is vital, particularly when working with leaders who specialize in distorting other people's choices.

Chapter 16

Choosing the future

What decisions lie in store for leaders and their coaches?

In this final chapter, we can at last turn our full attention to choosing the future, which, as I've argued, is a fundamental aspect of the art of leadership and the profession of coaching it. This is particularly important today because we stand at an unprecedented point in history where we are able to know more about the future than ever before, due to huge advances in the natural science, information processing, and other technologies. This probabilizing knowledge suggests that major change is on its way. Some of the choices involved in this may be trivial but others are of the most extreme significance, which no leader can ignore, as they may even pose threats to the continuation of human society, as we have come to understand it.

In this book, I have tried not to shy away from controversial issues that affect leadership and coaching and this is not the time to start doing so. In a spirit of informed speculation, therefore, let's draw on the work of futurologists, social and natural scientists and other researchers to try to anticipate some of the choices which leaders will have to make, for us and with us, in the coming decades. This information search on the near future will examine substantive issues such as increased competition, climate change, population growth, inequality, and new technology. How will the would-be interactional leader negotiate the perilous tightrope created by choices in these areas? And what can leadership coaching do to respond to the new challenges on the horizon. If leaders and their coaches think that working with the dilemmas caused by the Great Recession has been difficult, I'm tempted to say: 'you ain't seen nothing yet!'

Interactional leadership in the corporate world

Let's begin with some relatively foreseeable choices in the corporate sphere. Certain challenges for the future interactional leader will remain the same: the need for superb strategizing around innovation, excellent product and service development and first-class resourcing and delivery. But the temporal and spatial dimensions of these choices will alter as we enter what could be the most competitive period in the entire history of capitalism. Even now the time of change is accelerating at breath-taking speed. Giant companies can rise and fall in a matter of years – witness the rapid ascent over the past decade of mobile phone titans Apple and Samsung and the vertiginous descent of Nokia and Blackberry.

In this era of hyper-competition for corporates, the need to get major choices right first time around is likely to become even more critical, for there may be no second chance. The value of choice-focused leadership will increase accordingly. Picking winners among new technologies and services and responding nimbly to emergent and unexpected successes will be a high-wire act as never before, requiring a delicate balance between vision and resources, as well as exceptional persistence and, quite possibly, increased ruthlessness in cutting losses.

This new pressure on time will be intensified by geo-economic shifts that will challenge the first-mover dominance the West has enjoyed for centuries. This is already happening, as China moves towards the number one spot in the world economic league and the UK drops down it (World Bank, 2014). Britain's economic status is likely to continue to get closer to its relative population size (i.e. 1 per cent of the world's population). Even the European Union (EU), currently the world largest economic unit, has less than 10 per cent of the world's population, compared to the 40 per cent living in the emergent economies of Brazil, Russia, China and India.

Increased globalization is an opportunity to reject parochial nationalisms and fully embrace diversity. Companies will become increasingly transnational, making cross-cultural adeptness and the ability to think – and feel – globally prerequisites for successful leadership. Corporate leaders may continue to make the most of the West's universal brands, which give it a measure of cultural leadership, but the competition from emerging markets in terms of knowledge and innovation, not just in manufacturing, is likely to be fiercer than ever before.

CAPIT: five global choice arenas which will affect all organizational leaders

The above scenarios assume that intense competition between the nations and corporations of the world will continue to be the driving force of economic and social development. But there is a series of threats on the horizon which could utterly change this model and require a completely new degree of international and inter-corporate cooperation. These factors will test the balancing expertise of every leader, as they gradually impinge on the choice-making of corporations, governments, public sector and non-profit organizations – and ultimately on all consumers and citizens.

The factors which I have in mind can be grouped under the mnemonic CAPIT, which, incidentally, is related to the Latin root word for 'chief' or 'leader'. They are: Climate change, Ageing, Population, Inequality, and Technology. These arenas of choice contain many of the dialectics of the future, including the interaction between humans and the environment, rich and poor, young and old, and people and machines. The consequences of getting these choices wrong are almost too horrific to contemplate, which is precisely why in the coming years they have to be faced by our leaders – and by ourselves.

Climate change

Climate change will provide some of the most serious choices leaders will have to make over the coming years and some of the most controversial. As of January 2014, the EU is committed to preventing carbon emissions exceeding 450 parts per million (ppm) by 2030, in the belief that this would make it possible to stabilize the warming of the planet's surface air temperature at about two degrees Celsius higher than at the beginning of the industrial revolution. To have a reasonable chance of meeting this target, climate scientists insist that as much as 80 per cent of all known reserves of coal, oil and gas will have to be kept in the ground (Berners-Lee and Clark, 2013).

That means that radical choices will have to be made in the very near future, even in the EU, let alone in some parts of the developing world, where targets are often lower or non-existent. If the 450 ppm target is not met, climate scientists warn that that global warming could become an uncontrollable, runaway phenomenon leading to increases of four degrees or more by the end of the century. This does not sound that much in terms of daily fluctuations in temperature but relatively small amounts of average temperature change bring huge impacts on the planet. In fact, an increase of four degrees is warmer than anything experienced on the planet for 25 million years, when sea levels were some 75 metres higher than today (Hansen, 2009).

Four degrees of warming – which is now the consensus forecast among climate scientists, according to Clive Hamilton (2010) – could eventually raise land temperature by eight degrees or more (as most warming is absorbed by oceans). This would mean a dramatic increase in droughts, desertification and heatwaves, like the one which killed 70,000 people in Western Europe in 2003 (Robine *et al.*, 2008), as well as in the continued acidification of the oceans. The impacts, in terms of extreme weather events, could be devastating with increased rain and flooding, more severe cold spells, and a greater prevalence of high-velocity storms and hurricanes. Other events (so-called 'positive feedbacks') could accelerate the frequency of these impacts, underlining the non-linear nature of climate change. For example, in July 2013 a group of eminent climatologists warned that the melting of the summer Arctic ice, which is occurring much more quickly than forecast even 30 years ago, could result in the release of 'plumes' of highly polluting methane gas from the permafrost under the East Siberian Sea. They estimate that the environmental cost of this could be as much as $60 trillion (Whiteman *et al.*, 2013).

Faced with such potential catastrophes, it is psychologically easy to understand why a substantial minority of the public continue to deny that global warming is caused by human activity. To some extent, we believe what we want to believe, so why would anyone want to give credence to a scenario that has such devastating consequences for future generations? But with the world's leading climate scientists saying that it is 'extremely likely' that climate change is anthropogenic (IPCC, 2013) and a 97 per cent consensus among peer-reviewed papers expressing an opinion on the subject (Cook *et al.*, 2013), there is a disconnect between scientific and public opinion, which leaves our corporate and political leaders at a strategic crossroads. Taking a clear position on climate science will be the starting point. Scepticism has become an article of faith for some politicians, as it has for some corporate leaders. But can they afford to ignore the source of knowledge, which has produced the technological infrastructure of the modern world? According to one opinion poll, 66 per cent of the general public trust scientists on climate change but only 6 per cent trust 'business people' (Ipsos-Mori, 2012), which suggests that corporate leaders are unwise to cherry-pick the good bits of science and discard the rest.

Caught in this vice of choices, authenticity will be an increasing challenge for leaders. 'Green washing', that is, paying mere lip service to environmentalism, will not be enough. As sociologist Anthony Giddens (2011: 56) says, 'We have no hope of responding to climate change unless we are prepared to take bold decisions.' As the planet continues to warm, adaptation will also be vital. Faced by changes in the world's human geography, immensely difficult decisions will have to be made between areas that can be defended and those which have to be abandoned. At the same time, new possibilities will open up, as previously barren northern latitudes such as Siberia became increasingly habitable.

Introducing a low-carbon economy is one possible response to the problem of climate change. This will require courageous strategic choices by leaders, as it will probably result in a radical reduction in the consumption of products and services. As environmentalist Bill McKibben (2010) argues, making do with less could become the new norm, with people repairing, rather than replacing, products and the rapid spread of barter-like local exchanges in trades and services. Will corporate leaders see this as an opportunity for new forms of consumption, or try to defy it, refusing to accept diminutions of revenues and operational scale? For some, abandoning the ethos of 'big is better', and 'continuous growth' will not be easy. One unintended consequence of reduced consumption could be an end to the 'tyranny of choice', which I referred to in Chapter 3. Instead of agonizing between 100 cereals in a supermarket, we may struggle to find one type of cereal – or even a supermarket at all. For some people, this may be a relief.

Ageing

Another huge shift in the landscape of the near future is around the interaction between the young and the old. At present one in six people living in the UK is over 65; by 2050 this number will have risen to one in four (Parliament UK, 2014). Declining fertility rates and increased life expectancy are likely to widen the disparity between young and old. Already Germany has considerably more people aged over 65 than under 14 and the difference is even greater in Japan, where the 65-plus generation is projected to reach 37 per cent of the total population by 2060 (International Futures, 2014). In fact, according to the United Nations (2014), by 2050 there will be one child under 14 for every three people over 60 in Europe, whereas in Africa the reverse will be true, three children for every elderly person.

These changes are happening so fast – virtually within a generation – that it is hard to visualize their consequences. But it represents a historically unprecedented challenge for leaders in terms of the consumption of goods and service, property ownership, pension and care provision and, of course, careers and the structure of work. In the UK spending on the elderly will rise from 14 per cent of GDP to almost a fifth by 2050, according to an Office of Budget Responsibility report (2013). This means a huge new market for health care products and medical and care services. To take one slightly frivolous example, Japan is now producing more 'adult diapers' than nappies for children (Yamaguchi, 2012).

Immigration will probably have to continue to rise, if society is to care for the elderly. The same Office of Budget Responsibility report states that six million more immigrants (140,000 a year) will be needed by 2050 in the UK, if the national debt is to remain at a sustainable level. This is an example of the immense population movements that can be expected over the coming decades. These will create massive opportunities for culturally diverse goods and services but also potential social tensions and border problems for those organizational leaders policing these momentous changes.

With pension provision increasingly limited, there will be many more elderly workers in the labour force, working into their seventies and beyond. Will the younger generation benefit from working alongside experienced co-workers? Or will they feel that they are losing out on employment, at the same time as they have to fund the pension and healthcare costs of an 'over-privileged' baby boomer generation? HSBC chief economist Stephen D. King (2013) even suggests that we could be facing the equivalent of a Peasants Revolt by the young against the old, unless the older generation starts making major concessions. From an interactional perspective, this potentially negative dialectic of the future could have a positive outcome. If leaders and others can find a way to enlist people of every age in a common cause, we might break down some of the inter-generational barriers which have only developed in the West relatively recently (Watson, 2010).

Population growth

The world's population is growing at an astonishing rate. It currently stands at 7.2 billion and is forecast to increase to about nine billion by 2050. It took Homo sapiens some 200,000 years to achieve a population of one billion, a landmark reached in about 1800, but it will take barely another decade and a half to increase the world population by the same amount. In many ways, this is an amazing achievement for humanity but it brings with it threats to civilization that some experts put into the same category as global warming. Microsoft's head of computational science, Stephen Emmott, is one of them. He emphasizes the colossal strain on the world's resources caused by supporting a population of nine billion. In his estimation, agricultural production will need to double by 2050, which is why the world's land is being bought up by corporates and nations at a dizzying speed. Emmott is unequivocal about what is at stake: 'we really do need a food revolution, urgently,' he writes. 'Because without it one billion of us are almost certainly going to starve' (Emmott, 2013: 162).

Water is another massive challenge for our growing global population. Currently, it takes 3,000 litres of water to produce a hamburger and 72,000 litres to produce a computer chip. Water stress, in the form of severe droughts and desertification, is already on the rise. Groundwater over-drafting has led to the reduction of the water table in many areas of the world (e.g. India and California), necessitating the digging of ever deeper wells. Already there are 2.5 billion people in the world who have inadequate access to water and 768 million with no access to safe water at all (WHO/UNICEF, 2013). Conflicts over water, involving organizations of every kind, are probable; water wars between nations may even be a possibility (Dyer, 2008).

Will political leaders decide that Chinese-style child-restriction policies are the solution to reducing population growth? Will there be tax breaks for those who decide not to have children? Corporate leaders may find themselves incentivizing their employees not to have children, as 'family-unfriendly' policies become the organizational norm. Or does this strategy simply go against our human genetic inheritance to such an extent as to be futile? One thing is sure, painful personal and professional choices will have to be made by every leader. Making the right decisions around the infrastructure, logistics, security and financing necessary to sustain our new world population is likely to tax our leaders – and their coaches – for years to come.

Inequality of wealth

Another a key dialectic of the future, which leaders will have to confront, is the growing gulf between the rich and the poor across the world. In the UK, the proportion of national pay going to the top 1 per cent in 2013 has doubled since 1979 to 14.5 per cent (High Pay Centre, 2013). In the USA, the pattern is more extreme with the richest 1 per cent possessing 35 per cent of national wealth, while the poorest 80 per cent own just 11 per cent of it (Domhoff, 2013). In fact, according to a recent Oxfam report, 85 individuals now own as much as the world's poorest 3.5 billion people, while 1 per cent of the global population own over 60 times as much as the bottom 50 per cent (Fuentes-Nieva and Galasso, 2014). Among developed nations, the USA, UK and Australia have almost twice the income inequality of Japan and the Scandinavian countries, as measured by the differential between the top 20 per cent of income earners and the bottom 20 per cent (Wilkinson and Picket, 2010).

Income inequality costs a society in all sorts of ways. Wilkinson and Picket (2010) have argued that when 'the spirit level' of society is dangerously tilted, harm is done to all levels of society – not simply the poorest. They produce compelling evidence – though this is inevitably disputed by some – that a whole range of factors are exacerbated by income inequity, including community life, mental health, drug and alcohol use, physical health, obesity, criminal violence and imprisonment rates.

How will this division of wealth affect corporate leadership choices around markets and products? It may mean that more companies focus exclusively on the rich and the super-rich. After all, we live in a world where a new billionaire is created on average every 48 hours (Forbes.com, 2013). As for the bottom 20 per cent of earners, will the tax payer-funded public sector and charities have to pick up the pieces for caring for a sector of the population, who may find it increasingly hard to find even low-paid jobs?

Most political, corporate and public sector leaders are likely to be well within the top one per cent of earners. The issue is of particular relevance to UK CEOs, whose earning differential in relation to the average incomes of their employees had grown from a factor of 20 in 1965 to over 200 in 2011, according to one report (Mischel and Sabadish, 2012). What implications are there for high-level choice-making, when today the average FTSE 100 chief executive earns over £4 million a year? (Groom, 2013). Does this reduce his motivation to succeed, especially if he is guaranteed a pay-off in the case of failure? Or does it increase his incentive to perform well, as many would argue? It certainly puts more pressure on the selection and development of chief executives – and on organizational boards to provide the most productive environment for their boss's decision-making.

In these circumstances, it is not inconceivable that one of the roles of the leadership coach will be to try to keep the CEO and her executive team in touch with ordinary employees, from whom they are increasingly separated by their first-class lifestyles. Or will coaches, too, seek to share in this division of wealth, setting higher and higher fees? If the gulf between rich and poor turns into a binary opposition between 'them and us', these kinds of choice may become critical in shaping a coach's career path and ethical framework.

Technology

Finally, as if this array of potential leadership choices were not challenging enough, I want to look at some of the extraordinary possibilities thrown up by the new technologies which may change our world over the next few decades. It is highly likely that areas such as artificial intelligence, robotics, nano-technology, bio-technology and human augmentation will continue to develop at a galloping pace. The time of technological development continues to be compressed, in part because Moore's law of doubling of computer power about every two years continues to hold good (Brynjolfsson and McAfee, 2014). Today's cheap smart-phone exceeds the computational resources on Apollo 11, while Sony's

PlayStation 3 which appeared in 2007 had the computing power of a 1997 supercomputer (Watson, 2010).

We are approaching an era of exponential growth, in which technological innovations that in the past might have taken centuries will be completed in years or even months. Some would say we are already there, which means that our preference to conceive growth in linear terms makes it increasingly difficult to imagine the deeply discontinuous, quantum leaps that may take place just a few years from now. Cars that drive themselves, wars fought by robots, transport to Mars and beyond: these are choices we can imagine because they are already imminent in what has been called 'the second machine age' (Brynjolfsson and McAfee, 2014). But it is the unknown and unimaginable technological choices of the near future, which are likely to make most stringent strategic and practical demands on interactional leaders.

What I want to focus on here are the rapid advances being made in medical science and bio-technology. These may bring huge benefits to those suffering from many disabilities and diseases but ultimately these developments could pose major dilemmas about the very meaning of being human. Ray Kurzweil, a polymath futurologist has a particularly compelling vision of the impact of future technology on the experience of being human, expressed in his phrase 'when humans transcend biology' (Kurzweil 2005). He quotes Marshal McLuhan for support: 'First we build the tools, then they build us' (Kurzweil, 2006: 14). Kurzweil envisages a state, in a matter of decades, in which humans will benefit from synthetic organs, which replace the need for organ donors, brain-computer interfaces and bionic limbs, all monitored and repaired by nano robots in the bloodstream. This could enable humans to live to the age of 150 and beyond with remarkably healthy, constantly replenished bodies and powerfully enhanced brains.

The advantages of this medical progress may be immense but it could also lead us to cross a kind of Rubicon of human identity. For business leaders, especially in healthcare and related industries, the opportunities are undeniable but so are the tough choices. For example, will this technology be available to everyone or only to those who can afford it? If the latter is the case, the gulf which already exists between the health of the rich and poor is likely to widen even further. Indeed, could we reach a point where we may question whether we can talk about 'augmented' and 'unaugmented' humans as being members of the same species?

Other technologies conjure up the possibility of extraordinary choice-focused coaching conversations in the not-so-distant future. Robotics in particular will become an increasingly popular theme, as leaders have the option to automate more jobs. Downsizing conversations will take on a different, even more agonizing, tenor as a CEO contemplates replacing her entire factory floor staff with robots, substituting automated voice synthesizers for her call centre operators, or even outsourcing her executives to supercomputer-based decision-making centres. Some of these choices may be more individual. With an upcoming offsite in his branch in China's Guangdong Province, the London-based CEO may have to decide whether to attend the event in person or participate as a hologram. And what about his language skills? Should he have neuro-surgery to implant a chip into his brain which provides him with instant fluency in Cantonese or simply rely on the real-time translation device in his watch, as usual?

Technology: the solution to it all?

Optimists will say that some of the caution I have expressed above is misplaced and that almost all of the future threats I have outlined in this chapter can be solved by science and technology. This may be the most popular option for many leaders. Geo-engineering might be able to remove CO_2 from the atmosphere, genetically modified crops could feed the world, while a huge building programme for desalination plants solves the water crisis, to say nothing of other technologies not yet even on the drawing board. This would mean massively increased research and development budgets, new government subsidies for innovation, the fast tracking of scientists through the education process, and so on. Is this too much to hope for? Emmott (2013: 167), referring to the problems posed by over-population, thinks so; for him 'technologizing our way out of this doesn't look likely'. And yet we shouldn't entirely discount the human ability to perform extraordinary feats when up against it. If this endeavour is not driven by a facile optimism, it might just work. Coaches would be charged with the task of helping scientists and leaders of innovation to go beyond the imaginable, as they race against time to achieve breakthrough solutions. If saving human civilization is the motivation, what cannot be achieved?

Who will be choosing – and how?

Whatever the precise challenges of the coming years, is it likely that interactional leadership will become widespread and leaders generally rise to the occasion? Will global warming or population growth finds its Nelson Mandela or will 'the best lack all conviction/While the worst are full of passionate intensity', as the poet WB Yeats (1933) once lamented? Certainly, for the choice-focused leader developing a strong vision will be more important than ever. That means engaging with choices before many of their implications become visible, and it surely requires intelligent and realistic resourcing in order to produce sustainable results (some things never change). Embracing contradiction will also be vital, especially in a situation that is framed by the profound paradox of a human society, at the very pinnacle of achievement, which is in danger of becoming the victim of its own staggering success. And perhaps the ethics of freedom, in the form of preserving a range of positive options for future human generations, will become the touchstone for many of the choices which will have to be made.

The psychology of leadership choices in these circumstances can only be imagined. Emotional factors are bound to play a role, as high impact decisions will have to be made. Panic may become the norm, as stress symptoms jeopardize sober judgment. Will a sprit of negativity become dominant as the prospect of loss of various kinds induces paralyzing caution or will an equally unbalanced Pollyannaish optimism take hold? It may be that an epidemic of choice-avoidance will set in (perhaps it already has), as leaders do all in their power to get out of making difficult choices, which only leaves starker decisions for their successors. And how does the balance between self and others hold up when leaders are forced to make choices between their own immediate interests and the well-being of a wider world community, some of whose members have not yet been born?

We can speculate on what methods will be used to make these choices. Data-processing may play an even more important role in policy, as computers sift through vast quantities of data framing a particular choice, producing comprehensive cost-benefit analyses and recommendations. Decision-modelling and choice science in general are likely to become more authoritative, perhaps offering leaders a way out of taking direct responsibility for hugely consequential choices. Specialist decision-making consultancies may spring up. More than ever, there will be pressure for leadership teams and boards to establish themselves as effective choice-making environments for chief executives. Perhaps there will be a move toward more multilateral team models in organizations, with a greater emphasis on consensus and other forms of distributed decision-making. Leaders may seek to engage the stakeholders on their interactional maps through direct voting, so that collective responsibility for momentous decisions can be established, ensuring greater group commitment and diminished individual blame.

Political choice-makers may find themselves in a similar dialectic between the few and the many. The mechanisms of democracy in the coming decades may take the populist route, with electronic voting opening up new possibilities for mass participation in public policy-making and even issue-by-issue referenda. This may facilitate tough choices – or prevent them from ever being made. Or maybe political leaders will to go to the opposite extreme, declaring a wartime-type emergency and taking it upon themselves to make the decisions that count, perhaps by initiating rule by unelected technocrats, as some European countries did in response to the Eurozone crisis of 2010–11.

Leadership choices in the future: the importance of time

The time dimension of these future choices could be our biggest challenge. We are looking at problems which have taken long periods in the past to accumulate – many millennia in the case of population growth – but which may have to be resolved quickly in the very near future, through decisions, which as always, can only be made in the present. Is time against us, in more ways than one? Part of the problem is the short-term nature of leadership. Given the four to five year cycle of the political leader and the similar tenure of the average chief executive, what incentives are there for pursuing policies, the results of which may only become apparent over decades or even centuries? Polices like the carbon tax advocated by the pioneering climate scientist James Hansen (2009) could involve enormous short-term unpopularity. It will not be easy for a politician to get elected on a platform of radical change or a corporate leader to persuade his shareholders and other stakeholders of the viability of a policy which might mean radically reduced revenues. Yet if prevarication prevails and the time lag between the phases of the achievement cycle is too long, the results if and when they come may be too late. Whichever way you look at it, we may be entering a unique period in human history, in which our ability to deal with time could be the most decisive factor of all.

Conclusion: choices for the future of leadership coaching

Compared to the choices we have just examined, some of the decisions which leadership coaches have to make in the future seem mundane. But I want to conclude this book with some reflections on changes which I believe coaching has to make if it is take on a greater role in relation to the future leader's choices. Some of these changes only lie partially in the hands of coaches, such as my suggestion that choice-focused support for the chief executive or the board could become part of a company's governance code, or even the increased use of group coaches by politicians. Other choices lie fairly and squarely in the hands of the coaching profession, such as more conclusive research into the practice of coaching. I believe it is particularly important for coaching to discover what many coaches have in common in their everyday practice. This, I strongly suspect, would paint a relatively harmonious picture of coaching practice, quite distinct from the broken mirror of theoretical differences formed by the scores of competing coaching models which currently make up the profession.

This theoretical diversity, although a tribute to the creativity and free spirit of coaching, presents a bottleneck for the progress of the practice. In part, it is a result of a rejection of theorizing, which makes it difficult for different coaching models to engage with each other in constructive criticism. This is linked to another deficiency, the lack of an overarching theory of coaching, which according to John Bennett (2006) still hampers coaching's transformation from a business into a full profession. One of my motives for articulating interactional leadership coaching theory has been to provide a frame of reference for others to develop similarly comprehensive and multi-disciplinary models of leadership coaching. Concentrating on choice-making, I would suggest, provides a real focus for the practice. And perhaps interactional thinking, based on existential, phenomenological and dialectical philosophy, can move us on from the eighteenth century empiricist-rationalist assumptions still used by conventional psychology. These assumptions are typified by cognitive behaviourism, which, arguably, has at its core two deeply incompatible theories of human consciousness.

It may be that the future for coaching lies in the use of fewer specialized, external coaches and an increase in internal coaching in organizations. The trend towards distributed coaching may accelerate, where expert coaching skills are adopted by employees and citizens, so that there is always a coach at hand. But there is also a need to see leadership coaching as a specialism, which in certain respects is different from other forms of coaching at work. Perhaps too few coaches work with leaders, leaving a self-selecting elite to specialize in this field. At the same time, too much of the focus of psychological coaching is of a generalized nature that covers everything from psychotherapy to workplace coaching. Coaches need to be psychologically grounded but they also need to engage with business practice and leadership theory, which itself needs to look at the multiplicity of leadership roles.

It will not be easy for coaches to fully engage with the choices that leaders will make in the future. Coaches are not there to advise but to facilitate, unless, that is, they transparently declare some other purpose from the outset. I believe it is important to maintain an approach which is neutral, unprejudiced and unbiased, although inevitably this will be affected by a new zeitgeist and the organizational legislation and regulation which it may bring. In the end, coaches cannot determine the outcome of a leader's choices – nobody can do that. All they can do is to help a leader develop the art of balance by assisting her to connect with her reality and the interactional factors which frame it. If, in this way, coaching can make even a small improvement to the quality of the choices which leaders will make around the huge challenges that we all face in the coming years, it can more than justify itself as a profession.

References

Adler, R. (2001) 'Women in the executive suite correlate to high profits', Pepperdine University. Available online at www.w2t.se/se/filer/adler_web.pdf (retrieved 6/1/14).
Aesop (1998) *The Complete Fables*, trans. O. Temple, London: Penguin Books.
American Express OPEN (2013) 'State of women-owned business report', 4 April 2013. Available online at www.americanexpress.com/us/small-business/openforum/keywords/state-of-women-owned-businesses-report/ (retrieved 22/4/14).
Anderson, J.L. (1997) *Che Guevara: A revolutionary life*, New York: Bantam.
Ariely, D. (2008) *Predictably Irrational: The hidden forces that shape our decisions*, New York: HarperCollins.
Arthur, C. (2013) 'Google Chairman Eric Schmidt defends tax avoidance policies', *The Guardian*, 22 April. Available online at: www.theguardian.com/technology/2013/apr/22/google-eric-schmidt-tax-avoidance (retrieved 2/2/14).
Avolio, B., Walumbwa, F. and Weber, T (2009) 'Leadership: Current theories, research, and future directions', *Annual Review of Psychology*, 60: 421–49.
Benjamin, T. (2005) 'Persistence and Determination: Interview with Martin Sorrel', CNN.com, 16 December. Available online at: http://edition.cnn.com/2005/BUSINESS/12/15/boardroom.sorrell/index.html?eref=sitesearch (retrieved 11/3/13).
Bennett, J. (2006) 'An agenda for coaching-related research: A challenge for researchers'. *Consulting Psychology Journal: Practice and Research*, 58: 240–9.
Berners-Lee, M. and Clark, D. (2013) *The Burning Question: We can't burn half the world's oil, coal and gas, so how do we quit?* London: Profile Books.
Blair, T. (2001) *A Journey*, London: Arrow Books.
Blakey, J. and Day, I. (2009) *Where Were all the Coaches When the Banks Went Down? Advanced skills for high performance coaching*, Shirley: 121 Partners Ltd.
Bluckert, P. (2006) *Psychological Dimensions of Executive Coaching*. Maidenhead: Open University Press.
Blumenthal. K. (2012) *Steve Jobs: The man who thought different*, London: Bloomsbury.
Bonnstetter, B. (2013) 'The skills most entrepreneurs lack', *Harvard Business Review* blog, 1 April. Available online at http://blogs.hbr.org/2013/04/the-much-needed-skills-most-en/ (retrieved 19/4/14).
Bossidy, L. and Charan, R. (2009) *Execution: The discipline of getting things done*, New York: Crown.
Bowden, M. (2012) *The Finish: The killing of Osama Bin Laden*, New York: Grove Atlantic.
Bower, T. (2008) *Branson*, London: Harper Perennial.

Bradshaw, T. (2014) 'Steve Jobs promised "holy war" on Google, court hears'. FT.com, 2 April. Available online at: www.ft.com/cms/s/0/95e91db0-b9c8-11e3-957a-00144feabdc0.html (retrieved 2/4/14).
Branson, R. (2006) *Screw it, Let's Do it: Lessons in life*, London: Virgin Books.
Brynjolfsson, E. and McAfee, A. (2014) *The Second Machine Age: Work, progress and prosperity in a time of brilliant technologies,* New York: Norton and Co.
Burns, J.M. (1978) *Leadership,* New York: Harper & Row.
Campbell, J. (2012) *The Iron Lady: Margaret Thatcher: From grocer's daughter to Iron Lady,* abridged by D. Freeman, London: Vintage Books.
Cohen-Solal, A. (1987) *Sartre: A Life,* trans. A. Cangoni, New York: Pantheon Books.
Collins, J. (2001) *Good to Great: Why some companies make the leap... and others don't,* New York: Random House.
Conger, J. A. (1990). 'The dark side of leadership', *Organizational Dynamics,* 19(2): 44–55.
Cook, J. Nuccitelli, D., Green, S., Richardson, M., Winkler, B., Painting, R., Way, R., Jacobs, P. and Skuce, A. (2013) 'Quantifying the consensus on anthropogenic global warming in the scientific literature', *Environmental Research Letters,* 8(2). Available online at: http://iopscience.iop.org/1748-9326/8/2/024024/article (retrieved 20/2/14).
Cotter, J. (1996) *Leading Change, Boston,* Harvard Business School Press.
Cummings, J. (2009) 'Joe Biden, "the skunk at the family picnic"', Politico.com. Available online at: www.politico.com/news/stories/0909/27211.html (retrieved 12/1/14).
Damasio, A. (2006) *Descartes' Error: Emotion, reason and the human brain,* London: Vintage Books.
Danner, M (2006) 'Iraq: The war of the imagination', *New York Review of Books.* Available online at: www.nybooks.com/articles/archives/2006/dec/21/iraq-the-war-of-the-imagination (retrieved 19/4/14).
Descartes, R. (2008) *Discourse on the Method: Of correctly conducting one's reason and seeking truth in the sciences,* trans. I Maclean, Oxford: OUP.
De Beauvoir, S. (1948) *The Ethics of Ambiguity,* trans. B. Frechtman, Citadel Press: New York.
Domhoff, W. (2013) 'Power in America: Wealth, income and power'. Available on www2.ucsc.edu/whorulesamerica/power/wealth.html (retrieved 20/1/14).
Dotlich, D.L., Cairo, P.C. and Rhinesmith, S.H. (2006) *Head, Heart and Guts: How the world's best companies develop complete leaders,* San Francisco, CA: Jossey-Bass.
Dunford, R. and Palmer, I. (1996) 'Metaphors in popular management discourse: The case of corporate restructuring', in *Metaphors and Organizations,* D. Grant and C. Oswick (eds). London: Sage.
Drucker, P. (2002) *The Discipline of Innovation,* Harvard Business Review, 80(8): 95–102.
Dyer, G. (2008) *Climate Wars,* Toronto: Random House Canada.
Dyke, G. (2005) *Inside Story,* London: Harper Perennial.
Dyson, J. (1997) *Against the Odds: An autobiography,* London: Orion Business Books.
Dyson, J. (2014) 'Stop kicking out bright foreigners, or put British jobs at risk'. FT.com, 2 February. Available online at: www.ft.com/cms/s/0/34226450-8a76-11e3-9c29-00144feab7de.html#axzz2zKDEFM6N (retrieved 4/2/14).
Eagly, A. and Carli, L. (2007) *Through the Labyrinth: The truth about how women become leaders,* Boston, MA: Harvard Business School Press.
Emmott, S. (2013) *10 Billion,* London: Penguin Books.
Ferrandis, J. (2013) 'Fabra prescinde del entrenador personal contratado para mejorar su

liderazgo', *EL Pais,* 30 May. Available online at: http://ccaa.elpais.com/ccaa/2013/05/30/valencia/1369908170_790666.html (retrieved 19/4/14).

Forbes.com (2013) 'Full list: The newest 210 billionaires of 2013'. Available online at: www.forbes.com/sites/ricardogeromel/2013/03/04/full-list-the-210-newest-billionaires-of-2013 (retrieved 20/4/14).

Freud, S. and Breuer, J. (1955) *Studies on Hysteria,* trans. A. Richards, London: Hogarth Press.

Fuentes-Nieva, R. and Galasso, N. (2014) 'Working for the few: Political capture and economic inequality', Oxfam briefing paper 178. Available online at: www.oxfam.org/sites/www.oxfam.org/files/bp-working-for-few-political-capture-economic-inequality-200114-en.pdf (retrieved 20/2/14).

Garratt, B. (2010) *The Fish Rots from the Head: Developing effective board directors,* London: Profile Books.

Garten, J. (2001) *The Mind of the CEO: One-to-one with the world's top business Leaders,* London: Penguin Books.

Gigerenzer, G. (2008) *Gut Feelings: Short cuts to better decision making,* London: Penguin Books.

Gilbert, D. (2007) *Stumbling on Happiness,* New York: Harper Perennial.

Giddens, A. (2011) *The Politics of Climate Change,* 2nd edn., Cambridge: Polity Press.

Goffee, R. and Jones, G. (1998) *The Character of a Corporation: How your company's culture can make or break your business,* London: HarperCollins.

Goffee, R. and Jones, G. (2006) *Why Should Anyone be Led by You? What it takes to be an authentic leader,* Boston, MA: Harvard Business School Press.

Goleman, D., Boyatzis, R. and McKee, A. (2002) *Primal Leadership*: *Realizing the power of emotional intelligence,* Cambridge, MA: Harvard Business School Press.

Greenleaf, R. K. (1977) *Servant Leadership: A journey into the nature of legitimate power and greatness,* New York: Paulist Press.

Groom, B. (2013) 'Share price windfall reignites debate over executive pay', *Financial Times,* 9 June. Available online at www.ft.com/cms/s/0/f93083de-d055-11e2-a050-00144feab7de.html#axzz2zitVfYum (retrieved 20/4/14).

Hackman, J.R. (2009) 'Why Teams don't work, interview by D Coutu', *Harvard Business Review,* 87(5): 98–105.

Hall, E.T. (1984) *The Dance of Life: The other dimension of time,* New York: Anchor Books.

Hall, L. (2013) 'Profile: Peter Burditt', *Coaching at Work,* July/August: 20–23.

Hamel, G. (2000) *Leading the Revolution,* Boston: Harvard Business School Press.

Hamilton, C. (2010) *Requiem for a Species: Why we resist the truth about climate change*: Abingdon: Earthscan.

Hampden-Turner, C. (1990) *Charting the Corporate Mind: Graphic solutions to business conflicts,* New York: Free Press.

Hansen, J. (2009) *Storms of my Grandchildren: The truth about the coming climate catastrophe and our last chance to save humanity,* London: Bloomsbury.

Harvey, M. (2012) *Interactional Coaching: Choice-focused learning at work,* London: Routledge.

Heaney, S. (2001) 'Poetry's Power Against Intolerance', *The New York Times,* August 26, 2001. Available online at: www.nytimes.com/2001/08/26/opinion/26HEAN.html (retrieved 2/4/14).

Hegel, G.W.F. (1931) *The Phenomenology of Mind,* trans. J.B. Baillie, London: Macmillan.

Hegel, G.W.F. (1975) *Hegel's Logic*, trans. W. Wallace, Oxford: Clarendon Press.
Heidegger, M. (1962) *Being and Time,* trans. J. Macquarrie and E. Robinson, Oxford: Blackwell.
Heidegger, M. (2001) *Zollikon Seminars: Protocols-Conversations-Letters,* trans. F. Mayr and R. Askay, Evanston, IL: Northwestern University Press.
High Pay Centre (2013, 4 March) 'Top to Bottom' report. Available online at: http://highpaycentre.org/pubs/top-to-bottom-new-high-pay-centre-report-outlines-the-potential-for-wealth (retrieved 20/1/14).
Hofstede, G., Hofstede, G.J. and Minkov, M. (2010) *Cultures and Organizations: Software of the mind: Intercultural cooperation and its importance for survival,* New York: McGraw Hill.
Howell, J. (2013) *Snapshots of Great Leadership,* London: Routledge.
International Futures (2014) 'Population forecast for Japan'. Available online at: www.ifs.du.edu/ifs/frm_CountryProfile.aspx?Country=JP (retrieved 23/1/14).
IPCC (2013) 'Climate Change 2013: The physical science basis', Intergovernmental Panel on Climate Change. Available online at www.ipcc.ch/report/ar5/wg1/ (retrieved 20/2/14).
Ipsos-Mori (2012) 'Climate Week poll on public attitudes regarding climate change', 2 February. Available online at www.ipsos-mori.com/researchpublications/researcharchive/2916/Public-attitudes-regarding-climate-change.aspx (retrieved 25/1/14).
Isaacson, W. (2011) *Steve Jobs*, New York: Simon & Schuster.
Janis, I. (1972) *Victims of Groupthink*, Boston: Houghton Mifflin.
Janis, I. and Mann, L. (1977) *Decision Making: A psychological analysis of conflict, choice and commitment*, New York: The Free Press.
Kahneman, D. (2011) *Thinking, Fast and Slow*, London: Allen Lane.
Kang, E. and Zardkoohi, A. (2005), 'Board leadership and firm performance,' *Corporate Governance: An international Review*, 13(6): 785–99.
Kant, I. (1999) *Critique of Pure Reason*, edited and translated by P. Guyer and A. Wood, Cambridge: Cambridge University Press.
Kant, I. (2012) *Groundwork of the Metaphysics of Morals*, trans. M. Gregor and J. Timmermann, Cambridge: Cambridge University Press.
Kanter, R.M. (2006) 'Innovation: The classic traps, *Harvard Business Review'*, 84(11): 73–83.
Katzenbach, J. and Smith, D. (1993) *The Wisdom of Teams: Creating the high-performance organization*, Cambridge, MA: Harvard Business School Press.
Kershaw, I. (2007) *Fateful Choices: Ten decisions that changed the world 1940–41*, London: Allen Lane.
Kets de Vries, M. (2003) *Leaders, Fools and Imposters: Essays on the psychology of leadership*, Lincoln, NE: iUniverse.
Kierkegaard, S. (1980) *The Concept of Anxiety*, trans. R. Thomte, Princeton, NJ: Princeton University Press.
Kingdon, M. (2012) *The Science of Serendipity: How to unlock the promise of innovation in large organizations*, Chichester: Wiley.
King, S.D. (2013) *When the Money Runs Out: The end of Western affluence*, New Haven, CT: Yale University Press.
Kirton, M. (1989) 'A theory of Cognitive Style'. In *Adaptors and Innovators: Styles of creativity and problem solving*, M. Kirton (ed.), London: Routledge.

Klein, G. (1999) *Sources of Power: How people make decisions*, Cambridge: MIT Press.
Knight. F. (1921) *Risk, Uncertainty and Profit*, Boston: Hart, Schaffner and Marx. Available online at www.econlib.org/library/Knight/knRUP (retrieved 10/2/14).
Kotter, J. (1996) *Leading Change*, Boston, MA: Harvard Business School Press.
Kurzweil, R. (2005) *The Singularity is Near: When humans transcend biology*, New York: Viking Penguin.
Langworth, R. (ed.) (2008) *Churchill by Himself: The definitive collection of quotations*, New York: Public Affairs Books.
Law, H. (2010) 'Coaching relationships and ethical practice'. In S. Palmer and A. McDowall (eds) *The Coaching Relationship: Putting people first*, London: Routledge.
Leighton, A. (2012) *Tough Calls: Making the right decisions in challenging times*, Random House: London.
Leimon, A., Moscovici, F. and Goodier, H. (2011) *Coaching Women to Lead*, London: Routledge.
Lewin, K. (1947) 'Change frontiers in group dynamics: Concept, method and reality in Social Science; social equilibria and social change', *Human Relations*, 1(1): 5–47.
Lewin, K., Lippit, R. and White, R.K. (1939) 'Patterns of aggressive behavior in experimentally created social climates', *Journal of Social Psychology*, 10: 271–301.
Lindblom, C. (1959) 'The science of "muddling through"', *Public Administration Review*, 19(2): 79–88.
Locke, J. (1997) *Essay Concerning Human Understanding*, R. Woolhouse (ed.), London: Penguin Classics.
Magee, D. (2003) *Turnaround: How Carlos Ghosn rescued Nissan*, New York: HarperBusiness.
Mandela, N. (1994) *Long Walk to Freedom*, London: Little, Brown and Company.
Martin, I. (2013) *Making it Happen: Fred Goodwin, RBS and the men who blew up the British economy*, London: Simon & Schuster.
Matisse, H. (1995) *Matisse on Art*, J. Flam (ed.) Berkeley: University of California Press.
Mazzucato, M. (2013) *The Entrepreneurial State: Debunking public vs. private sector myths*, London: Anthem Press.
McKibben, B. (2010) *Eaarth: Making a life on a tough planet*, New York: Times Books.
McLean, B. and Elkind, P. (2004) *The Smartest Guys in the Room: The amazing rise and scandalous downfall of Enron*, London: Penguin Books.
McNeil, B.J., Pauker, S.G., Sox, H.C. and Tversky, A. (1982) 'On the Elicitation of Preferences for Alternative Therapies,' *New England Journal of Medicine*, 306: 1259–62.
Mintzberg, H. (1990) 'The manager's job: Folklore and fact', *Harvard Business Review*, 68(2): 163–78.
Mischel. L. and Sabadish, N. (2012) 'CEO pay and the top 1%: How executive compensation and financial sector pay have fuelled income inequality', *Economic Policy Institute*, May 2012. Available online at www.epi.org/publication/ib331-ceo-pay-top-1-percent/ (retrieved 23/1/14).
Moore, C. (2013) *Margaret Thatcher: The authorised biography, Volume One: Not for turning*, London: Allen Lane.
Munk, N. (2004) *Fools Rush In: Steve Case, Jerry Levin and the unmaking of AOL Time Warner*, New York: HarperBusiness.
Odean, T. (1998) 'Are investors reluctant to realize their losses?' *Journal of Finance*, 53: 1775–98.

Office for Budget Responsibility (2013) 'Fiscal Sustainability Report, July 2013'. Available online at: http://budgetresponsibility.org.uk/fiscal-sustainability-report-july-2013/ (retrieved 21/2/14).
Padgett, C. (2012) *Corporate Governance: Theory and practice*, Basingstoke: Palgrave Macmillan.
Parliament UK (2014) 'The Ageing Population'. Available online at: www.parliament.uk/business/publications/research/key-issues-for-the-new-parliament/value-for-money-in-public-services/the-ageing-population/ (retrieved 1/3/14).
Pascale, R.T. (1984) 'Perspectives on strategy: The real story behind Honda's success', *California Management Review*, 26: 47–72.
Peters, T. (1987) *Thriving on Chaos: Handbook for a management revolution*, New York: Alfred A. Knopf inc.
Petit, P. (2003) *To Reach the Clouds*, London: Faber and Faber.
Pomper, G. (2001) 'The 2000 Presidential Election: Why Gore lost', *Political Science Quarterly*, 116(2): 201–23.
Popper, K. (1963) *Conjectures and Refutations: The growth of scientific knowledge*, London: Routledge and Kegan Paul.
RBS (2014) 'RBS issues trading update, 27 January 2014'. Available online at: www.rbs.com/news/2014/01/rbs-issues-trading-update.html 2014 (retrieved 18/4/14).
Richards, S. (2010) *Whatever it Takes: The real story of Gordon Brown and New Labour*, London: Fourth Estate.
Roberts, R. (1989) *Serendipity: Accidental discoveries in science*, New York: John Wiley and Sons.
Robine, J.-M., Cheung, S., Le Roy, S., Van Oyen, H., Griffiths, C, Michel, J.-P., Herrmann, F. (2008) 'Death toll exceeded 70,000 in Europe during summer of 2003', *Comptes Rendus Biologies*, 331(2): 171–8.
Rogers, C. (1961) *On Becoming a Person: A therapist's view of psychotherapy*, London: Constable.
Rosenthal, E. (2005) *The Era of Choice: The ability to choose and its transformation of contemporary life*, Cambridge, MA: MIT press.
Rosinski, P. (2003) *Coaching across Cultures: New tools for leveraging national, corporate and professional differences*, London: Nicholas Brealey.
Salecl, R. (2010) *The Tyranny of Choice*, London: Profile Books.
Sampson, A. (1999) *Mandela: The authorised biography*, London: HarperPress.
Sandberg, S. (2013) *Lean In: Women, work and the will to lead*, New York: Alfred. A. Knopf.
Sartre, J.-P. (1947) *Situations I*, Paris: Gallimard.
Sartre, J.-P. (1948) *Existentialism and Humanism*, trans. P. Mairet, London: Methuen Library.
Sartre, J.-P. (1958) *Being and Nothingness: An essay on phenomenological ontology*, trans. H. Barnes, London: Routledge.
Sartre, J.-P. (1976) *The Critique of Dialectical Reason*, trans. A. Sheridan-Smith, London: New Left Books.
Sartre, J.-P. (1992) *Notebooks for an Ethics*, trans. D. Pellauer, Chicago, IL: University of Chicago Press.
Schafer, M. and Crichlow, S. (2010) *Groupthink versus High-Quality Decision Making in International Relations*, New York: Columbia University Press.
Schumpeter, J. (1994) *Capitalism, Socialism and Democracy*, London: Routledge.

Schwartz, B. (2004) *The Paradox of Choice: Why more is less*, New York: HarperCollins.
Seldon, A. (2005) *Blair*, London: The Free Press.
Shakespeare, W. (1995) *Henry V*, Arden Shakespeare, third series, T.W. Craik (ed.), London: Bloomsbury.
Shakespeare, W. (1997) *Macbeth,* Arden Shakespeare: second series, K. Muir (ed.), London: Thomson Learning.
Shakespeare, W. (2001) *Othello*, Arden Shakespeare: third Series, E. Honigman (ed.), London: Thomson Learning.
Shakespeare, W. (2005) *Hamlet*, Arden Shakespeare, third series, N. Thompson and A Taylor (eds), London: Thomson Learning.
Slaughter, A.-M. (2012) 'Why women still can't have it all', *The Atlantic Magazine*. Available online at: www.theatlantic.com/magazine/archive/2012/07/why-women-still-cant-have-it-all/309020/ (retrieved 7/1/14).
Spinelli, E. (1994) *Demystifying Therapy*, London: Constable.
Spinelli, E. (1997) *Tales of Un-Knowing: Therapeutic encounters from an existential perspective*, London: Duckworth.
Tappin, S. and Cave, A. (2008) *The Secrets of CEOs: 150 global chief executives lift the lid on business, life and leadership*, London: Nicholas Brealey.
Theakston, K. and Gill, M. (2011) 'The Postwar Premiership League', *Political Quarterly*, 82(1): 67–80.
Tuckman, B. (1965) *'Developmental sequence in small groups'*, Psychological Bulletin, 63(6): 384–99.
Tversky, A. and Kahneman, D. (1974) 'Judgment under Uncertainty: Heuristics and biases', *Science*, 185(4157): 1124–31.
Uhlig, R. (2010) *Genius of Britain: The scientists who changed the world*, London: Collins.
UK Parliament (2014) 'The Ageing Population'. Available online at: www.parliament.uk/business/publications/research/key-issues-for-the-new-parliament/value-for-money-in-public-services/the-ageing-population/ (retrieved 1/3/14).
United Nations (2014) 'World Population Ageing 1950–2050'. Available online at: https://unp.un.org/Details.aspx?pid=2956www.un.org (retrieved 25/1/14).
Vlasic, B. and Stertz, B. (2000) *Taken for a Ride: How Daimler-Benz drove off with Chrysler,* New York: HarperBusiness.
Vroom, V and Jago, A. (1988) *The New Leadership: Managing participation in organizations,* Englewood Cliffs, NJ: Prentice Hall.
Watson, R. (2010) *Future Files: A brief history of the next 50 years*, Nicholas Brealey Publishing: London.
Welman, P. and Bachkorova T. (2010) 'The issue of power in the coaching relationship'. In S. Palmer and A. McDowall (eds) *The Coaching Relationship: Putting people first*, London: Routledge.
Whiteman, G., Hope, C. and Wadhams, P. (2013) 'Climate Science: Vast costs of Arctic change', *Nature*, 499(July): 401–3:
Whitney, J. and Packer, T. (2000) *Power Plays: Shakespeare's lessons in management and leadership,* New York: Simon and Schuster.
WHO/UNICEF (2013) 'Progress on sanitation and drinking water, 2013 update', Available online at: http://apps.who.int/iris/bitstream/10665/81245/1/9789241505390_eng.pdf (retrieved 10/1/14).
World Bank (2014) 'GDP Ranking, April 2104 update'. Available online at: http://data.worldbank.org/data-catalog/GDP-ranking-table (retrieved 1/2/14).

Wilkinson, R. and Pickett, K. (2010) *The Spirit Level: Why equality is better for everyone,* London: Penguin.

Williams, J. and Dempsey, R. (2013) 'The rise of executive feminism', *Harvard Business Review* blog. Available online at: http://blogs.hbr.org/2013/03/the-rise-of-executive-feminism/ (retrieved 20/4/14).

Wilson, N. (2009) 'Women in the boardroom help companies succeed', *The Times*, (19 March).

Wilson, T. and Schooler, J. (1991) 'Thinking too much: Introspection can reduce the quality of preferences and decisions,' *Journal of Personality and Social Psychology*, 60: 181–91.

Yamaguchi, Y. (2002) 'Elderly at Record', bloomberg.com. Available online at: www.bloomberg.com/news/2012-05-09/elderly-at-record-spurs-japan-stores-chase-1-4-trillion.html (retrieved 22/1/14).

Yeats, W.B. (1933) *Collected Poems*, London: Macmillan.

Yukl, G. (2002) *Leadership in Organizations,* 5th edn., Upper Saddle River, NJ: Prentice-Hall.

Index

360-degree surveys 162

achievement cycle 5, 6, 10–11, 12, 27, 36, 37, 165; cross cultural leadership and 82–5; defining the team: role of 91–2; delivery: executing the strategy 15–16, 55–6; entrepreneurial leader and 85, 86, 88; portraits: from Steve Jobs to Hamlet 133–46; potential leaders 100, 104; resources: transforming the possible into the probable 14–15, 55; strategy: choosing the future 12–13, 54–5; techniques of coaching 54–6; thought leaders 110, 112, 113, 117; *see also* non-delivering leader, coaching; non-resourcing leader, coaching; non-strategizing leader, coaching
acquisitions 18, 30, 122, 140
action focus 15
adaptors 113
Adler, R. 104
Aesop 19
Africa 172
ageing 169–70, 171–2
agriculture 173, 176
altruism 58
ambiguating and disambiguating: springing the certainty snare 61
ambiguity 18, 22, 24, 33, 35, 58, 165–6; of choice 151–2, 154, 157; starting a business 85; undialectical ethics: price of rejecting 152–4
amnesia defence 23
anatomy of choice 10
ancient Greeks 21
Anderson, J.L. 128
anger 29, 153, 162; non-resourcing leader case study 46–7
anxiety 35, 93, 112, 113, 153

AOL 140
Apple 13, 87, 112, 134–6, 169
Ariely, D. 73
Arthur, C. 153
Asia 22, 66
Atlee, Clement 140
Australia 83, 84, 173
authenticity 23–4, 73, 111, 143, 150, 155–7; climate change 171; language of 158
auto industry 13, 83, 175
availability heuristic 29
avoidance: choice 30–1, 32, 177; tax 153; uncertainty 82, 83
Avolio, B. 24
awareness, choice 11–12, 31

balance sheet, decisional 31
balancing art of choice-focused leader 25, 35; dialectics of change 26–7, 50; realm of visionary juggler 26
balancing positivity and negativity: 'challenge' in coaching 154–5; coaching: support and challenge 60
bankruptcy 122, 138, 140
Bay of Pigs invasion 127–8
BBC 112
Benjamin, T. 75
Bennett, J. 178
Berners-Lee, M. 170
Biden, Joe 129–30
Bin Laden, Osama 129
Blackberry 169
Blair, Tony 19, 127, 130, 140, 141–2, 143
Blakey, J. 154–5, 160
blame culture 50, 113
Bluckert, P. 161
Blumenthal, K. 135
board 162, 166, 167, 177, 178; chair of

Index   189

89–90, 122, 126, 160, 162; coaching *see* board coaching
board coaching 120, 178; case study 122–4; choice-focused board 122; group coaching: basic processes 120–1; leading upwards: individual support for leader 126–7
Bonnstetter, B. 85
Bossidy, L. 36
Bowden, M. 129, 130
Bower, T. 137, 138
Bradshaw, T. 136
brain scans 162
brainstorming 54, 111
brand reputation 14–15
Branson, Richard 137–8
Brazil 169
Brown, Gordon 127, 141, 142–3
Brynjolfsson, E. 174, 175
Burditt, Peter 161
Burns, J.M. 37, 110
Bush, George W. 128–9
Bush, George H.W. 130

Campbell, J. 106, 127, 141
car industry 13, 83, 175
carbon tax 178
Carter, Howard 113
Carter, Jimmy 129
case studies: board 122–4; cross-cultural issues 83–5; difficult leader 163–6; entrepreneur 87–9; gender 73, 106–8; global leader 83–5; group coaching 122–7; non-delivering leader *see separate entry*; non-executive leader *see separate entry*; non-resourcing leader *see separate entry*; non-strategizing leader *see separate entry*; potential leaders 101–4, 106–9; succession leadership 108–9; team leaders 94–6, 97–9; thought leaders 116–19
Castro, Fidel 127–8
certainty snare 35–6, 152; ambiguating and disambiguating: springing 61; non-resourcing leader case study 47
chair of board 89, 122, 126, 160, 162; case study 89–90; *see also* board coaching
challenge and support in coaching 60; 'challenge' in coaching 154–5
change 37; dialectics of 26–7, 50
Cheney, Dick 128–9
chief executive 122, 126, 140, 167, 174, 178; and board or management team *see* group coaching; and chair of board 89, 160
China 169
Churchill, Winston 36
climate change 169–71
Clinton, Bill 108
coaching in practice: case studies *see separate entry*; practical techniques of coaching *see separate entry*; research 178
cognitive behaviourism 178
Cohen-Solal, A. 110
Coleridge, Samuel 144
collaborative leadership case study: balancing self and others 101–3
collective versus individual values 82
collectively-led or multilateral teams 94, 96–7, 177; case study 97–9; *see also* group coaching
Collins, J. 22, 24
communication leadership 25
communicative leadership: subject matter expert 118–19
competition 168–9
compulsive attitude to work 18
confidentiality 167
conflict 125, 173
Conger, J. 134, 160
consensus-hunting 31
consultants, external 32
consultative decision-making 31
Cook, J. 171
Cooks, Tim 135
corporate culture 14
corporate governance 139, 166–7; codes 89, 122, 178
corporate responsibility 14–15
corruption 154
Cotter, J. 36
counter-voices 92, 95–6, 120, 121, 128, 141; for coach 167
creative destruction 153
creative and intellectual leadership *see* thought leaders
Cuba 127–8
cultural differences 172; cross-cultural leadership and achievement cycle 82–5; long-term and short-term orientations 22, 66
Cummings, J. 129–30

Damasio, A. 29
Danner, M. 129

De Beauvoir, S. 151
democratic voting 31
depression 18
Descartes, R. 29, 32
destruction, creative 153
dialectical teams 93, 114
dialectics of change 26–7, 50
difficult leaders, coaching 160–1; case study 163–6; corporate governance 166–7; importance of supervision in balancing coach's choices 167; requirements 161–2; role of the organization 166; 'Soprano Syndrome' 162–6, 167
directional strategy 12–13
discrimination 23
Disney 126
do no harm 153
do nothing to anyone that you would not wish done to you 153–4
Domhoff, W. 173
dot-com boom 157
Dotlich, D.L. 36
Drucker, P. 115
duality: chief executive and chair of board 89, 160
Dunford, R. 158
Dyer, G. 173
Dyke, G. 111, 112
Dylan, Bob 110
Dyson, James 13, 115, 136–7, 138

Eagly, A. 105
Einstein, Albert 110
Eisner, Michael 126
Emmott, S. 173, 176
emotion 10, 18, 33, 35, 36, 144, 162, 176–7; decision-making interaction of reason and 28–9; non-resourcing leader case study 46–7; rationalizing to disclose distorting bias of 59
emotionalizing 60
empathizing 61, 153; non-delivering leader case study 74, 75
empirical studies 36–7
Enron 89, 138–40, 154, 157
entrepreneurial leader 85–6; achievement cycle and 85, 86, 88; case study 87–9; coaching 86–7
estrangement of life at the top 60
ethical dimension 22, 27, 37, 51, 137, 139, 149–50; ambiguity of choice 151–2, 154, 157; authenticity 23–4, 73, 111, 143, 150, 155–8, 171; 'challenge' in coaching 154–5; choice, engaging with 150; coach, ethics of 154, 174; codes 152, 154; do no harm 153; ethical choices involve situational interaction of self and others 150–1; freedom, ethics of 151, 156–7, 164–5, 176; Golden Rule 153–4; know thyself 152; law and morality 159; practical techniques of coaching 58; principles of interactional ethics 150–2; respecting freedom of choice 23; 'Soprano Syndrome' 162–6, 167; taking responsibility for choices 23, 32, 156, 158; undialectical ethics: price of rejecting ambiguity 152–4
Europe 172
European Union 169, 170
Eurozone crisis 177
evasion, choice 32
exhaustion 18
external consultants 32

Fabra, Alberto 130
Facebook 87
'fantasy hire': getting recruitment right 49
Fastow, Andy 139
fees for coaching 86–7, 174
Ferrandis, J. 130
firefighters 29
foreign policy 120, 127, 141; coaching for politicians 130; group helps political leader 129–30; influence of leadership group 127–9
fractional teams 93
France 84
Franklin, Benjamin 31
freedom: of choice 23; ethics of 151, 156–7, 164–5, 176
Freud, S. 162
Fuentes-Nieva, R. 173
Fuld, Dick 160
funnelling skills 56, 140
future, choosing the 168, 176–8; CAPIT: five global choice arenas which will affect all organizational leaders 169–76; interactional leadership in corporate world 168–9; leadership coaching 178–9; technology: solution to it all 176

Garratt, B. 89
Garten, J. 21

Gates, Robert 129
gender 73, 100, 104–6, 125; board membership 122; case study 106–8
Germany 84, 104, 120, 171
Ghosn, Carlos 83
Giddens, A. 171
Gigerenzer, G. 57
Gilbert, D. 12, 20, 28
global interactional leader 81–2; cross cultural leadership and achievement cycle 82–3; Marlene: 'I'm only creating a strategy for 37 countries!' 83–5
globalization 169
Goffee, R. 24, 116
Golden Rule 153–4
Goleman, D. 36
Goodwin, Fred 18–19, 25
Google 114, 135–6, 153
Gore, Al 108
governments 121, 158; coaching for politicians 130; foreign policy 120, 127–30; leading upwards: individual support for leader 127
Greeks, ancient 21
green washing 171
Greenleaf, R.K. 37
Groom, B. 174
group coaching 120, 167; basic processes 120–1; case study: board of directors 122–4; case study of conflict in management team: negative opposition 124–7; choice-focused board 122; leading upwards: individual support for leader 126–7; *see also* team leader
Groupthink 122, 127–8
Guevara, Che 128
gut feeling 31

Hackman, J.R. 92, 93
Hall, E.T. 105
Hall, L. 161
Hamel, G. 157
Hamilton, C. 170
Hamlet: to lead or not to lead? 145–6
Hampden-Turner, C. 26
Hansen, J. 170, 178
harm, do no 153
Harvey, M. 11, 17, 53, 102, 155
healthcare 172, 175; case study of conflict in management team 124–7
Heaney, Seamus 140
Hegel, G.W.F. 23, 27, 32, 33, 34, 151

Heidegger, M. 23, 32, 34, 57, 150
herd mentality 57
hierarchy of choice 9–10
hindsight 11, 151
Hobson's choice 32
Hofstede, G. 22, 82, 83
Homer 26
Honda 13, 113
Howe, Geoffrey 141
Howell, J. 156
Husserl, E. 33

ideas dimension *see* thought leaders
imbalances, addressing *see* oppositional enquiry
immigration 172
India 169, 173
individual support for leader: leading upwards 126–7
individual versus collective values 82
individually-led or unilateral teams 94; case study 94–6, 99; *see also* group coaching
inequality 169–70, 173–4
intellectual leadership *see* thought leaders
inter-generational barriers 172
interactional self 5, 6, 17, 27, 37; others: interpersonal dimension 19–20, 57; practical techniques of coaching 56–8; self: personal dimension 17–19, 56; time dimension 20–2, 57–8
intuition 29; emotionalizing 60
inversion of choice 30
iPhone 135
Iproniazid 113
Iraq 128–9, 141–2
Isaacson, W. 11, 112, 126, 134
isolation of life at the top 60
iTunes 135
Ives, Jonny 135

Janis, I. 31, 122, 127–8, 158
Japan 84, 171–2, 173
Jobs, Steve 11, 13, 112, 126, 134–6, 138
juggler, visionary 26

Kahneman, D. 11, 29, 30
Kang, E. 89
Kant, I. 33, 35, 151, 153
Kanter, R.M. 114
Katzenbach, J. 93
'keeping door open' decision-making style 73

Kennedy, John F. 12, 128
Kershaw, I. 120
Kets de Vries, M. 161–2
Kierkegaard, S. 28, 32, 35
King, S.D. 172
Kingdon, M. 114
Kirton, M. 113
Klein, G. 29
Knight, F. 85
know thyself 152
Kotter, J. 140
Kurzweil, R. 175

language of authenticity 158
Langworth, R. 36
Latin America 22, 82
Law, H. 154
law and morality 159
Lay, Ken 89, 139, 156
leadership theories: new synthesis 36–7
Lear, King 144
Lehman Brothers 160
Lehrer, J. 29, 32
Leighton, A. 5, 21, 111
Leimon, A. 104
Lewin, K. 61, 91
Lindblom, C. 11
listening 19, 48–9
Locke, J. 33–4
long-term and short-term orientations 22, 66
loss aversion 30, 60

Macbeth: delivery without vision 144–5
McKibben, B. 171
McLean, B. 139, 154
McNeil, B.J. 30
macro- and micro-choices 30
Magee, D. 83
Major, John 142, 143
Malaysia 137
Mandela, Nelson 12–13, 21, 140, 151, 156
manipulative behaviour and ethics of freedom 151
map, interactional 19–20, 57, 177; entrepreneurial leader 87–8; group coaching 121; non-delivering leader 71–2; non-resourcing leader 44–5, 51; non-strategizing leader 64–5
market research 50, 51
Martin, I. 18, 25, 122
Matisse, Henri 100
maximizing 31

Mazzucato, M. 115, 135
mergers 30, 140
Merkel, Angela 104
meta-level of choice 11, 31, 91, 94
micro- and macro-choices 30
Microsoft 87, 135
mind guards 128
Mintzberg, H. 36
mirage choice 32
Mischel, L. 174
Moore, C. 106
moral relativism 150–1
morality *see* ethical dimension
Morton's fork 32
muddling through 10–11
multilateral or collectively-led teams 94, 96–7, 177; case study 97–9; *see also* group coaching
multirole dimension 24–5, 27, 36, 37, 141; practical techniques of coaching 58–9
Munk, N. 140
Murdoch, Rupert 138
mustard gas 113

narratives 111
National Health Service (NHS) 149; case study of conflict in management team 124–7
negative and positive aspects of choice, interaction of 29–30
negative upwards leadership 127
negativity and positivity, balancing: 'challenge' in coaching 154–5; coaching support and challenge 60
neuroscience *see* psychology and neuroscience of choice
Nissan 83
Nixon, Richard 158
Nokia 169
non-actualizing leader portrait 138–40
non-choices 32
non-contradiction, law of 33–4, 153
non-delivering leader, coaching 70–1, 77; actualisation and time 75–6; Deborah's vision 71–2; delegator trips up 72–3; failure as the secret to whole cycle success 74; gender issue 73; 'getting your hands dirty': key achievement choices 74–5
non-delivering leader portrait 138–40
non-executive directors 123
non-executive leader 89; case study 89–90

non-resourcing leader, coaching 41–2, 51–2; building leadership profile 51; building leadership team 47–8; coaching objectives 45; emotional patterns 46–7; 'fantasy hire': getting recruitment right 49; interactional mapping 44–5, 51; leadership psychology 46; listening 48–9; new channels and platforms 50–1; paradox of leadership coaching 43–4; revolution in creativity and communication 49–50; vision 42–3
non-resourcing leader portraits 133–7
non-strategizing leader, coaching 62–3, 69; achievement choices: putting the vision to work 68–9; 'collapsed vision' 63–4; crossing the Rubicon: the vision emerges 66–8; interactional mapping 64–5; rebuilding self-confidence and regaining a sense of self 65–6
non-strategizing leader portrait 137–8

Obama, Barack 129–30
Odean, T. 30
Odysseus 26
omission bias 30
open future coaching 101
openness 23, 156, 161
opportunity costs 31
oppositional enquiry 59; balancing positivity and negativity 60; emotionalizing 60; non-delivering leader case study 74; non-strategizing leader case study 65–6; rationalizing 59
oppositional logic 34–5, 45, 112, 113, 124, 126
organizational culture: ethical 154; fragmented 116; stories 111
Othello: the fallible resourcer 144
over-confidence 18–19, 60, 152

Padgett, C. 89, 166
paradox of leadership coaching 43–4, 160–1, 167
paralysis by analysis 55–6
Pascale, R.T. 13
pensions 172
person-centred therapy 162
personality 18, 85, 162; Interactional Styles Outliner (ISO) 46, 56, 82; non-resourcing leader case study 46; non-strategizing leader case study 65–6

Peters, T. 113
Petit, Philippe 26
pharmaceutical industry 13, 113
philosophical background 32–3, 37; certainty snare 35–6, 47, 61, 152; implications for choice-making 35; law of non-contradiction 33–4, 153; oppositional logic 34–5, 45, 112, 113, 124, 126
Pixar 13, 135
politicians 106, 108, 140, 149, 177–8; coaching for 130; fate of the successor: Major and Brown 142–3; group influence 120, 121, 127–30; Thatcher and Blair: hubris of vision 141–2
Pomper, G. 108
Popper, K. 34–5
population growth 169–70, 172–3, 176
positional strategies 13, 55, 63, 100
positive and negative aspects of choice, interaction of 29–30
positivity and negativity, balancing: 'challenge' in coaching 154–5; coaching support and challenge 60
potential leaders 100, 146; case study: balancing self and others in collaborative leadership 101–3; case study: 'talking the talk' versus 'the religion of doing it' 103–4; rising star 101
power distance 82
practical techniques of coaching 53–4; achievement cycle 54–6; ambiguating and disambiguating: springing the certainty snare 61; empathizing 61; ethical dimension 58; interactional self 56–8; multirole dimension 58–9; oppositional enquiry 59–60; *see also* case studies
prechoices 30; rationalizing: helps to prevent 59
pro-bono coaching work 86–7
psychoanalysis 162
psychology and neuroscience of choice 28, 162, 178; choice avoidance 30–1, 32, 177; methods of choice-making 31; positive and negative aspects of choice 29–30; reason and emotion in decision-making 28–9; varieties of choice 31–2
public sector 141, 149, 174; case study of conflict in management team: negative opposition 124–7

radar operators 29
rationality 10, 18, 32, 33, 35, 36; emotionalizing 60; interaction of reason and emotion in decision-making 28–9
Reagan, Ronald 31, 130
reciprocity 153
recruitment: 'fantasy hire' 49; non-executive directors 123
relativism, moral 150–1
renunciation, principle of 11, 134
responsibility for choices, taking 23, 32, 156, 158
reversible choices 30, 32
Richards, S. 127, 142
risk: starting a business 85–6
Roberts, R. 113
Robine, J.-M. 170
Rogers, C. 162
Rosenthal, E. 30
Rosinski, P. 85
Royal Bank of Scotland (RBS) 18–19, 25, 122
Russia 169

Salecl, R. 10, 30
sales model of interactional skills 102
Sampson, A. 13
Samsung 169
Sandberg, Sheryl 105
Sartre, J.-P. 9, 23, 28, 32, 33, 34, 35, 93, 110, 125, 150, 152, 162
Scandinavian countries 173
Schafer, M. 31, 128, 130
Schlesinger, Arthur 128
Schmidt, Eric 153
Schremp, Jurgen 15
Schumpeter, J. 153
Schwartz, B. 28, 29, 30, 31
Seldon, A. 141
self-confidence 18; entrepreneurs 85; regaining a sense of self and rebuilding 65–6
self-knowledge 18, 46, 52, 53, 56, 144, 152, 156
servant leadership 37
Shaheen, Jeanne 105
Shakespeare, William 133, 143–6
short-term and long-term orientations 22, 66
Skilling, Jeffrey 138–40
Slaughter, A.-M. 105
social capital 14, 105
social institutions 151

Sony 174–5
'Soprano Syndrome' 162–6, 167
Sorrel, Martin 21, 75
Soviet Union 120
Spinelli, E. 152, 162
Stalin, Joseph 120
stories 111
stress 29, 176–7
subject matter expert: communicative leadership 118–19
succession planning 25, 108–9
sunk costs 30
supervision of coaches 167
support and challenge in coaching 60; 'challenge' in coaching 154–5

Tappin, S. 160
tax: avoidance 153; carbon 178
team leader 91, 141; choices of the team: self-others interaction and team formations 93–4; counter-voices 92, 95–6; defining the team: role of achievement cycle 91–2; multilateral or collectively-led teams 94, 96–9, 177; setting the bar high: dialectical team 93, 114; time dimension 92–3; unilateral or individually-led teams 94–6; *see also* group coaching
technical leadership 24–5
technology 169–70, 174–6
Thatcher, Margaret 106, 127, 140–1, 142
Theakston, K. 140, 142
theories on leadership: new synthesis 36–7
thought leaders 110, 146; actualizing: delivering the end product 115; clearing the way for creativity 115–16; communicative leadership: the subject matter expert 118–19; ideas dimension of leadership: every leader should be a thought leader 111; leading innovation and creativity 112; possibilizing: lighting the spark 112–14; probabilizing: resourcing creativity 114–15; universities, think tanks, research laboratories, institutes and consultancies 116
time dimension 20–2, 33, 34, 130; cairos 21, 55; competition 168–9; cross-cultural leadership 82; ethical choices 151; future, choosing the 177–8; gender 105, 107; global leaders 81–2; gut feeling 31; non-delivering leader case

study 75–6; non-resourcing leader case study 50–1; practical techniques of coaching 57–8; teams 92–3
Time-Warner 140
tough love 153
transactional leader 37
transformational leader 37
trust 19, 45, 156
Tuckman, B. 92
Tversky, A. 29
tyranny of choice 30–1, 171

U-turn 32
Uhlig, R. 136, 137
UKTV 114
uncertainty 85–6, 146; avoidance 82, 83; integrity under conditions of 156
unilateral or individually-led teams 94; case study 94–6, 99; *see also* group coaching
United Kingdom 82, 83, 84, 169, 171; Corporate Governance Code 89; gender 104; immigration 172; inequality 173, 174
United Nations 172
United States 82, 83, 84, 127–30, 173; chair of board 89; gender 104; scientific research 114–15
universal moral principles 150–1
universities 116; case study 116–18

varieties of choice 31–2
Viagra 13, 113
Virgin 137–8
virtual teams 92
visionary juggler 26

Vlasic, B. 15
Vroom, V. 36

Wallenda, Karl 26
Warfarin 113
water 173, 176
Watergate scandal 158
Watson, R. 172, 175
wealth, inequality of 169–70, 173–4
Wells, Frank 126
Welman, P. 152
what if choices 31
white lies 24
Whitelaw, Willie 127, 141
Whiteman, G. 170
Whitney, J. 143, 146
whole-cycle leadership 16, 36, 83, 100, 102
Wilkinson, R. 173, 174
Williams, J. 104
Wilson, N. 122
working groups 93
Wozniak, Steve 134, 135

Yamaguchi, Y. 172
Yeats, W.B. 176
Yukl, G. 37

zombie leadership 13, 69; achievement choices: putting the vision to work 68–9; 'collapsed vision' 63–4; crossing the Rubicon: the vision emerges 66–8; interactional mapping 64–5; rebuilding self-confidence and regaining a sense of self 65–6

eBooks
from Taylor & Francis

Helping you to choose the right eBooks for your Library

Add to your library's digital collection today with Taylor & Francis eBooks. We have over 50,000 eBooks in the Humanities, Social Sciences, Behavioural Sciences, Built Environment and Law, from leading imprints, including Routledge, Focal Press and Psychology Press.

Choose from a range of subject packages or create your own!

Benefits for you
- Free MARC records
- COUNTER-compliant usage statistics
- Flexible purchase and pricing options
- 70% approx of our eBooks are now DRM-free.

Benefits for your user
- Off-site, anytime access via Athens or referring URL
- Print or copy pages or chapters
- Full content search
- Bookmark, highlight and annotate text
- Access to thousands of pages of quality research at the click of a button.

Free Trials Available

We offer free trials to qualifying academic, corporate and government customers.

eCollections

Choose from 20 different subject eCollections, including:

- Asian Studies
- Economics
- Health Studies
- Law
- Middle East Studies

eFocus

We have 16 cutting-edge interdisciplinary collections, including:

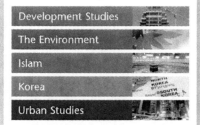

- Development Studies
- The Environment
- Islam
- Korea
- Urban Studies

For more information, pricing enquiries or to order a free trial, please contact your local sales team:

UK/Rest of World: **online.sales@tandf.co.uk**
USA/Canada/Latin America: **e-reference@taylorandfrancis.com**
East/Southeast Asia: **martin.jack@tandf.com.sg**
India: **journalsales@tandfindia.com**

www.tandfebooks.com